Some notes of praise for THE MONASTIC JOURNEY

"Fortunately for us, Thomas Merton was a master of expression who left a large legacy of spiritual writing. . . . This collection speaks directly to monks and religious, but, as with all his writings, Merton had others also in mind. These pages, he wrote, will have meaning not only for monks, but 'indeed for all Christians, since the monastic life is traditionally regarded as the pure Christian life, the perfect life in Christ.' . . . May his words be a continuous source of inspiration to us as we, fellow travellers on the same journey, strive to live such a life."—*Spiritual Book News*

"This handsome volume, expertly edited, presents Merton's most matured reflections on monasticism during the last 10 years of his life. These essays are of specific value to Christian monks, especially Catholic. But the essential motifs and meanings in these writings are no less significant to others. . . . Merton explicates on the nature, role and vocation of a contemplative and also explains very succinctly such terms as chastity, charity, obedience and poverty."

—*The Courier-Journal*

"[Merton's] mind overran the whole terrain of the world and life. His humor and warmth were infectious, his simplicity and openness a delight. For people who wish to get in touch with his thoughts and feelings about monasticism, this reader is recommended."—*The Christian Century*

"In [this book] I personally renewed an old friendship with Merton's clear and powerful exposition of the essentials of spirituality. . . . Merton brings us back sharply to the only foundation of any authentic and perduring growth in the love of God and man, Christ himself."—*Twin Circle*

"[This] is the kind of Merton book which ought to become for us the point and locus of his continuing significance. . . . One hopes that *The Monastic Journey* will help retain and restore contemplative integrity in our time."—*Church World*

THE MONASTIC JOURNEY

The Monastic Journey

THOMAS MERTON

Edited by Brother Patrick Hart

•

[Text Complete and Unabridged]

IMAGE BOOKS

A Division of Doubleday & Company, Inc.
Garden City, New York

Image Book edition by special
arrangement with Sheed Andrews
and McMeel, Inc.

Image Book edition published
September 1978
Copyright © 1977 by the Trustees of
the Merton Legacy Trust

ISBN: 0-385-14094-0

CONTENTS

Acknowledgements 8

Foreword by Brother Patrick Hart 9

Preface by the Trustees of the Merton Legacy Trust 15

PART ONE   *The Monastic Vocation*

What is the Monastic Life? 19

Basic Principles of Monastic Spirituality 28

Monastic Peace 62

PART TWO   *Monastic Themes*

The Humanity of Christ in Monastic Prayer 121

Conversion of Life 145

Monastic Attitudes: A Matter of Choice 162

PART THREE   *The Solitary Life*

Project for a Hermitage 179

Wilderness and Paradise 189

The Solitary Life 197

APPENDIXES

Monastic Renewal: A Memorandum 213

A Letter on the Contemplative Life 218

Contemplatives and the Crisis of Faith 224

Notes 231

Select Bibliography 236

ACKNOWLEDGEMENTS

Grateful acknowledgement is made to the following for permission to reprint copyrighted material: The Abbey of Gethsemani for 'Basic Principles of Monastic Spirituality' (1957) and 'Monastic Peace' (1958); Stamperia del Santuccio for 'The Solitary Life' (1960); *Cistercian Studies* for 'As Man to Man' (1969). The Editor also wishes to express his appreciation for permission to reprint other material in this volume, some of which appeared in *Monastic Studies*: 'The Humanity of Christ in Monastic Prayer' (1964); and *Cistercian Studies*: 'Conversatio Morum' (1966), 'Monastic Attitudes: A Matter of Choice' (1967), 'Wilderness and Paradise: Two Studies' (1967) and 'Contemplatives and the Crisis of Faith' (1967). The lines from 'The Quickening of St John the Baptist' and the quotation from *The Asian Journal of Thomas Merton* are reprinted with permission of the publisher, New Directions.

FOREWORD

At the Center for the Study of Democratic Institutions in Santa Barbara shortly before embarking on his Asian journey, Thomas Merton encountered a group of university students. One of them, a French revolutionary student, challenged him with the statement: 'We are monks, also'. Merton reflected on this later during the course of his trip and commented on it in the talk he gave at Bangkok just a few hours before his death. 'The monk', he remarked, 'is someone who takes up a critical attitude toward the contemporary world and its structures.' The monk in this context is in protest against modern society like the Egyptian desert dweller of the fourth century who fled the Roman culture of his day. But these students, among so many others, are also seeking the mystical dimension in religion, which they find sadly lacking in 'organized religion' in the churches of the West. Thomas Merton, in his writings on the monastic and contemplative life, however, always emphasized the mystical aspect of religion, the interior journey.

It is true, in a sense, that to be a monk is not the monopoly of a few cloistered monks and nuns, but rather, as Raymond Panikkar observed in his talk at Bangalore to the monastic leaders of Asia in October of 1973: 'Every human being has a monastic dimension, but this is realized in different ways and cultivated in different degrees of purity and awareness by different people'. If there is a monastic dimension in everyone, then perhaps the writings of Thomas Merton on the monastic journey will have meaning for many today living outside the monastery walls.

Over the years Merton wrote informative articles on the life of the monk directed to the interested lay person, as well as several full-length books, including *The Waters of Siloe*, *The Silent Life* and *Contemplation in a World of Action*, which became best-sellers. But Merton wrote many more es-

says and articles on the monastic journey, describing its beauties and demands, emphasizing the essentials of the life, the
basic values of silence, solitude, prayer, purity of heart,
among others, while at the same time remaining open to genuine renewal. Some of these essays were published by the
Abbey of Gethsemani in limited editions, while other articles
on monastic themes were circulated by way of monastic journals and reviews of a rather restricted publication in both
Europe and America, and are no longer readily accessible.

Since the death of Thomas Merton on 10 December 1968,
by accidental electrocution in Bangkok, Thailand, and the
subsequent renewed interest in his monastic witness and writings, it was suggested that the most significant of these texts
which had not as yet appeared in book form, and the pam-
phlets which were allowed to go out of print, be made available once again to a wider audience.

The articles selected and edited for this volume were written during the last decade of Merton's life, and hence reflect
his mature thought on both community monastic living and
the solitary life, which was a lifelong preoccupation. The first
three essays attempt to describe something of the mystery of
the monastic vocation, and were published originally in pam-
phlet form by the Abbey of Gethsemani. Together they form
a strong statement on the basic verities of the monastic way
of life.

The remainder of the volume is composed of articles written for monastic journals on various themes proper to the
monastic journey, such as 'The Humanity of Christ in Monastic Prayer', 'Conversion of Life', 'Monastic Attitudes: A
Matter of Choice' and 'Wilderness and Paradise: Two
Studies'.

Several hitherto unpublished works are also included in
this volume: 'Monastic Renewal: A Memorandum' and 'Project for a Hermitage'. Another manuscript on 'The Solitary
Life', printed by Victor and Carolyn Hammer of Lexington,
Kentucky, 'pro manuscripto' on their hand press in an ele-
gant but limited edition, is no longer in print. This deeply
moving monograph in praise of the hermit life fittingly brings
the volume to a close. It expresses eloquently Merton's view

of the monastery as having its windows opened out onto the
desert.

Finally, three appendixes are added: in addition to the unpublished memorandum on monastic renewal referred to
above, there is a letter Merton penned to the Abbot of the
Cistercian monastery of Frattocchie near Rome in response
to Pope Paul's personal request for a 'Message of Contemplatives to the Modern World'. The third appendix, 'Contemplatives and the Crisis of Faith', constitutes the final message which was eventually promulgated at the Synod of
Bishops which met in Rome during October of 1967. It must
be read in conjunction with the letter. This joint work of
Dom J. B. Porion, Procurator General of the Carthusians,
Abbot André Louf, Cistercian Abbot of the monastery of
Sainte-Marie-du-Mont in northern France, and Father
Thomas Merton, was first published in French in the Vati-
can daily, *L'Osservatore Romano* on 12 October 1967, and
later in English translation in *Cistercian Studies*.

Rereading these pages in preparation for publication, I am
amazed at the evolution in Merton's thinking on the monastic life in the Church, and his growing hesitancy about proclaiming it in too triumphalistic tones to the world. The modesty of the monk appeals to us today even more than when
these essays were first written. As he grew older and wiser in
the monastic way, he became more convinced of the need of
expressing love and mercy and compassion toward others, as
he experienced God's overwhelming love and mercy in his
own life. This growth in compassion led him to embrace the
whole world, as can be seen by his great love and concern for
all suffering humanity, the more solitary his life became.

Following a long tradition, Merton viewed the monastic
life as a 'school of charity'. For him, the entire monastic ascesis with its detailed rules and regulations was oriented to
that end—the love of God and the love of neighbour. As he
wrote in one of the essays which appears in this volume on
the subject of monastic peace: 'St Bernard of Clairvaux expanded and implemented the thought of St Benedict when
he called the monastery a school of charity. The main object
of monastic discipline, according to St Bernard, was to re-

store man's nature created in the image and likeness of God; that is to say, created for love and self-surrender.'

In Christianity the basic experience or enlightenment is that we are loved by God, as St John wrote in his First Epistle: 'We love because He first loved us'. In other words, God took the initiative: it was not my idea to love God and neighbour, but rather my love is the answer, or response, to a call, an invitation, a vocation. The first thing then in Christianity is the belief that the world is loved by God.

Merton's view of the monastic vocation is basically that of the Christian life lived in a 'prepared' environment, to use the language of Dr Maria Montessori. If the heart of the Christian message is faith in God's love, then certainly the monastic life must be one of charity above all else. Otherwise monasticism would be completely devoid of meaning. The well-known maxim of St John of the Cross is as true of the monastic vocation as it is for the life of any Christian: 'At the evening of our lives we shall be judged on love'.

Many men and women today are interested in a life of prayer, building community and a personal experience of God, the inward journey. And they are the ones who are asking for Merton books and essays on the monastic life. They suggest (and I am in complete agreement in this respect) that Merton was at his best when writing on the monastic and contemplative life, *because he lived it*, he experienced its demands and its joys. In a word, he knew it from the inside.

The monastic journey, in many ways, turns out to be everyone's journey through life. Thomas Merton emphasized this in a special statement he made for the jacket of *A Thomas Merton Reader* in 1962: 'The Christian is, I believe, one who sacrifices the half truth for the sake of the whole truth, who abandons an incomplete and imperfect concept of life for a life that is integral, unified, and structurally perfect. Yet his entrance into such a life is not the end of the journey, but only the beginning. A long journey must follow: an anguished and sometimes perilous exploration. Of all Christians the monk is, or at least should be, the most professional of such explorers. His journey takes him through deserts and paradises for which no maps exist. He lives in strange areas of solitude, of emptiness, of joy, of perplexity and of admiration.'

Thomas Merton noted in his *Asian Journal,* the last book he was to write before his death: 'It is the peculiar office of the monk in the modern world to keep alive the contemplative experience and to keep the way open for modern technological man to recover the integrity of his own inner depths'. May his words be a continuous source of inspiration to us as we, fellow travellers on the same journey, strive to live such a life, aware of its fragility and imperfections as well as its great potential for growth in the love of God and neighbour.

BROTHER PATRICK HART
Abbey of Gethsemani

PREFACE

When Thomas Merton set up—some years before his death—a Trust to handle his literary Estate, one of its main purposes was to ensure wherever possible, that his books and writing would be kept in print and thus available to the general public. The Trustees, therefore, were most grateful to Brother Patrick Hart, O.C.S.O., when he suggested putting together this volume of Merton's writing on monasticism none of which is currently available in book form. We would like to take this opportunity of thanking Brother Patrick for his careful editing of the material and the work involved in collecting it for publication.

Our real journey in life is interior,
it is a matter of growth, deepening,
and an ever greater surrender to the creative
action of love and grace in our hearts.

The Asian Journal of Thomas Merton

Night is our diocese and silence is our ministry
Poverty our charity and helplessness our tongue-tied sermon.
Beyond the scope of sight or sound we dwell upon the air
Seeking the world's gain in an unthinkable experience.
We are exiles in the far end of solitude, living as listeners
With hearts attending to the skies we cannot understand:
Waiting upon the first far drums of Christ the Conqueror,
Planted like sentinels upon the world's frontier.

'The Quickening of St John the Baptist'
(on the Contemplative Vocation)

The Collected Poems of Thomas Merton

The monk is a man who completely renounces the
familiar patterns of human and social life and follows
the call of God into 'the desert' or 'the wilderness',
that is to say, into the land that is unknown to him and
unfrequented by other men. His journey into the
wilderness is not a mere evasion from the world
and its responsibilities. Negative reasons cannot
adequately account for the monastic journey into
solitude. Monastic renunciation is the answer to a
positive call from God, inexplicable, not subject to
scientific demonstration, yet able to be verified by
faith and the spiritual wisdom of the Church.

Thomas Merton on the Monastic Journey

PART ONE

The Monastic Vocation

WHAT IS THE MONASTIC LIFE?

Encounter and Questions

Life is made of encounters. A true encounter stimulates questions and answers. When you meet an interesting stranger you find yourself alert and curious. Who is this person? You seek to discover something of the mystery of his identity and of his history. At the same time if he inspires confidence, if he seems to be a person of unusual depth and experience, you begin to open up to him and to share with him the secret of your own life. In this way, a true personal encounter brings us not only knowledge of another, fellowship with another, but also a deeper comprehension of our own inner self.

To encounter not a person, but a religious community of persons—a monastic community—is an unusual experience. Not only is a monastic community a very unique and original body of men, with a religious and historic character that arouses interest and challenges the modern mind, but at the same time the encounter with such a community has rules and limitations of its own.

You can see the buildings, listen to the monks in choir. You may speak to a brother in the gatehouse. You may make a retreat in the guesthouse, visit the monastery enclosure, speak to the guest master and retreat master. But here already restrictions appear. Women are not even allowed into the enclosure. Men may enter the enclosure but are not allowed normal communication with all the monks. In fact, you rarely see the ordinary members of the community at close quarters. Why these restrictions? Why do the monks keep silence among themselves and refrain from talking to outsiders? Why do the monks stay in their enclosure instead of teaching, preaching and performing other active works which are usually associated with a life dedicated to God?

What kind of lives do these silent men live, anyway? Are they happy? Do they find their existence more meaningful in the monastery, or do they secretly regret not only the pleasures and comforts of the outside world, but also its responsibilities, its challenges and its fulfilments?

Monasticism Today

The monastic life is a life of renunciation and total, direct worship of God for his own sake. Is this still to be regarded as something a reasonable man will undertake in the twentieth century? Is it simply an escape from life? Is it a refusal of fellowship with other men, misanthropy, evasion, delusion?

A monk must understand the motives which have brought him to the monastery, and he must re-examine them from time to time as he grows in his vocation. But a defensive, apologetic attitude is not in accordance with the monastic life. A monk would be out of character if he tried to argue everybody into admitting that his life is justified. He expects merely to be taken as he is, judged for what he is, because he does not waste time trying to convince others or even himself that he amounts to anything very special.

The monk is not concerned with himself so much as with God, and with all who are loved by God. He does not seek to justify himself by comparing himself favourably with other people: rather, he sees himself and all men together in the light of great and solemn facts which no one can evade. The fact of inevitable death which puts an end to the struggles and joys of life. The fact that the meaning of life is usually obscure and sometimes seemingly impenetrable. The fact that happiness seems to elude more and more people as the world itself becomes more prosperous, more comfortable, more confident of its own powers. The fact of sin, that cancer of the spirit, which destroys not only the individual and his chances of happiness, but whole communities and even nations. The fact of human conflict, hate, aggression, destruction, subversion, deceit, the unscrupulous use of power. The fact that men who refuse to believe in God, because they think that belief is 'unreasonable', do in fact surrender without reason to baser forms of faith: they believe blindly in every secular myth, whether it be racism, communism, nationalism, or one of a thousand others which men accept today without question.

The monk confronts these perplexing facts. And he confronts the religious void in the modern world. He is well aware that for many men, as for a certain philosopher (Nietzsche), 'God is dead'. He knows that this apparent 'death' of God is in fact an expression of a disturbing modern phenomenon, the apparent inability of man to believe, the death of supernatural faith. He knows that the seeds of this death are in himself, for though he is a believer, he too sometimes must confront, in himself, the possibility of infidelity and failure. More than anyone else he realizes that faith is a pure gift of God, and that no virtue can give man room for boasting in the sight of God.

What is this so-called 'death of God'? It is in fact the death of certain vital possibilities in man himself. It is the death of spiritual courage which, in spite of all the denials and protestations of commonplace thinking, dares to commit itself irrevocably to belief in a divine principle of life. It is the seeming death of all capacity to conceive this as a valid possibility, to reach out to it, grasp it, to obey the promptings of the Spirit of divine life, and surrender our heart and mind to the Gospel of Jesus Christ.

A monk has made this surrender, knowing what it costs, knowing that it does not absolve him from the doubts and struggles of modern man. But he believes that he possesses the key to these struggles, and that he can give his life a meaning that is valid not only for himself but for everyone else. That meaning is discovered in faith, though not in arguments about faith. Certainly faith is not opposed to reason. It can be shown to be rational, though it cannot be rationally 'proved'. But once one believes, one can become able to understand the inner meaning of one's belief, and to see its validity for others. Both this belief and this eventual understanding are special gifts of God.

What Is a Monk?

In almost all the great religions of the world we find special groups of men and women who separate themselves from the ordinary life of society, take upon themselves particular and difficult obligations, and devote themselves to one task above all: to deepening their understanding and practice of their own religion in its most basic implications.

In Hinduism, the monk seeks deliverance from the earthly round of time and delusion by ascetic and mystical purification. In Buddhism he seeks enlightenment as to the ground of his own being. In Judaism, shortly before the time of Christ, the monks of Qumran lived in the full eschatological consciousness of Old Testament prophecy. In Islam, though the Sufis are not 'monks', they have traditionally sought the deepest ecstatic experience of union with God. In Christianity the monk seeks before all else to live out his faith in and according to the Gospel of Jesus Christ by renouncing himself, taking up the cross of self-denial and following Christ. He unites himself with the hidden years of labour spent by Jesus in Nazareth, or he follows Jesus into the desert sharing the Master's solitary prayer.

The Catholic monastic life is the response to Jesus Christ's call to penance and prayer in the Gospel. All Christians seek to save their souls by following Christ. Monks, however, paying strict attention to the injunctions of the Master, seek to observe more closely and more faithfully such words as the following:

'Take heed to yourselves lest your hearts be overcharged with surfeiting and drunkenness, and the cares of this life, and that (last) day come upon you suddenly. . . . Watch therefore, praying at all times that you may be accounted worthy . . . to stand before the Son of Man.' (Luke 21.34–6)

'If anyone will come after me, let him deny himself and take up his cross, and follow me. For he that will save his life shall lose it, and he that shall lose his life for my sake shall find it. For what does it profit a man if he gain the whole world and suffer the loss of his own soul?' (Matt. 16.24–6)

'If you will be perfect, go, sell what you have and give to the poor, and you shall have treasure in heaven, and come, follow me.' (Matt. 19.21)

'If any one love me, he will keep my word, and my Father will love him, and we will come to him and will make our abode with him. . . . Abide in my love. If you keep my commandments you shall abide in my love, as I have kept my Father's commandments and abide in his love.' (John 14.23, and 15.9–10)

'And the multitude of the believers had but one heart and one soul, neither did any one say that any of the things which he had was his own: But all things were common unto them.' (Acts 4.32)

The monk takes the Gospel with the deepest seriousness. He is bound, by his faith in Christ, to develop a *special awareness* of the spiritual possibilities and hazards of human life. 'Take heed to yourselves . . .' The monastic life is a life which, by means of discipline and renunciation, delivers man from the heedlessness and irresponsibility, the spiritual insensibility and the lack of freedom which come from immersion in cares, pleasures and self-seeking.

The monk strives to learn that *spirit of sacrifice* by which, basing himself on trust in Christ and on faith in the nearness and power of Christ, he can let go of himself, abandon concern for his own life and his own fulfilment, in order to surrender to a deeper, invisible principle. The Holy Spirit becomes mysteriously present as a source of life and light to the man who, for the love of Christ, no longer seeks to follow the guidance of his own individual caprice and his own will.

The monk strives to penetrate the deep meaning of all the words of Christ, to keep them in his heart night and day, pondering on them. (Luke 2.19)

The monk seeks union with Christ by obedient and faithful love. He believes that by love he abides in Christ and Christ abides in him. (John 15.1–5) This mysterious union of the Christian with Christ can and does become more than a matter of blind faith. In the monastic life, faith opens out into a spiritual light of understanding which is however pro-

portionate to the monk's humility and purity of heart. (See
Matt. 5.3–12)

Purity of Heart

The discipline of the monastic life is all directed to one end:
the development of this 'purity of heart' which is a condition
of peace, self-forgetfulness, humility, unconcern with the images and preoccupations of a life dominated by servile care.

Purity of heart is not, however, the result of an individualistic exploit, something that is attained merely by in-
trospection, self-examination, and earnest efforts to make spiritual progress, regardless of the needs of others. Purity of
heart in the monastic sense cannot be developed without
humble fellowship in the charity of Christ. That is why monastic community life, with its constant demands for self-for-
getting service and charity, is the chief means for bringing
the heart of the monk to a state of peace, gentleness, faith
and simplicity.

However, the monk lives his common life in a spirit of
inner solitude. That is why in certain monasteries, like those
of the Cistercians, special emphasis is placed on silence and
prayer.

But the monastic life of silence and prayer should never
create a sense of conflict between love of God and love of
one's brother. When these two get in the way and impede
one another, it is a sign that one is not living fully and wisely
as a true monk, in the spirit of faith. But it may be quite
difficult, in practice, to learn to live a communal life of fellowship while at the same time meditating and worshipping
God in one's heart. One of the signs of a Cistercian vocation
is the ability to reconcile these two apparently conflicting
trends in a life of silence and simplicity among brothers.

Prayer, Praise and Labour

The monk is a man of prayer and of praise. His life of
prayer is centred in the Liturgy of the Church, the chanting
of Psalms, and the Eucharistic Sacrifice.

The Liturgy is the royal road of the monk to God. That is why St Benedict said that 'nothing is to be preferred to the work of God' (*Opus Dei*). The centre of the Liturgy is the Mass, the renewal of Christ's sacrifice by Christ Himself, Victim and High Priest, in the midst of His Chosen People. To understand what the Liturgy really is, we must understand the true nature of Christianity. What is Christianity but the mystery of Christ in us, the mystery of Christ in His Church, the mystery of our salvation and union with God in Christ Jesus?

St Paul shows us the true meaning of 'the mystery which has been kept in silence from eternal ages which is manifested now'. (Rom. 16.25) This mystery is our incorporation in Christ. It is the holy and eternal design of God the Father to save us in Christ His Son, to 'bless us with spiritual blessings in heavenly places in Christ . . . that He might make known the mystery of His will, according to His good pleasure . . . to *re-establish all things in Christ*, that are in heaven and on earth, in Him.' (Eph. 1)

The 're-establishment' of all things in Christ means the spiritualization of all creation through contact with the sacred humanity of the Word. The Man-God Jesus Christ reigns in heaven. But He is present and He acts on earth in the members of His Body, the Church. All who are incorporated in Christ by faith and baptism share with Him His divine sonship, and enter with Him into the mystery of His divine life and power.

Now it is by the power of His Cross that we are saved, and our life in Christ comes from our participation in His death and resurrection. But the Cross and Resurrection of Christ are something more than a historical memory. They are a present fact, mystically actualized by the Liturgy, or the 'sacred action' which we call the Mass. The Mass is a sacred mystery, a divine and human action in which God and man participate in one common love-feast of sacrifice and reconciliation.

Jesus clearly promised that He would be truly and objectively present in His Church, as its ruler, sanctifier and teacher but particularly in this most concrete and most spiritual of all actions: His own High-priestly sacrifice of the Mass.

Christ Jesus is then our priest and our victim, and it is He who mystically offers Mass among us, just as truly present in the midst of the faithful today as He was in the midst of His disciples at the Last Supper.

From this great centre of the Mass, the Liturgy reaches out to sanctify every moment of the Christian day, by the canonical hours of the Divine Office—the Church's sacrifice of praise.

Man has a body and a soul, and both need to play their proper parts in his daily life. The body must be fed and clothed, and for this purpose man must labour with his hands, till the soil, hew timber, care for his livestock, make his clothing, warm his home and keep it simply furnished. But more important is the nourishment of man's soul by study, reading, meditation and even by the contemplation of divine things. Finally, man must raise his spirit to God in thanksgiving, prayer, repentance and adoration. Not one of these aspects of man is forgotten in the monastery. The Rule of St Benedict takes full account of human nature and provides for man a healthy and happy life which St Benedict has called a 'school of the Lord's service'. Here there is indeed toil and sacrifice, but much more there is the satisfaction of duty well done. Finally, and above all, there is the supernatural joy of one who has given all his time and all his thoughts to God, and lives as a faithful child of his heavenly Father.

The Monastic Family

The monastic community life is patterned on that of Disciples around the Master. Christ is the true head of the community. Faith brings the monk to Him, through the Holy Spirit, for strength, guidance, support, inspiration and courage. But the Master is visibly represented in the midst of His disciples by a human person, the Father Abbot. The Abbot, chosen from among the monks by vote, is an older and more experienced priest who is capable of administering the affairs of the monastery and taking care of the spiritual and material needs of the monks. All the monks obey him according to their vow, in a spirit of faith, and under his direction they carry out the work that needs to be done for the common good.

Some of the monks become priests, and some of these will carry out necessary spiritual functions in the community or in the retreat house. The priests are trained to act as spiritual directors, professors of theology, and to fulfil other especially responsible functions. However, the priest is not ordained merely to do a job. His priesthood is an added perfection in his monastic life of prayer.

Others in the community remain monks without going on to receive Holy Orders. These may devote more of their time to choral prayer and study, or they may devote more time to manual work, with less time in choir. But all the members of the community engage in prayer, manual work, and meditative reading or study. The proportions may differ in individual cases.

In the past there were two clearly distinct categories of monks: the choir monks and the so-called laybrothers. Canonically the laybrothers were on a different level from the choir monks. But now the status has been unified, all have the same privileges and are juridically equal. But the difference of functions remains, since some monks are more attracted to manual than to intellectual work, and others are better endowed for choral service. Rigid uniformity has never been the true monastic ideal: on the contrary, there must be room for a diversity of gifts and attractions, and no one must attempt to coerce men into a mould for which they are not fitted by nature or by grace.

Men of every type, profession, temperament, from every level of society and from all races and nations, are bound together in the monastery by ties of faith and charity. They have learned by experience that they are all sons of a common Father in Heaven. Here there are no racial or social distinctions. All are one in Christ, and all can join with the psalmist in singing: 'Behold how good and pleasant it is for brothers to dwell together in unity.' (Ps. 132.1)

BASIC PRINCIPLES OF
MONASTIC SPIRITUALITY

There can be no doubt that the monastic vocation is one of the most beautiful in the Church of God. The 'contemplative life', as the life of the monastic orders is usually called, is a life entirely devoted to the mystery of Christ, to living the life of God Who gives Himself to us in Christ. It is a life totally abandoned to the Holy Spirit, a life of humility, obedience, solitude, silence, prayer, in which we renounce our own desires and our own ways in order to live in the liberty of the sons of God, guided by the Holy Spirit speaking through our Superiors, our Rule, and in the inspirations of His grace within our hearts. It is a life of total self-oblation to God, in union with Jesus Who was crucified for us and rose from the dead and lives in us by His Holy Spirit.

But beautiful as this life may be, simple and exalted as the tradition of the monastic Fathers may show it to us, monks are human and human frailty tends always to diminish and to distort the wholeness of what is given to us by God. This is all the more to be regretted when some persons full of goodwill and generosity embrace the monastic life, only to find their goodwill dissipated in futilities and in routine. Instead of living the monastic life in its purity and simplicity, we always tend to complicate it or to pervert it with our own limited views and our own too human desires. We place exaggerated emphasis on some partial aspect of the life, thus unbalancing the whole. Or we fall into that spiritual myopia which sees nothing but details and loses sight of the great organic unity in which we are called to live. In a word, if the rules and observances of the monastic life are to be properly understood, we must always keep in view the real meaning of monasticism. In order not to be confused by the means

which are given to us, we must always relate them to their
end.

The great ends of the monastic life can only be seen in the
light of the mystery of Christ. Christ is the centre of monastic living. He is its source and its end. He is the way of the
monk as well as his goal. Monastic rules and observances, the
practices of monastic asceticism and prayer, must always be
integrated in this higher reality. They must always be seen as
part of a living reality, as manifestations of a *divine life*
rather than as elements in a system, as manifestations of duty
alone. The monk does more than conform to edicts and commands which he cannot understand—he abandons his will in
order to live in Christ. He renounces a lower freedom for a
higher one. But if this renunciation is to be fruitful and
valid, the monk must have some idea of what he is doing.

The purpose of these notes is to examine briefly the great
theological principles without which monastic observance and
monastic life would have no meaning. The truths we present
here must necessarily take a very condensed form. Anyone
who wishes to understand them must read them medita-
tively and in the presence of God.

Although these pages have been written for monks, and in
particular for Cistercian novices and postulants, they will
have meaning for all religious and indeed for all Christians,
since the monastic life is traditionally regarded as the pure
Christian life, the perfect life 'in Christ', a sure way to the
summit of that ordinary perfection of charity to which Jesus
has called all those who have left the world to follow Him to
heaven.

What Do You Seek?

If we want to live as monks, we must try to understand
what the monastic life really is. We must try to reach the
springs from which that life flows. We must have some notion of our spiritual roots, that we may be better able to sink
them deep into the soil.

But the monastic vocation is a mystery. Therefore it cannot be completely expressed in a clear succinct formula. It is a gift of God, and we do not understand it as soon as we receive it, for all God's gifts, especially His spiritual gifts, share in His own hiddenness and in His own mystery. God will reveal Himself to us in the gift of our vocation, but He will do this only gradually.

We can expect to spend our whole lives as monks entering deeper and deeper into the mystery of our monastic vocation, which is our life hidden with Christ in God. If we are real monks, we are constantly rediscovering what it means to be a monk, and yet we never exhaust the full meaning of our vocation.

When we enter the monastery, we may or may not have some notion why we have left the world. We can give some answer, more or less clear, to the question: 'Why have you come here?' This question is one which we should ask ourselves again and again in the course of our monastic life; 'What are you doing here? Why have you come here?' Not that it is a question whose answer we have known but tend to forget. It is a question which confronts us with a new meaning and a new urgency, as we go on in life.

Sometimes we hesitate to ask ourselves this question, afraid that by doing so we might shake the foundations of our vocation. The question is one which ought never to be evaded. If we face it seriously, we will strengthen our vocation. If we evade it, even under a holy pretext, we may perhaps allow our vocation to be undermined.

The monk who ceases to ask himself 'Why have you come here?' has perhaps ceased to be a monk.

What are some of the answers we give to the question: 'Why have you come here?' We reply—'To save my soul', 'To lead a life of prayer', 'To do penance for my sins', 'To give myself to God', 'To love God'. These are good enough answers. They are religious answers. They are meaningful not only for what they say, but for what they imply. For, on the lips of a Christian, such statements must eventually mean much more than they actually say. As they stand, they give evidence of good subjective dispositions, but they by no means lead to a full understanding of the monastic life. For the monastic life is not defined merely by the fact that it enables us to save our soul, to pray, to do penance, to love God. All these things can be done outside the monastery and *are* done by thousands.

But neither is Christian monasticism adequately defined as a quest of perfection. A Zen Buddhist, in Japan, for example, may enter a monastery to seek a life of retirement and spiritual discipline. He is perhaps seeking the highest reality. He is seeking 'liberation'. Now if we enter the monastery seeking the highest reality, seeking perfection, we must nevertheless realize that for us this means something somewhat more than it can ever mean for a Zen Buddhist.

Our monastic life must therefore develop so that our concept of the end for which we are striving becomes more clearly and more specifically Christian.

It makes much more sense to say, as St Benedict says, that we come to the monastery to *seek God*, than to say that we come seeking spiritual perfection.

The end which we seek is not merely something within ourselves, some personal quality added to ourselves, some new gift. It is God Himself.

To say 'Why have you come here?' is the same as saying 'What does it mean, to seek God? How do you know if you are seeking Him or not? How can you tell the difference between seeking Him and not seeking Him, when He is in fact a hidden God, *Deus absconditus?*'

When Moses spoke to God saying: 'Show me thy face' the Lord answered, 'Man shall not see me and live'. (Exod. 33.20)

Yet Jesus tells us that eternal life is to know the one true God, and Jesus Christ whom He has sent. (John 17.3) This knowledge of God which is eternal life is not arrived at by pure speculation. We come to know God by being born of God and living in God. We cannot really know Him only by reading and study and meditation.

We can come to know God only by becoming His sons and living as His sons. 'As many as received Him, He gave the power to be made sons of God, to them that believe in

His name, who are born not of blood, nor of the will of the flesh, nor of the will of man, but of God.' (John 1.12–13)

We can live as sons of God, we can know God only if we live in charity.

'Dearly beloved, let us love one another, for charity is of God. And every one that loveth is born of God, and knoweth God.' (1 John 4.7)

But this charity is not just a natural love for one another. We do not become sons of God by the mere fact of living together in a society dedicated to a common purpose, sharing common interests with one another. Do not even the gentiles so? The charity that unites us is the charity of Christ—in the strict sense of a love *exercised* by the Sacred Heart, not just as the broad sense of a love patterned on His love. We sing at the *Mandatum—congregavit nos in unum Christi amor*— the love of Christ's heart for us (not just our love for Him) has drawn us together. We could not love Him unless 'He had first loved us'.

We become sons of God by being born again in Christ—by baptism—and we live and grow and bring forth fruit only by 'remaining in Christ'.

'Abide in me and I in you. As the branch cannot bear fruit of itself unless it abide in the vine, so neither can you unless you abide in me.' (John 15.4) Thus we arrive at the real heart of our monastic vocation.

Our monastic life is a life in Christ, a life by which we remain in Christ, sharing His life, participating in His action, united with Him in His worship of the Father.

Christ is our life. He is the whole meaning of our life, the whole substance of the monastic life. Nothing in the monastery makes sense if we forget this great central truth.

But who is Jesus? He is the Son of God, He is the word who was made flesh and dwelt among us. The monastic life, like all Christian life, the life of the Church, prolongs the mystery of the incarnation on earth, and enables men to receive into their souls, in great abundance, the light and the charity of Christ. We come to the monastery to live more fully, more perfectly and more completely *in Christ*.

Therefore we can conclude that we come to the monastery

to seek Christ—desiring that we may find Him and know Him, and thus come to live in Him and by Him.

And as we begin to find Him, we begin to realize at the same time that we have already been living in and by Him—for 'He has first loved us'.

The Word Was Made Flesh

The whole meaning of the monastic life flows from the mystery of the incarnation. We come to the monastery, drawn by the action of the Holy Spirit, seeking eternal life. Eternal life is the life of God, given to us in Christ.

We come seeking truth. Christ said: 'I am the truth'. We come seeking life. He is also the way, and the life. We come seeking light. He is the 'light of the world'. We come seeking God. In Him 'dwells all the fullness of the Godhead corporeally'. (Col. 2.9)

In Christ God has *revealed* Himself to us, and *given* Himself to us:

'The word was made flesh and dwelt among us, and we saw His glory, the glory as it were of the only begotten Son of the Father, full of grace and truth.' (John 1.14)

'By this has the charity of God appeared towards us because He has sent His only begotten Son into the world, that we may live by Him.' (1 John 4.9)

The question 'Why have you come here?' is then the question Jesus asked in the garden of the agony; '*Whom do you seek?*' We seek Jesus of Nazareth, Christ, the son of the living God, who descended from heaven for the love of us, who died for us on the Cross and rose from the dead and sits, alive, at the right hand of God the Father, filling us with His life and directing us by His spirit, so that He lives and breathes and works and acts and loves in us. Our purpose in life is then to grow in our union with the risen Christ, to live more and more deeply the life of His body, the Church, to continue on earth the incarnation which manifests the love of God for men, so that we may share the glory of God with Christ in heaven.

The word was made flesh. *Verbum caro factum est.* This truth is the foundation stone of our monastic life. It is not just a truth which we know, and periodically meditate on. It is a truth which we must live by. Our whole life and all our activities must be steeped in the light which flows from it—that light is the radiance of God Himself. The Word is the splendour of the Father's glory. He is the image of the invisible God and the exemplar of all God's creation. All things, all living beings, all inanimate creation, all spirits and intelligences, are created in Him, are sustained in Him, live in Him and by Him.

'In Him were all things created, in heaven and on earth, visible and invisible, whether thrones or dominations or principalities or powers: all things were created by Him and in Him. He is before all, and by Him all things consist.' (Col. 1.16–17)

When St Benedict saw all creation gathered together 'as though in one ray of the sun' he saw all things in the light of the word 'without whom was made nothing that is made' and who 'enlightens every man that comes into the world' (John 1.3, 9). This is the end to which we tend, to see the glory of the word incarnate, 'the glory as of the only begotten of the father, full of grace and truth' (John 1.14). We seek to see, and know, and love all things in Him—the world, the angels, our brothers; the Father and the Holy Spirit. This is the answer to the question, 'Why did you come here, Whom do you seek?'

He is All. And in order to see Him who is All, we must know and find ourselves in Him. We must find all things in Him. We must find the Father in Him.

The word was made *flesh*. Incarnation! He took a human body and soul to Himself so that the word dwelt among us as a man. The word did not assume flesh as a disguise, as a mere garment which could be cast off and thrown away. He became a man. Jesus, a man, is God. His body is the body of God. His flesh is so full of the light and power of God that it is completely and totally divine.

And this Man-God, Jesus Christ, has become for us our

new world, a new creation, in which all things are to be 'recapitulated'.

Dom Vonier says: 'The incarnation is adequately appreciated only by those to whom Christ's humanity is the marvel of marvels, a superb creation in which they have their being, in which they live, work, die, and in which they hope to rise again and in which they find the fullness of the Godhead as Moses found the fire in the bush.' (*Complete Works of Abbot Vonier*, 'The Christian Mind'—vol. 1, p. 12.)

Jesus did not assume human nature only in order to die for us on the cross and elevate us above 'matter'. The sacred humanity of Christ reigning and active in heaven, is a *permanent principle* of sanctification, spiritualizing all that is brought in contact with Him by His Church.

If the word was made flesh, and if the body of Christ remains as a permanent source of sanctity, then bodily creation is not evil. God when He created the world, 'saw that it was good' (Gen. 1) because it was made in Him and kept in existence by Him.

If our life is a search for Jesus, the word made flesh, we must realize that we are not to act like pagan mystics, who repudiate the visible world as pure illusion, and who seek to black out all contact with sensible and material things. On the contrary, we must begin by learning *how to see and respect the visible creation* which mirrors the glory and the perfections of the invisible God.

Visible creation is held in being by the word. But the word Himself has entered into material creation to be its crown and its glory. The divine king has entered in His own creation with a body which is the summit of all created being. The body of Christ is something greater and more wonderful than all the angelic creation, because it is hypostatically united to the word, and St Paul reminds us that we must prefer Him to all the angels.

'Beware lest any man cheat you by philosophy and vain deceit; according to the tradition of men, according to the elements of the world, and not according to Christ. For in Him dwells all the fullness of the Godhead corporeally.' (Col. 2.8–9)

If therefore we seek Jesus, the word, we must be able to see Him in the created things around us—in the hills, the fields, the flowers, the birds and animals that He has created, in the sky and the trees. We must be able to see Him in nature. Nature is no obstacle to our contact with Him, if we know how to use it.

The Church uses material things in her liturgy because she knows that they speak eloquently of God—she uses lights, incense, vestments, music. Above all she uses material things not only as symbols, but as means by which the grace of God is directly applied to our souls in the sacraments.

The word, who was made flesh, continues to make Himself present in His perfect sacrifice, under the consecrated species of bread and wine.

If we are to live as Christians, as members of the incarnate word, we must remember that the life of our senses has also been elevated and sanctified by the grace of Christ—we must learn to use our senses to see and hear and appreciate the sacramental aids to holiness which the Church has given us. Hence the place of art, chant, and so on, as accessories to the liturgy. We must be able to use our *imagination* in reading the Scriptures. We must respond to the living and inanimate beings which all declare the wisdom and glory of God their creator.

We must, first of all, see all material things in the light of the mystery of the incarnation. We must reverence all creation because the word was made flesh.

We can afford to reverence humble and material things, because the Church, the body of Christ, remains in the midst of the world to sanctify it and shed upon all things the power of God's holy blessings. St Paul says: 'Every creature of God is good, and nothing is to be rejected that is accepted with thanksgiving. For it is sanctified by the word of God and prayer.' (1 Tim. 4.4–5)

The monk, a man of prayer, must learn that through his prayers, through the blessing that is spread abroad by the presence of a monastery, the world is sanctified and brought close to God. He must rejoice in the fact that by his hidden union with Christ he enables all things to come closer to their last end, and to give glory to their creator.

The monk must see the monastic community as Christ, living visible and present in the midst of His creation, and blessing all the surrounding country and all the things which the monks touch and use, leading all things to unite with us in praising God through His incarnate son. The material things which surround us are holy because of our bodies, which are sanctified by our souls, which are sanctified by the presence of the indwelling word (cf. St Bernard's sermons on the Dedication of a Church).

The created universe is a temple of God, in which our monastery is as it were the altar, the community is the tabernacle, and Jesus Himself is present in the Community, offering His homage of love and praise to the Father and sanctifying souls and all things.

Hence, in the monastic life, our senses are *educated* and elevated, rather than destroyed. But this education requires discipline. If our eyes are to be the eyes of the 'new man' (Christ) they must no longer look upon things with the desires and prejudices of the 'old man'. They must be purified by faith, hope and love. While mortifying our senses, monastic asceticism gives them a new life in Christ, so that we learn to see, hear, feel, taste, etc., as Christ, and even our senses are then spiritualized.

The Word of the Cross

All that we have said is only an introduction to the real mystery of our monastic vocation. God created the world, and saw that all things were good, for they subsisted in His word. The word was made flesh, and dwelt among us, and we saw the glory of God in Him. But is this all? If it is, then man has only to follow his natural instincts, make use of created things and he will easily and spontaneously find his way to God. But that is not the case. There are many obstacles to the 'spiritualization' of our life. To become 'new men' we have to struggle, fight, and even die.

We are fallen men, and the world has fallen with us. Man and the world were enslaved by the prince of darkness, and plunged into error and sin. Sin made it impossible for man to find his way back to God.

Although God's attributes are plainly visible in creation, man without God has, by his own fault, fallen into darkness and does not know God. 'Although they knew God they did not glorify Him as God or give thanks, but became vain in their reasoning and their senseless minds were darkened, for while professing to be wise they have become fools.' (Rom. 1.21–2)

Everywhere the New Testament puts us on our guard against the folly of a purely human kind of contemplation, and a purely human asceticism, which produce an illusion of holiness and wisdom, but cannot unite us with God or reconcile us with Him. Human ascetic and mystical techniques cannot save us from our sins. They keep us far from God, and take us ever further from Him because their illusion engenders in us a false confidence and pride. They are centred on man, not on God, they tend to glorify man, not God.

St Paul, in Romans, having pointed first to the pagan mysteries and other rites, then to the law and the asceticism of the Jews, exclaims that neither of these can deliver man from sin and reconcile him to God. He quotes the words of the psalms we sing so often, in order to prove it:

Jews and Greeks are all under sin—There is not one just man, there is none who understands; there is none who seeks after God. All have gone astray together, they have become worthless. There is none who does good, no not even one. Their throat is an open sepulchre; with their tongues they have dealt deceitfully. The venom of asps is beneath their lips; their mouth is full of cursing and bitterness. Their feet are swift to shed blood; destruction and misery are in their ways. And the path of peace they have not known. There is no fear of God before their eyes. (Rom. 3.10 ff; cf. Psalms 14, 52, 5, 139, 35 and Isa. 59)

St Paul concludes: 'All have sinned and all have need of the glory of God.' (Rom. 3.23)

The Old Testament tells us everywhere of a world that is displeasing to God, one which He is always on the point of destroying because of its wickedness.

And God seeing that the wickedness of men was great on the earth and that all the thought of their heart was bent upon evil at all times, it repented Him that he had made man on the earth. And being touched inwardly with sorrow of heart, He said: 'I will destroy man whom I have created from the face of the earth, from man even to the beasts, even to the creeping things to the fowls of the air for it repenteth me that I have made them.' (Gen. 6.5–7)

Such words as these give a tremendous urgency to our search for God, for Christ. We seek the incarnate word not only as the creator and exemplar of all things, but far more as the *redeemer*, the saviour of the world. The word was made flesh in order to die on the cross for the sins of mankind, and to reconcile fallen man to God.

The monk must always be conscious of the fact that without Christ, there would be no salvation, no happiness, no joy, because man would be irrevocably cut off from God, the source of all life and joy. He must realize, above all, how utterly useless is human effort to please God, without Christ. Man cannot save himself, no matter how heroic may be his sacrifices, without Christ. But on the contrary once the sacrifice of the cross is seen as our true salvation, then even the smallest act of charity becomes valuable and precious in the sight of God—even a cup of cold water.

The monk must be conscious of the infinite holiness of God, and of the offence which sin offers to that holiness. This consciousness of the holiness of God and of the offence of sin gives us the fear of the Lord which is the beginning of wisdom, and without which we cannot begin to pray as the Church would have us pray because we cannot have a true sense of spiritual realities. But we must at the same time have an unbounded confidence in the cross of Christ.

Here then is our situation—without Christ, we are entirely cut off from God, we have no access to Him, except in rites of natural religion which cannot save our souls of themselves (but we know that by the merits of the passion of Christ God will give His grace to everyone who does what he can to live according to the light of his conscience). *With* and *in* Christ, all our lives are transformed and sanctified, and the smallest acts of love have their value as propitiation for sin.

We need a saviour in whom we will be born again to a new life, and ascend into heaven. God so loved the world that He has given us His Son to be our saviour. The more we appreciate this fact the greater our gratitude and trust, the more will we enter into the knowledge of God in Christ and serve Him with all hearts.

Jesus said—'No one has ascended into heaven except him who has descended from heaven, the son of man who is in heaven. And as Moses lifted up the serpent in the desert, even so must the son of man be lifted up, that those who believe in Him may not perish, but may have life everlasting.' (John 3.13–14)

All men need a saviour, and all have received Him in Christ who has died that all may be saved. 'All are justified freely by His grace through the redemption of Christ Jesus.' (Rom. 3.24)

Whom, then, do we seek in the monastery? Not only God our Father and creator—for even if we seek Him we cannot find Him without Christ. We seek Christ our saviour and redeemer, in Whom we are reconciled to the Father. Or rather, we seek the Father in Him; for as St Paul says:

God was truly in Christ reconciling the world to Himself.

and

Christ died for all in order that all who are alive may live no longer for themselves but for Him who died for them and rose again. (2 Cor. 5.19, 14)

We seek Christ Crucified as our redemption, as our strength, our wisdom, our life in God. (1 Cor. 1.23–4)

We cannot fully understand this if we do not understand the love and compassion of Christ for us in our weakness. It was the Pelagians who saw the cross only as a challenge and an inspiration, not as a power, a source of life and strength. Christ is not just a sublime hero whom we must strive every nerve to imitate—He is a loving saviour who has come down to our level to give us His strength. He willed to identify Himself with our weakness in Gethsemani and on the cross.

We seek Jesus not only as our personal, individual salvation, but as the salvation and the unity of all mankind. The original solidarity of man, on which our perfect happiness and fulfilment depend, was destroyed by sin and man cannot find peace and unity within himself, or in society, until he is reconciled to God in Christ. Christ is our peace, with one another, with ourselves, and with God. Therefore we seek Him as the saviour of the world, as the Prince of Peace, who will restore the unity of mankind in his kingdom of peace.

The redemption which Jesus came to bring, was offered to all by His death on the cross: we receive our redemption by mystically dying together with Him and rising with Him from the dead, 'since one died for all, therefore all died.' (2 Cor. 5.14)

The monk who prays in the fear of God and thanks God for the infinite love with which He has sent His Son to redeem us, realizes not only that Jesus died for him individually, but that He died for the Church. That He loved the Church and came to unite all mankind to God in a unity of spirit to the Father in Himself, 'Christ also loved the Church and delivered Himself up for her, that He might sanctify her in a bath of water by means of the word.' (Eph. 5.25)

This is the 'word of the cross' (or the doctrine of the cross) which is 'foolishness to those who perish, but to those who are saved, that is to us, it is the power of God.' (1 Cor. 1.17)

This doctrine is the heart of our whole life of prayer and penance.

If we understand these things, we will understand the Divine Office, and see what we are praying for. In the Psalms we are constantly contemplating, in mystery, the great reality of our redemption in Christ. We are thanking God for that redemption, we are pleading for the whole Church, and for those who do not know God. We are begging God to forgive sin, and to save those who are immersed in the darkness of sin. We are begging that we may all come to the vision of His glory, and that His Christ may be glorified in us.

More than that, we come to realize that it is Jesus Himself, praying in us, Who continues, in our Divine Office, His work of redeeming the world. The monk is united with Jesus as a saviour, in the Office, and above all in the Mass.

Children of the Resurrection

Christ having died on the cross and risen from the dead, 'dieth now no more'. He sits at the right hand of the Father, and has become for us a 'life-giving spirit'. (1 Cor. 15.45)

Just as Adam, when he came from the hand of the creator, was to be the head of the human race and the principle of natural life, so Christ when He entered into His glory by the resurrection, became the head of a new mankind, joined to Him in one mystical body, and vivified by contact with His sacred humanity which had now become 'life-giving spirit'. That is to say that the humanity of the word reigning in heaven as the 'Christ' or the 'Anointed' of the Father sends into our souls and bodies the divine spirit.

Our monastic life does not consist merely in having Jesus for a saviour whom we thank and adore, while He reigns in heaven or in the Tabernacle—it is a life which is nourished by constant spiritual contact with the glorified humanity of Christ the saviour, who lives in us by His grace and is thus the principle of our supernatural life—'life-giving spirit'.

Our point of contact with the risen saviour is faith in His cross. By faith we submit our minds and hearts entirely to Him and to the power of the divine life of charity. Charity then becomes the principle of a new activity, of the good works by which we serve the living God—we are then 'cleansed from *dead works*'—the things we do have a totally new and spiritual character in Christ. They give glory to God, they build up the Body of Christ, they merit for us an increase in our union with Him who is our holiness.

Contact with the risen humanity of Christ is true holiness. Growth in holiness is growth in our union with the risen Christ. But Christ lives and acts in His Church. Growth in union with the Church, deeper participation in the prayer life of the Church, in her sacramental life, in her other activities, gives us a deeper sharing in the life and mind and prayer of Christ Himself. The life of a monk is immersed in the depths of the Church's life in Christ. The monk is essentially a *vir ecclesiae*.

Our spiritual life is the life of the Spirit of Christ in His Church. It is the life that flows from contact with Christ as 'life-giving spirit'. To have a truly spiritual life is then to think and love and act not just as Christ *would* act in a given situation, but as He precisely *does* act, by His grace, in us, at the moment. It is to live and act with the mind of the Church, which is the mind of Christ.

In other words, our life in Christ is something more than imitation from afar, a moral reproduction in our lives, of a pattern offered by Jesus in the Gospels. We do not simply open a 'Life of Christ' and then by our own power and ingenuity and good will put into effect, humanly, the things which we read. Such efforts are necessary, but unless they are on an entirely supernatural plane they have little fruit for our spirit.

Our life in Christ, our actions in Christ, are those in which Christ, living within us by grace, inspires our thoughts and acts by the movements of His Holy Spirit of love springing up from within the depths of our own souls.

Speaking of this spiritual life as divine wisdom, St Paul points out that we cannot know the things of God unless we receive the spirit of God, who gives us a deep insight into the hidden secrets of the mind and will of God. (1 Cor. 2.9–12) To be thus taught and moved by the Holy Spirit is to have the 'mind of Christ'. (1 Cor. 2.16)

But the wisdom of the Spirit, which gives us the 'mind of Christ,' is entirely opposed to another wisdom, the wisdom of the 'flesh' and of the 'sensual man who does not perceive the things that are of the Spirit of God, for it is foolishness to him and he cannot understand because it is examined spiritually.' (1 Cor. 2.14)

Jesus insisted that we had to be born again to the life of the spirit precisely because: 'It is the spirit that gives life, the flesh profits nothing' (John 6.64). 'That which is born of the flesh is flesh, and that which is born of the spirit is spirit.' (John 3.6) And St Paul adds: 'What a man sows that he will also reap. For he that sows in the flesh from the flesh shall also reap corruption. But he who sows in the spirit from the spirit will reap life everlasting.' (Gal. 5.8)

We are caught in a bitter conflict between the flesh and the spirit. Jesus has delivered us from sin, but not from the weaknesses and concupiscences of the flesh. We have to reproduce in our life the cross of Christ so that having died sacramentally to sin in baptism and penance, we may also put to death sin in our flesh by restraining our evil desires and bad tendencies. This is the basis for our life of monastic asceticism.

Hence our whole monastic life implies an obligation to discipline ourselves and renounce ourselves in order to live in and by the Spirit of Christ. The ascetic life is both negative and positive, and the positive element of Christian asceticism is the more important. St Paul sums up the whole meaning of Christian asceticism with such phrases as these:

Walk in the Spirit and you will not fulfil the lusts of the flesh. (Gal. 5.16)

You see that he first says 'Walk in the Spirit'—the positive side of asceticism—and the negative part follows as a logical consequence, as an immediate effect, 'you will not fulfil the lusts of the flesh'.

They who belong to Christ have crucified their flesh with its passions and desires. If we live by the Spirit, by the Spirit let us also walk. (Gal. 5.24–5)

Therefore, brethren, we are debtors not to the flesh, that we should live according to the flesh, for if you live according to the flesh you will die, but if by the spirit you put to death the deeds of the flesh you shall live. (Rom. 8.12)

Note the expression *'debtors* to the flesh'. The flesh is like a usurer—who gives a little in order to take everything—constantly strengthening his hold on the one in his power, and exacting a more and more servile submission.

Let us consider what St Paul means by the works of the flesh. When the Bible speaks of flesh and spirit, it does not mean to oppose the material element in man to his spiritual element, as if the body were evil and only the soul were good. On the contrary, both terms refer to the whole man, body and soul. The whole man is 'flesh' if his body and his selfish passions dominate his soul. The whole man is 'spirit' if his soul is subject to the Spirit of Christ and his body is subject to the soul. To live 'in the Spirit' therefore does not mean living without a body. It means suffering temptation and trial. It means labour, and all the normal conditions of man's life on earth.

'The inclination of the flesh, which is death' (Rom. 8.5) leads us to all kinds of sin. Not only to sins of sensuality and carnal lust, but also to sins against religion—like witchcraft, magic, superstition, idolatry, and especially to sins against charity, sins which divide us against our brother, like envy, enmities, jealousies, contentions, factions, parties, anger, and even murder. (See Gal. 5.19–21) The works of the flesh which are most stressed by St Paul are those which divide the body of Christ into factions.

'Since there are jealousy and strife among you, are you not carnal and walking as mere men?' (1 Cor. 3.3)

'If you have bitter jealousy and contentions in your hearts, do not glory and be liars against the truth. This is not the wisdom that descends from above, it is earthly, sensual, devilish.' (James 3.14–15)

The Pharisees were ascetics, yet theirs were 'dead works,' they lived 'in the flesh' and were enemies of the cross of Christ.

The action of the Holy Spirit in our lives produces joy and peace, unity with our brethren, and in order to do this the Spirit teaches us obedience and humility. This explains the great importance of these fundamental virtues in the Rule of St Benedict. In studying and keeping the Holy Rule we must realize the function of these virtues is not only to gain merit for our souls and to exercise us in self-discipline, but also and above all *to unite us with Christ in His body the Church*. They are virtues without which we cannot begin to keep His commandment that we 'abide in Him'.

The Benedictine ascesis of silence, obedience, solitude, humility, manual labour, liturgical prayer, is all designed to unite us with the Mystical Christ, with one another in charity, and its aim to bring our souls under the complete dominance of the Holy Spirit. The Benedictine way of humility in the common life is precisely the best way to help us 'walk in the Spirit'. St Benedict himself indicates this (end of ch. 7).

If we follow our monastic lawgiver, we will taste the fruit of the Spirit which is: 'charity, joy, peace, patience, kindness, goodness, faith, modesty, continency'. (Gal. 5.22)

St Benedict in his Rule makes it quite clear that the whole aim of the Benedictine life is to form Christ in us, to enable the Spirit of Christ to carry out, in our lives, actions worthy of Christ. We reproduce His obedience and humility when, like Him, we can truly say: 'I did not come to do my own will, but the will of Him who sent me'. (2nd degree of humility) We reproduce His passion when, like Him, we are made 'obedient unto death' (3rd degree of humility), when we suffer all things patiently and perseveringly for love of Him (4th degree of humility) and when we are, like our divine saviour, reduced to nothing, a 'worm and no man' (7th degree of humility). Having ascended all the degrees of humility, our hearts are empty of self, and God Himself can produce the likeness of Christ in us by the action of His Spirit, who brings joy and consolation in all the aspects of the monastic life: *delectatio virtutum quae Dominus jam in operario suo mundo a vitiis et peccatis, Spiritu Sancto dignabitur demonstrare.* (Rule, c. 7)

Sons and Heirs of God

The positive side of monastic asceticism is always more important than the negative.

What matters most is not so much what we deny ourselves and give up (the flesh), but the new life which develops in us in proportion as we are emptied of self (the life of the Holy Spirit). In any case, we could not carry on the work of emptying ourselves and purifying ourselves unless the Spirit of God helped our weakness. (Rom. 8.29)

When we arrive at the purity of heart which is the fruit of monastic asceticism, of humility and obedience, then the Spirit of God, who has gained possession of our hearts, 'gives testimony to our spirit that we are the sons of God'. (Rom. 8.16) Not only that, but we receive a conviction of the truth that we have entered with Christ, in mystery, into all the good things of God. We are heirs of God and joint-heirs with Christ. (Rom. 8.17) We are sons of God because we are led by the Spirit of God. (Rom. 8.14) And to be led by the Holy Spirit is to live in joy, confidence, exultation and interior liberty, for the spirit of divine sonship is a spirit of freedom. It is not, and cannot be, a spirit of bondage and fear. The spirit of freedom is the spirit of the heavenly Jerusalem, the Church. It is the freedom with which Christ has made us free. (Gal. 4.21–31)

We have a holy obligation to defend this freedom and joy, and to live always in the Spirit, not allowing ourselves to be caught 'under the yoke of slavery' (Gal. 5.1) to the 'elements of this world'. (Col. 2.8) We must not allow ourselves to be enslaved by the flesh in any form—whether sensuality, or licence, or self-love, or disobedience, or purely human forms of religious observance—for example the formalism and vain observance which accompany self-will and pride in our religious life.

If we are sons of God, then the Spirit of God prays in us, and St Paul says this is necessary, for by ourselves 'we do not know what we should pray for as we ought'. (Rom. 8.26)

The prayer of the Holy Spirit in His Church, the prayer that is always sure of reaching the very depths of the heart of God and giving Him infinite glory, is the *Liturgy*. In the liturgy, Christ Himself is present as high priest in the midst of His holy people. The prayer of the Church is the prayer of

Christ. It is the prayer of salvation, sanctification, and redemption.

Pius XII says that in the liturgy 'Through His Spirit in us, Christ entreats the Father' (*Mediator Dei*). He adds: 'In assuming human nature, the divine word introduced into this earthly exile a hymn which is sung in heaven for all eternity. He unites to Himself the whole human race and with it sings this hymn of praise to God' (*Mediator Dei*). At every liturgical function, Jesus the head of the Church is present with His whole mystical body, offering praise to the Father and sanctifying the souls of men.

Therefore it is clear that in the liturgy we find Jesus as our redeemer and sanctifier. But it is above all in the Mass, which is the very heart of the liturgy, that we discover Christ Himself, and ourselves in Him.

The Mass, particularly the Conventual Mass, is the very heart of the monastic life because in it the monastic community and all the persons who go to make it up, unite with Christ the high priest in the very mystery of His great redemptive act which is made present upon the altar. At every Mass Christ is present to us as immolated and risen from the dead, and the Church is immolated and rises with Him. At every Mass, the new life of the Spirit, the life of the sons of God, is renewed in us as we participate in the sacrifice of the divine high priest, the Lamb of God who takes away the sins of the world.

The Mass is the very heart of our monastic sacrifice of ourselves to God. At every Mass and Communion we *live* the very essence of our monastic immolation of ourselves with Christ. At the Consecration we *renew our total surrender to the will of God* in and with Jesus crucified. At Mass we enter into the holy of holies, the sanctuary of heaven, with Him. At Mass, the whole body of Christ stands before the face of the heavenly Father and adores His infinite holiness, makes perfect reparation for all sin, thanks Him for all His gifts and above all thanks Him for His great glory.

In so doing, the Church also petitions Him for mercy and for grace and for all the temporal blessings that we need in order to live as sons of God. Above all, in Communion we are sacramentally united to the risen and glorified saviour, the principle of our life 'in the Spirit'. We are also united to one another more closely in the Spirit of Christ, because by our Communion we grow in charity.

It is in the Mass and the liturgy that we are most truly and perfectly monks, because it is there that we most fully live our life in Christ, finding Him whom we have come to seek, submitting in and with Him to the Father's will.

Now our *manual labour* gives practical expression to our obedience. We see every assignment as the will of God. We put aside our own tastes, our own will and our own opinions and hasten to do the work assigned to us as Jesus Himself hastened to do the will of the Father. We say with Him: 'my meat is to do the will of Him that sent me'.

Also in manual labour we become helpers and co-operators with God the creator and administrator of the world—we become instruments of his divine providence—we help Him change and renew the face of the earth. We are agents and tools of the creator Spirit. Like Adam, we are privileged to be the gardeners of God's creation, and to contemplate God in and through the creatures we work with.

Finally, by our manual labour, we help to feed and clothe ourselves and our brethren and we also contribute to the support of the poor. We are thus not only carrying out the Father's will, in obedience, but in charity we are feeding and clothing Christ who comes to us hungry and naked and poor.

In order to live the liturgy, we must give ourselves to *Lectio Divina* (spiritual reading). Here too, we seek and find Christ. Here as in the liturgy we find Him in His word. 'For the word of God is living and efficient and keener than any two-edged sword, and extending even to the division of soul and spirit, of joints also and of marrow, and a discerner of the thoughts and intentions of the heart.' (Heb. 4.12) In our search for God, we quickly come to realize that He is found in His words, for they alone before the incarnation of the word Himself, could bridge the abyss that separates us from His infinite holiness. The word of God is filled with His infinite creative power: He spoke, and all things were made. His word has power to save our souls: we must purify our hearts in order to 'receive the ingrafted word that is able to save your souls'. (Jas. 1.22)

Hence the need of monastic silence, in order that the monk may be 'swift to hear and slow to speak' (Jas. 1.19) God spoke His eternal word in silence, and He wishes us to receive His words in silence. If we are merely speculative students of Scripture, breaking the words of God up into scientific fragments and deafening our spirit with the noise of human argument—which is too often the noise of the 'flesh' with its spirit of factions and divisions—then we cannot hear the word who speaks to us silently in the words of God.

The monk will always remember that 'He who is of God hears the words of God' (John 8.47) and he is always attuned to the coming of God in His words, since each morning he sings in the invitatory of Vigils (Ps. 94), 'Today if you should hear His voice, harden not your hearts.'

What does the Holy Spirit say to us in our reading of Scripture? He teaches us to see in Scripture the great themes which we have been treating as fundamental in the monastic life—the word made flesh, the divine redeemer uniting to Himself a 'perfect people' living in Him, by His Spirit, and united through Him to the Father. More particularly the Holy Spirit enlightens us, in our reading, to see how *our own lives* are part of these great mysteries—how we are one with Jesus in them. And then the Holy Spirit opens our eyes and attunes our hearts to the future, the consummation of all and the glory of Christ in His Church.

Both in his *Lectio Divina* and in his liturgical praise, the monk prays as an individual and as a member of Christ, listens to God as a person and as a member of the Church. Liturgy demands of us the sacrifice of what is merely individualistic and eccentric in our lives, that we may rise above ourselves to the supra-personal level of the bride of Christ. In the liturgy we must sacrifice and lose something of ourselves in order to find ourselves again on a higher level. But the liturgy can never make us mere automatons praising God like machines. On the contrary, liturgical praise is the *collective interior prayer* of persons who are fully conscious of themselves as members of Christ. There is and can be no contradiction between liturgy and personal prayer. If our liturgical prayer is not also *personal* and *interior*, if it does not spring spontaneously from our own freedom and our own interior spirit, from the inviolable sanctuary of our own deepest will, then it is not a prayer at all. In order that our liturgical prayer may always have this interior and personal quality, we must frequently enter into the inner chamber of our own heart outside the time of choral prayer, and pray to the Father in secret. This is necessary if we are to keep alive the spontaneity and freedom which are the most precious contribution we can bring to the liturgy, and without which our liturgical prayer will be a 'dead work'.

Liturgy, *Lectio Divina*, and private contemplative prayer all work together to deepen our life in Christ, and all have an absolute importance which cannot be replaced. No one of them, by itself, can satisfy all the interior needs and aspirations of the monk's soul. No one of them must ever be allowed to crowd out the others. In all of them the monk seeks and finds Christ, but if he seeks Christ in the liturgy alone, then the liturgy will become formalism. If he seeks Him in private contemplation alone, then his contemplative prayer will become illuminism—or will degenerate into daydreaming or even sleep. If he seeks Him in work alone, he will fall into the sin of activism.

In short, all the monk's prayer life is and must be a life of *prayer in the Spirit*. The Spirit of Christ, while praying in us in the liturgy, 'Reminds us of everything Jesus has said'. The same Spirit who drove Jesus into the desert that He might be tempted by the devil, leads us into the wasteland of interior trial in which our love is tested and purified. Finally, the Spirit of sonship, enables us to experience our union with the Father in the Son, crying out within us 'Abba, Father'. Our prayer life is mature when, in prayer, the Spirit of God, having purified our love and made us obedient and humble, raises us up to God our Father in a spirit of liberty and confidence, because the *experience of His mercy* makes us sure that we are His sons. (Read Rom. 5.1–5)

The whole ascetic life of the monk, in all its aspects both positive and negative, is summed up in his consecration of himself, his whole life, all that he has and all that he is, to God, by his five monastic vows. The life of the monk is the life of the vows. One of the most important of these vows is that of conversion of manners (conversion of life), which is not properly understood if we regard it merely as a special vow to 'tend to perfection'. Conversion of manners means striving to change one's whole life and all one's attitudes from those of the world to those of the cloister. By conversion of manners we definitely consecrate our whole life to the service of God as monks, men who have turned their backs on the world, who have substituted the humility, chastity, poverty, renunciation of the cloister for the ambitions, comforts, pleasures, riches and self-satisfaction of the world. Obedience means the renunciation of our own will, in order to carry out in our whole life the will of another who represents God. Stability means renouncing our freedom to travel about from place to place, and binds us to one monastery until death. Poverty and Chastity are not explicitly mentioned in the Rule of St Benedict because they were considered by him to be included in conversion of manners, but they form an essential part of the monk's obligations.

Spouse of Christ

The monastic life of humility, obedience, liturgical prayer readings, penance, manual labour, contemplation, tends to ever purify the soul of the monk and lead him to intimacy with Christ in that sacred virginity which makes him worthy of marriage with the word of God. This spirit of virginity is the true essence of the contemplative life which is our vocation.

We are not contemplatives by the mere fact of living an enclosed and penitential life. We can indeed be more active, more restless and more distracted in the cloister than we would be in the active life, if we do not possess the interior virginity of spirit, the silence and peace of soul, which enable us to find God in His word, to listen to the words of Christ, to move with the breathings of the Holy Spirit within us.

The virginity of spirit to which we are called is a purity of heart in which our souls preserve their baptismal innocence, or the innocence of the second baptism of our vows, and offer themselves in perfect purity to God. Virginity of soul does not preclude temptations and trials, but the deep spirit of faith which it implies enables us always to rise above the flesh and its storms in order to meditate on the incorruptible beauty of the word. St Augustine defines virginity as: *in carne corruptibili incorruptionis perpetua meditatio* ('In corruptible flesh, perpetual meditation of what is incorruptible'). The life of the virgin soul that is the spouse of Christ is a life lived in the pure, limpid radiance of the word Himself.

Spiritual virginity is not arrived at by violence or strain. The first step is the total acceptance of our self, our whole being, as God has willed us to be—the acceptance of all the parts of our being—body and soul, mind and instinct, emotions and will, in order to give all to God in the harmony of a balanced and spiritualized personality.

The purpose of our monastic vows is to stabilize us in a life of union to the will of God, to keep us unceasingly united to His will in all things until death. The vows therefore protect us in our striving for virginity of spirit. They are one of the great means to that virginity. Chastity preserves us from being tainted by the flesh. Poverty keeps our soul unspoiled by the desire of material possessions or by anxiety about ourselves. Stability makes us renounce the urge to travel and to change our way of life. Obedience protects us from the corruption of self-will. Conversion of manners aims directly at spiritual virginity—by orienting our whole life to God in faith and love—the vow of *conversatio morum* is a vow to live 'in the Spirit'.

The virginity of spirit which keeps us united to the word is the perfection of the monastic life. By it, the monk not only renounces human marriage, but rather lays hands upon the supernatural and mystical reality of which marriage is only an external symbol—the union of love which joins the soul to God 'in one spirit'. Virginity of spirit keeps the soul in constant contact with the holy word of God, the sanctity of God Himself. Above all, sacred virginity makes visible the union of the Church with Christ her divine spouse. Pope Pius XII says:

> The most delicate fruit of virginity is this that virgins make tangible as it were the perfect virginity of their Mother the Church and the sanctity of her intimate union with Christ. . . . The greatest glory of the virgins is undoubtedly to be the living images of the perfect integrity of the union of the Church and her divine spouse. (*Sacra Virginitas*)

This is the end and the perfection of the monastic vocation: to find Christ, the word, to cling to Him in the purity of perfect love and unalterable peace, and to say with the bride in the canticles: 'I found Him whom my soul loveth: I held Him: and I will not let Him go.' (Cant. 3.4) From this it is clear that the whole monastic life is lived in and with Mary the Virgin Mother who has given us the word incarnate. She is the model and the summary of all monastic spirituality, and the Fathers could call her the 'rule of monks'— *Maria regula monachorum*.

A life 'in the Spirit' is then a life of spiritual virginity, in which we are moved not by our own desires, tastes, aptitudes, feelings and nature, but by the will and love of God. In such a life, we are completely conformed to the Virgin Mother of God, who by the perfect simplicity of her faith received into her immaculate heart the full light of the word and, having clothed Him in her virginal flesh, by the action of the Holy Spirit, gave Him to be the saviour of the world.

Hence to live 'in the Spirit' is in effect to live in and by Mary, the bride of the Holy Spirit. Life in the Spirit is a life which she herself has obtained for us and given to us as mediatrix of all grace. The movements of our life in the Spirit are directed by her motherly heart. To acknowledge Mary perfectly as our queen is then to abandon ourselves entirely to the action of the Holy Spirit, who comes to us through her.

If Mary becomes our queen and our 'rule', the inspirations of the Holy Spirit will tend more and more to reproduce in our lives the virginal detachment and the pure love of God which led Mary to submit her whole being entirely to the will of God. We will be led by the Holy Spirit to make our religious consecration a true replica of Mary's *fiat*. We will not only give ourselves to God *aliquo modo* but we will give ourselves *as she did*.

Spiritual virginity therefore implies an emptiness of self, a forgetfulness of self, which can only exist in so far as we renounce all deliberate complacency in anything that is not willed by God—and when doing His will, rest not in the thing we do but in Him for whom we do it.

In this way, we see that spiritual virginity is impossible as long as we remain concerned with ourselves, our plans, our ideas, or even with our ideals—*a fortiori* with persons and objects for their own sakes.

Many souls in religion do good things and lead lives that are more or less virtuous, they avoid faults and strive for perfection, but in all that they do they are motivated more by their own desires and their own will than by the will of God. They think of Him of course, but unconsciously they keep Him in the background. Rather than being *moved by* His will, they do what they think fit and then offer it to Him for His approval. They do not think first and foremost—'What does God want of me?' but rather 'What do I want?' and then they dutifully ask 'Does God permit it? Will He accept it?' Their life is a conscientious effort to do what they want to do, in such a way as to avoid offending God. But this is not virginity of spirit. The virgin spirit is not 'married' to its own will or its own plans. It is free—unattached. It is available. It is expendable. God can come at any moment and find the will empty and free, waiting for His initiative. That is all that matters!

Spiritual virginity is not merely *emptiness* or *absence* of other beings. Here again, the positive aspect of virginity is the more important. Virginity does not consist merely in being free and detached from creatures, but in being *united to God*.

The perfection of spiritual virginity is then the mystical marriage of the soul with the word. Of this marriage, St Bernard says:

> The soul that loves God perfectly is married to Him. What is more delectable than this likeness between the soul and God? What is more to be desired than that charity which brings it about that, not content with the teaching of human masters, thou approachest, O soul, the Word himself, and remainest constantly united to Him, familiarly turning to Him in everything, consulting Him about all that goes on: thy intellect is as capable of knowing Him, now, as thy will is courageous in its desires. . . . This is no mere contract between the soul and the word, it is a perfect union in which the fact of willing and notwilling the same things makes one spirit out of two beings. (Sermo 83 *In Cantica*)

In order to be perfectly what God wants us to be we must be truly ourselves. But in order to be truly ourselves we must find ourselves in Christ—which can only be done if we lose ourselves in Him. This is our great vocation.

Conclusion

The monastic life is a *search for God* and not a mission to accomplish this or that work for souls. The monk fulfils his function in the Church in proportion as he finds God in the peculiar way that God makes possible for Him. Each of us will find God in his own way, but all of us together will find Him by living together in the Spirit, in perfect charity, as members of one another in Christ, recognizing the fact that Christ lives in us both as a community and as individuals. Our vocation is to live by the will of God in prayer and sacrifice that we may become able to see and glorify Christ in His Church and reach perfect union with Him by the action of the Spirit, in the sanctuary of our own souls. Thus we return, through Christ, to the Father of all.

We must never forget that we will not be able to do this unless we have really renounced the past and left the world for the love of God. It is not possible to be a monk and at the same time to live in the monastery in a spirit of compromise, retaining all the comforts and ambitions and concerns that characterize life in the world. Without a true *metanoia*, a true conversion of one's whole life, monastic discipline is an illusion. There must be a total reorientation of our entire being from the love of self to the love of God. The monk cultivates 'contempt' for the world in the sense in which the world is opposed to God. But at the same time, he retains his love for and concern with all those souls redeemed by Christ, who are struggling to find Him and serve Him even in the midst of the world—and above all for those who, loved and sought by Christ, never think of Him and have never, perhaps, heard His holy name.

The Monk in a Changing World

It would be an illusion to think that the monk could live entirely unrelated to the rest of the world. As an individual, it is true, he retains only a minimum of contact with worldly society. He lives in solitude, far from the cities of men. He does not go out to preach or teach. He remains in the cloister contemplating and praising God. Nevertheless, he is inextricably involved in the common sufferings and problems of the society in which he lives. From these sufferings and problems there is and can be no escape. On the contrary, they may perhaps be felt more acutely, because in a more spiritual form, in the cloister. Far from being exempted from service in the battles of his age, the monk, as a soldier of Christ, is appointed to fight these battles on a spiritual, hidden front—in mystery—by prayer and self-sacrifice. He cannot do this unless he is somehow in contact with the rest of the world, somehow identified with the others who suffer outside the cloister walls and for whom he is fighting in his solitude, fighting not against flesh and blood 'but against principalities and powers, against the rulers of the world of this darkness,

and against the spirits of wickedness in the high places.'
(Eph. 6.12)

Hence, though the monk is withdrawn from the world, he
preserves an intimate spiritual contact with those with whom
he is actually or potentially united 'in Christ'—in the Mystery
of our unity in the Risen Saviour, the Son of God. He feels
that he has them all in his heart and that they are in him
and with him as he stands before the throne of God. Their
needs are his own, their interests are his interests, their joys
and sorrows are his, for he has identified himself with them
not only by a realization that they all share one human nature, but above all by the charity of Christ, poured forth in
our hearts by the Holy Spirit who is given to us in Christ.

And so the monk must have some general idea of the
world in which he lives. He will not profit by losing himself
in the maze of political entanglements which is only on the
surface of history. He will perhaps understand the history of
his age better if he knows less of what takes up space on the
front pages of the newspapers. He will have a different, and
perhaps more accurate, perspective.

He must realize clearly that the world of the twentieth
century is in a state of crisis because it is going through a
change more sudden and more profound than anything that
has ever happened before. It is a complete upheaval of the
whole human race, and no one can say with assurance what
will be the final result of this transformation. One thing only
is certain, the world as we know it, society as we know it, will
be even more radically changed in the next fifty years than
they have been in the first half of the century. And this
means that by the end of the twentieth century our society
will be unrecognizable, by the standards of the nineteenth
century and of the ages which preceded it.

In this changing world the Church, against which the
gates of hell shall not prevail, has a permanent place. The
monk, an integral part of the mystical Christ, also has his
permanent place in the changing world of man. And this
means that in some respects the Church and the monastic
Order have to change, since they cannot keep in touch with
the rest of men otherwise. The changes will be superficial and

accidental, external, secondary. The deep hidden essence of
the Christian and monastic life will remain what it always
has been. But secondary attitudes, customs, observances, and
practices, have always changed with the times and will do so
again.

The monk in our world is then faced with a responsibility
towards God, towards himself, and towards the rest of the
world. He must see to it that his monastic life is firmly
rooted in the essential truths of Christianity, that he lives in
the mystery of Christ. Otherwise, if his monastic life and
ideal consist in what is secondary and accidental, all will van-
ish in the process of change. For we repeat it is certain that
the changes through which our world must pass will require
the sacrifice of many secondary and transient aspects of the
Christian and monastic lives. The essentials will emerge necessarily in all the greater clarity and strength after this transformation.

As examples of what is 'accidental' and 'secondary' in the
monastic life, we may include everything which is proper
only to a particular age or nation or culture—for instance the
custom of using Gothic architecture for monastic buildings,
or certain special forms of religious habit or certain fashions
in piety, such as devotion to a particular saint or attachment
to some devout practices which are not universal. Also the
outlook and spirituality of monks may vary, in accidentals,
from age to age.

But in its essentials—solitude, poverty, obedience, silence,
humility, manual labour, prayer and contemplation—monastic
spirituality does not change.

The transformation through which the world must pass
will not be merely political. It is indeed an illusion to think
that the forces which are at work in our modern society are,
above all, political. The great political movements of our
time, so complex and so often apparently so meaningless, are
the smoke screen behind which are developing the evolutions
of a spiritual war too great for men to wage by any human
plan. This is something that is going on in the whole of mankind, and it would go on even if there were no political
movements. The politicians are only the instruments of

forces which they themselves ignore. These forces are more powerful and more spiritual than man.

Behind and beyond the action of created forces, whether human or superhuman, we know that the Supreme Wisdom of God is working inexorably, through all these agents in combat with one another, for a solution that transcends the particularized interests of various groups and sections of mankind. The monk, hidden in the mystery of Christ, should be, of all men, the one most aware of this hidden action of the divine will. This he will surely be if he is a man of sacrifice, pure in heart, a man of prayer.

The monk should not imagine that in a chaotic age like ours his only function is to preserve the ancient attitudes and customs of his Order. These are necessary and valuable indeed in so far as they are vital and fruitful, and help us to live more freely and more consciously in the mystery of Christ. The past should live on, and the monk is indeed a preserver of the past. However, the monastery should be something more than a museum. If the monk *merely* keeps in existence monuments of literature and art and thought that would otherwise decay, he is not what he ought to be. He will decay with what is decaying all around him.

The monk does not, in fact, exist to preserve anything, be it even contemplation or religion itself. His function is not to keep alive in the world the memory of God. God depends on no one to live and act in the world, not even on His monks! On the contrary, the function of the monk in our time is to *keep himself alive by contact with God.*

While all the rest of the world bows down before money, power, and science, the monk spurns worldly expedients and gives himself in poverty, humility and faith to the Almighty. While all the rest of the world adores the machine and engages in a frenzied cult of work for its own sake, the monk, while living by the labour of his hands, remembers that man's highest and most fruitful activity is the spiritual 'work' of contemplation. While the world, enslaved by its own material needs and desires, drives itself mad with anxiety, the monk rises above anguish to dwell in peace in the 'Sabbath' of divine charity.

In our age in which everyone else is carried away with the exigencies of a great cultural and political struggle, the monk has, as his primary function, the duty to *be a monk*—to be a man of God, that is to say a man who lives by and for God alone. Only by doing this can the monk preserve what is rich and vital in his monastic and Christian tradition.

In order to be what he is meant to be, the monk must rise above the common ethical level of humanitarian paganism, and live the 'theological' life centred on God, a life of pure faith, of hope in God's providence, of charity in the Holy Spirit. He must live in the 'mystery of Christ'. He must see that Christ and His Church are one, and he must centre his whole life in this one faith and one direction, to the unity of the one Church of Christ.

In the darkness of the struggle, the monk must cling with all the powers of his soul to the teachings of the Church, to the authority and sanctifying power of the Church. He cannot depend on his own limited vision, or make crucial decisions on the basis of his own judgement. Now above all he must think and act with the Church.

In short—the monk's vocation at all times is to live in, and for, and by Christ. But most especially when the mystery of iniquity works most openly in the world, is it necessary for the monk to dissociate himself from all that is not spiritual and Christian, from all that tends to anything but God, in order to keep alive in the world that spiritual atmosphere without which all that is good and sane in human culture will die of asphyxiation.

In the night of our technological barbarism, monks must be as trees which exist silently in the dark and by their vital presence purify the air.

MONASTIC PEACE

Blessed Are the Peacemakers

Never before have men talked so much about peace, and never has there been so little peace in the world. What was said by the prophet Jeremiah of the men of his time applies even more truly to the men of our own: they have said, 'Peace, Peace', and there is no peace.

We prescribe for one another remedies that will bring us peace of mind, and we are still devoured by anxiety. We evolve plans for disarmament and for the peace of nations, and our plans only change the manner and method of aggression. The rich have everything they want except happiness, and the poor are sacrificed to the unhappiness of the rich. Dictatorships use their secret police to crush millions of men under an intolerable burden of lies, injustice and tyranny, and those who still live in democracies have forgotten how to make good use of their liberty. For liberty is a thing of the spirit, and we are no longer able to live for anything but our bodies. How can we find peace, true peace, if we forget that we are not machines for making and spending money, but spiritual beings and sons of the most high God?

Yet there *is* peace in the world. Where is it to be found? In the hearts of men and women who are wise because they are humble, humble enough to be at peace in the midst of anguish, to accept conflict and insecurity and overcome it with love, because they realize who they are, and therefore possess the freedom that is their true heritage. These are the children of God. We all know them. We do not have to go to monasteries to find them. They are everywhere. They may not spend their time talking about peace, or about God, or about Christ our Lord: but they know peace and they know God, and they have found Christ in the midst of battle.

They have surrendered their minds and their wills to the call of Christ, and in Him they have found reality.

For Christ Himself, as St Paul says, is our peace. He is the cornerstone on which God the Father has built the whole world and all that is real in it. He is the centre of all that exists. He is 'the image of the invisible God begotten before every creature, because in Him were created all creatures in the heavens and on the earth, both visible and invisible . . . all have been created in Him and through Him. He exists prior to all creatures and in Him they are all preserved in being. Further He is the head of the Church . . . for it pleased God the Father that in Him all fullness should dwell, and that through Him God should reconcile to Himself every being, and make peace both on earth and in heaven through His blood shed on the cross.'

When the New Testament speaks of 'the world' it speaks not of God's creation (which God saw from the beginning to be 'very good') but of the division in God's creation brought about by man's spirit of selfishness and dissension. St James describes the spirit of the world as a spirit of 'bitter jealousy and strife'. And St Paul adds: 'As long as there are jealousy and wrangling among you, are you not worldly and behaving in keeping with human standards?' That is why the world cannot give peace to anyone. The world is, by its very essence, struggle, conflict, division, dissension. For there to be peace in the world, men must renounce their selfishness in order to make peace, and we cannot make peace with others unless we are at peace with ourselves. But we cannot be at peace within ourselves unless we are able to make the sacrifices which peace demands. For the spirit of peace is brought into our hearts only by the willingness to renounce our petty selves and find our true selves beyond ourselves in others, and above all in Christ.

Hence Jesus Himself gives us the solution, when He comes to us bringing a 'peace which the world cannot give'. What is this peace? It is not a psychological stunt, not the effect of a few clever slogans, not a technique of self-control. The peace which Christ brings is not a thing, or a practice, or a technique: it is God Himself, in us. It is the Holy Spirit.

The peace which Christ brings is not a formula for individual escape, nor for egotistical self-fulfilment. There can be no peace in the heart of the man who seeks peace for himself alone. To find true peace, peace in Christ, we must desire others to have peace as well as ourselves, and we must be willing to sacrifice something of our own peace and happiness in order that others may have peace, and that others may be happy.

The peace which Christ brings is not the peace of a tyrannical 'order' which is disorder because in it all opposition is merely suppressed, and differences are violently wiped out. Peace does not mean the suppression of all differences, but their coexistence and fruitful collaboration. Peace does not consist in one man, one party, one nation, crushing and dominating everyone else. Peace exists where men who have the power to be enemies are, instead, friends by reason of the sacrifices they have made in order to meet one another on a higher level, where the differences between them are no longer a source of conflict.

All these things need to be said, even in a little book about life in a contemplative monastery. For unless the true meaning of peace is understood, the sense of the monastic life cannot be grasped at all. The monk is before all else a peacemaker. That is to say, he is always, and above all, like all priests and all religious, a servant of Christ, *Rex Pacificus*, the king of peace.

Failure to grasp this essential truth is to misunderstand the whole idea of the religious vocation, and of the Church, and of the Christian faith itself. For the life consecrated to God in religion is a life dedicated to perfect charity, and what is charity but the force which makes peace and manifests visibly in the world the mysterious invisible peace of a God who is charity?

When the Fathers of the Church commented on the words of Genesis, that man was made in the 'image of God', they understood that all mankind was intended to be as it were 'one man' so perfectly united in charity, as to reflect, on earth, the unity of the three divine persons in the one nature which is love itself. This unity, destroyed by selfishness and sin, was restored, objectively speaking by Jesus Christ, the 'new Adam'. Once Christ had risen from the dead, once He had sent the spirit of love and unity into the hearts of His disciples, it became possible again for the unity of divine love to be clearly manifested in the mystical body of those who are one as Christ and His Father are one, in the bond of the spirit of peace.

So, as Jesus said: 'All are to be one, just as you Father are in me and I am in you, so they too are to be one in us'. In the manifestation of this unity, the world must realize that Christ has come forth from the Father because the Father 'so loved the world as to give His only-begotten Son' to heal its wounds and its dissensions and unite it to Himself.

Therefore Christ not only unites to Himself those whom He has chosen and loved, but He makes them the ambassadors of His love and of His peace, peacemakers who are to bring His message of salvation and unity to all men. He says to His Father: 'The glory you have bestowed on me, I have bestowed on them that they may be one as we are one—I in them and you in me. Thus their oneness will be perfected. The world must come to acknowledge that I am your ambassador, and that you love them as you love me.'

All Christians, then, but especially priests and religious, are intended by God to be ambassadors of His love and peacemakers in the world, God wills them to be good Samaritans, bringing salvation to a world bleeding and dying from the wounds inflicted upon it by the robbers who have taken it upon themselves to make not peace but what they call 'history'.

All Christians, then, have as their first duty to be peacemakers, to make peace in their own heart, and to surrender themselves entirely to the Spirit of peace. Then, when they are entirely abandoned to His love, they will serve Him as He pleases and go wherever He sends them. They will hear, at all times, the voice of the Good Shepherd and the Prince of Peace, Who has pity on the multitudes who are as sheep without a shepherd. They will help Him to bring together the sheep which have been dispersed in the storms of this world, so that in the end there may be one fold and one shepherd.

There are many different ways in which a Christian can be a peacemaker. First of all, the most common and ordinary way, is the vocation to sanctity in the Christian family. Peace is the very essence of life of the home, and one reason why there is so little peace on the national level is that there is so little peace in families. The lay Christian should be, by rights, a lay apostle. He should build peace in his home, but he should spread peace in the community in which he lives and dedicate himself, as far as possible, to the cause of peace and order in his nation.

Then there are those called to the priesthood and to the apostolic life, whether as a religious or in the diocesan clergy. These all bring Christ to men in their words and their example, and above all in the sacraments which produce the peace and grace which they symbolize and unite us more closely to God and to one another in the spirit of Christ.

Finally, the contemplative life, by the very fact of its retirement from the world, and its withdrawal from direct participation in the struggles of the world, fights for peace on a higher and more spiritual level. The contemplative builds, in his monastery, a spiritual Jerusalem which is the image of the city of God in heaven. The presence of this 'city of spiritual peace' rising invisible in the hearts of men dedicated to God in the desert keeps alive on earth the essence of that peace which Christ brought to His Church. The contemplative builds, in his monastery, the perfect 'form' of the mystical body, a pattern to the rest of the Church. For it is the precise function of the contemplative monastery to be, in itself, a complete little 'Church', a self-contained 'mystical body' which manifests, to the rest of Christendom, the realization, on a small scale, of that which we all seek: unity in charity and peace, the communion of saints in the glorification of the Triune God. The monastery remains in the world, but not of the world, as a vision of peace, a window opening on the perspectives of an utterly different realm, a new creation, an earthly paradise in which God once again dwells with men and is almost visibly their God, their peace and their consolation.

Of course, the monastic community could not perfectly achieve this end if it were to remain too conscious of itself. The monastic Church does indeed offer the witness of sublime edification before the rest of the world. But the monk himself, to live in all truth as a man of peace, must forget himself and his potentialities for 'edification'. He must lose himself in God, in his community, and its prayer, and its work; he must lose himself in the simplicity of his own pure and transparent soul. He must forget that there is anything admirable in himself or in his monastery. He must do this, motivated not by a false and forced humility, but by the true humility which is reality itself speaking its own incontrovertible truth at all times in the depths of his own soul: a reality which, by reminding him of his own nothingness and of his own greatness at the same time, teaches him to find peace not in his own imagined strength or talent or virtue, but solely in the everlasting mercy of God.

These are perhaps 'deep' thoughts. But they are essentially simple. And above all it is necessary to begin with some such thoughts as these. They alone can keep everything in the right perspective. It is vain and absurd merely to retail the observances and customs of monks, and worse still to dramatize their essentially undramatic solitude, in order to arouse the curiosity or admiration of the world. Such talk would be contrary to the very spirit of the monastic vocation which loses all its justification as soon as the attention of men is drawn to the monks themselves, instead of being led, beyond them, to God.

Action and Contemplation

The monk is important more for what he *is* than for what he *does*. This is true, in fact, of every Christian. 'Being' always takes precedence over 'doing' and 'having'. We must first be sons of the heavenly Father. At least we must strive 'to be perfect as our heavenly Father is perfect'. Our works follow from this. We strive to do as He does, to love all men as He loves them. So by the fruits of charity our divine sonship will be known to men. The main thing, however, is not that our sonship should be recognized, but that we should *be* sons of God. Recognition is not important.

While in other vocations one may be called to execute this or that work in the Church—to preach, to teach, to nurse the sick, to feed the hungry—the monk is *not called to any particular work.* This must be properly understood. Too often the monastic life is contrasted with other lives on the basis of what the monk *does not* do. This comparison is false and misleading. It is not true to say that because the monk is not called to teach in school or nurse the sick, that he is therefore not called to perform works of charity and mercy. On the contrary, the mere fact that he is not bound to any *specific* enterprise, any *particular* project, means that the monk is called to *all* the works of charity at once, in a fuller and more eminent sense.

Instead of binding himself to do a particular and limited job, the monk leaves himself free for all charity, for the full, completely integrated life of the Gospel. This does not mean, of course, that the monk tries to practise all the counsels of charity at once (which would be impossible, since many of the counsels like almsgiving and poverty, are mutually exclusive). But the monk becomes a member of a little 'mystical body', the monastic community, which itself in one way or another carries out all the counsels. For although the monk himself possesses nothing, yet the products of his labour enable the monastery to give alms and to feed the poor. Although the individual monk may not practise hospitality, the monastery does so. The monastery gives the poor a share in the fruits of its labour. And though the members of the community may not preach to the faithful, the community itself does so in many ways, most of all by its example and by the eloquence of its worship.

The monk's great work is then to be a monk. But to be a monk he must live a life of perfect charity with his brethren in the cloister, all day long sharing the burdens and joys, the sorrows and rewards, the labours and the adoration of his monastic 'Church'. The monastic life is designed in such a way that all day long each member of the community must reproduce in his conduct and in his heart, the humility and obedience, the prayer and mercy, the wisdom and meekness of Christ. By doing this he and his brethren form 'one Person'—the mystical Christ—who carries out every kind of work of charity, in regard to those who come into contact with the monastic community from the outside. The monk's job is to collaborate with his brothers in forming 'one Person'—the mystical Christ, the monastic community.

In other words, it would be grossly misleading to say that in the active life, religious preach, teach and so on, while in the monastic or contemplative life they have no special work to do, except to pray.

This false contrast generates a kind of guilt complex which prompts monks to distort the true concept of the divine office so that the choral prayer is regarded as the 'special work' for which the monk has been called to the monastery, and to which he is directly assigned by the Church. This is a misunderstanding, because in fact the Benedictine monastery is not comparable to a monastery of an active congregation devoted to teaching. The brother who is called to carry out the work of teaching is called to do a precisely defined and well specified job. But the monk is not called to a *particular* task, as we have said above. He is called to *be a monk*, above and beyond particular and limited tasks. He is called to live in God, to sound the ultimate depths of his divine sonship, to be in all things a living member of a community which by its peace and unity fully represents Christ. If he narrows his horizons and fixes his gaze upon one particular function which he performs, and makes that function the proximate end for which he has come to the monastery, then he will be hampered and obstructed in carrying out his real 'job' which is to *be* what he is called—a man of God. Instead of simply 'being a monk' and praising God with all his heart, he will unconsciously centre his attention on the divine office as a 'performance'. This is a mistake. It ends inevitably in a more or less secular agitation and in inordinate concern with results and even with human applause. Certainly the monk will love his office more than anything *else* except the Mass—but that still does not mean that he exists 'for the sake of' his office. No, the office is only a part of an entire life of love lived 'for the sake of' love itself, that is to say lived for God. The office was made for the monk, not the monk for the office. He has not just come to the monastery precisely in order to praise God in choir and nothing else: but he praises God all the more freely and all the more fully because he is, in fact, in the monastery and because he is filled with unutterable gratitude to the mercy of God who has brought him there. If he keeps his eyes on God, the monk's adoration will be all the more pure—and more edifying besides.

The so called 'contemplative life' is not always too well understood even by those who are living it. To begin with, it is misleading to call the monastic life contemplative without further qualification.

The use of such a term is of course juridically correct. Church law distinguishes those Orders which are strictly enclosed and have no external or parochial ministry, from those others whose members engage, officially, in the 'active' or the 'apostolic' life. But the mere fact that one lives on the inside of a monastic enclosure does not make a man a 'contemplative'. We never find the word 'contemplation' in the Rule of St Benedict, and we shall see that this can be explained very simply by the fact that St Benedict was legislating for what, *in his time*, was called the 'active life'.

The Fathers of the Church used the term 'active life' (*bios praktikos*) for the life of ascetic purification and the practice of virtue which leads to the pacification of our passions and brings them under the control of the spirit. In fact, the whole function of the active life, in this sense, is to liberate a man from attachment to the things of the world, to deliver him from the confusion of a life subject to sin, and to place him in a state of peace and interior purity (*apatheia*) which disposes his soul for contemplation. Of course, if St Benedict legislates for beginners in terms of the 'active', or ascetic life, it is with a view to contemplation later on. The main point is that for St Benedict *both action and contemplation are necessary in the monastic life*. Both go together. As St Bernard

says, 'Martha and Mary are sisters and they must live together in peace in the same house'.

It should be clear from this that one does not enter a
contemplative monastery without embracing a great deal of
rather laborious activity. The postulant who expects that he
will be given a cell and a book, and will be left alone to 'contemplate' all day long is in for a rude awakening. He will find
the life extraordinarily busy. Indeed, it is a common problem
of monastic superiors and legislators to see that the life does
not sometimes become too busy, and that the individual
monk, in a fervour of misguided zeal, does not come to neglect the time allotted to reading and meditation and restful
absorption in God.

At the same time, there is another error to be avoided: it
consists in thinking that the monastic life of penance is a life
of numerous penitential practices. Here again, the emphasis
would be on 'doing' rather than on 'being'. The monk is certainly and essentially a penitent. And one cannot be a penitent
without 'doing' penance. But one may lose the monastic
spirit if he materializes his inner conversion to the point of
complicating everything with penitential devices.

The true penance of the monk is essentially and above all
in his monastic 'conversion of manners', the constant and
ceaseless effort to make himself over, by God's grace, from a
rugged and selfish individualist into a charitable and loving
member of Christ. This is a life work which cannot succeed
if the monk ignores the great monastic means, which are obedience and humility and charity and simplicity; in a word,
the renunciation of one's own ideas and interests for the
benefit of others. ('Let no monk follow what he judges useful
primarily to himself, but rather what is to the advantage of
others' says St Benedict in the Rule.)

Benedictine penance is serious and uncompromising, but it
always presupposes Benedict's own spirit of moderation,
simplicity and reserve. The monk will avoid every exaggeration that diverts his gaze from his real task in the monastery: his surrender to Christ by obedience, humility and
charity.

St Benedict practically defines a monk as one who 'seeks

God'. And this too must be properly understood. We all tend to be pagans at heart, and this blinds us to the true meaning of our Christian faith. There is a very great difference between seeking God as Christians, or as unconscious pagans. The pagan has no Christ, no Holy Spirit, perhaps even no personal God at all. He has to struggle upward to union with the 'Supreme Being'—the 'Absolute'—by sheer force of his own will and by his own fortitude, relying on his own battery of religious practices. His task is one of almost unbelievable difficulty—and this explains why pagan religions are all shot through with compromise and despair. Few men are able seriously to undertake the awful business of becoming, say, a yogi. Besides, with all the subtlety and heroism of the purest techniques of natural religion—what does man finally encounter? Not God—only himself. His purified, inner spiritual self, if you like, but still it is only himself.

St Paul tells us a very different story. 'Do not say in your heart, who shall ascend to heaven, (that is to bring Christ down); or who shall descend into the abyss (that is to bring Christ up from the dead). But what does the Scripture say? The message is near you, on your lips and in your heart, (that is the message of faith which we preach).'

Christian sanctity is not a Promethean exploit. We do not have to storm the walls of heaven and bring down the fire of God, we do not have to raid His treasure rooms in order to obtain the good things He has reserved for us. Prometheus was a hero in a myth which expressed the ultimate despair of all the pagan religions. But Christ really descended from heaven, taking on our flesh, reuniting the human race in Himself, giving all men light in His light, sending us His Spirit to unite us to the Father. Seeing that we would never come to Him, God has come to us. Seeing that we could never attain to Him, He surrendered Himself to us. Seeing that we could never, by our own powers, gain a right idea of his true nature. He has revealed Himself to us, and He has shown us how to comprehend Him not by knowing, but by loving. These are secrets which God alone could reveal to us, and He has done so by giving us Himself.

Consequently the Christian monk does not come to the

monastery to *acquire* something new and esoteric that no one else can have or appreciate. He does not come to excel all lesser men by his hidden knowledge and mysterious inner perfection. All this would be only a kind of self-exaltation which, as St Benedict points out, would lead him far from God and ruin him in the abyss of his own pride. The monk is just an ordinary Christian who lives, in the monastery, the ordinary Christian life: but he lives it in all its perfection. He lives it to the full. He puts aside everything else, he forgets every other concern, in order to *be* a Christian.

To be a Christian means to possess God and everything else in Christ. Hence the monk does not come to the monastery to 'get' something which the ordinary Christian cannot have. On the contrary, he comes there in order to realize and to appreciate all that any good Christian already has. He comes to live his Christian life, and thus to appreciate to the full his heritage as a son of God. He comes in order that he might see and understand that *he already possesses everything*.

This is the true secret of the monastic life. This is what it means 'to be a monk'. It means really to know Christ living in us, to know the Father, in the Son, through the Holy Spirit. To know that the three divine persons dwell in us all, to taste the ineffable wonder of that mutual surrender in which God gives Himself more fully to us by inducing us to abandon ourselves to Him. The true contemplative life is then simply a deep penetration and understanding of the ordinary Christian life which, for all that we call it 'ordinary' is the most wonderful of all miracles: God Himself living in us!

This throws a new light on the concept of seeking God. Many beginners in the monastic life are disturbed and anxious, indeed they upset their whole spiritual life, by struggling to grasp and to 'feel' God, as if they did not already possess Him invisibly in their hearts. Indeed, a monk who flings himself into a wild pagan conquest of the Absolute can end by driving God from his heart by the sheer violence of his own misguided efforts. We cannot know God except by becoming 'little ones'—little enough to grasp the wonder of the fact that He has done everything in giving Himself to us, and that only one thing remains for us—to thank Him and appreciate what He has done. This is the one thing necessary.

To do this one thing is to seek God and to find Him at the same time. Such is the key to the monastic life. For to 'do' this one thing, which is the whole object of the monastic vocation, one has to lay aside all the other 'doings' with which men are so mightily preoccupied—one must be humble enough to get along without such a lot of 'doing' and simply 'be' a son that is loved by the heavenly Father.

Until one has made this discovery, he cannot really begin to be a monk.

The School of Charity

Our Lord has told us that He came into the world that we might have life. And He also said that eternal life is the knowledge of God and of Jesus Christ, sent by the Father. Finally, through St John the Apostle, He tells us that: 'Everyone that loves is a child of God and knows God. He who has no love does not know God, because God is love. . . . No one has ever seen God, yet if we love one another, God abides in us and our love for Him reaches perfection'. The whole meaning of man's spiritual life is to be sought in love. But fallen man is born with his gaze centred upon himself. He is oriented away from God and away from love. To be born selfish is not an irreparable tragedy and indeed our sinfulness can be turned to great good, by the grace of God, if we will change our selfishness into love. But we cannot do this without the help of God Himself, and of other men.

The same apostle of Christ who tells us that God is love, and that love is the way to know Him, also tells us that there is no love in the 'world' (in the sense in which it is alienated from God) because the spirit of the world is opposed to the Spirit of God, and the children of the world cannot receive the Spirit of God or know Him unless their lives are transformed from within. When this transformation takes place, they are no longer children of this world but sons of God.

One who loves God may indeed remain in the world, but he must never be 'of the world'. However, those who wish to study and practise the purity of love, and learn the full meaning of love, have found a more excellent way. They form a Christian community in solitude, in the 'desert', isolated from the overwhelming confusion which 'the world' radiates in every direction. And there, under special conditions, they learn to love one another and worship God. When their weakness has been strengthened, when they have become perfect in love, then they may be strong enough to go out and meet the selfishness of the world, and overcome evil with good. Or perhaps they will simply continue to practise charity within the confines of their monastic community, and let the community itself speak out God's message, in the mystery of a fraternal unity and worship which bears witness to the presence of the risen Christ.

In any case, the monastery is a school of charity, in which men learn love, not out of books but in the book of life itself, which is the heart of the saviour, Jesus Christ. This is a living book, written not on sheets of paper but in God Himself, and reproduced in the hearts of men purified and moved by the Holy Spirit. The science of the saints, which is the main object of study in the monastery, is not learned in words but in deeds; it is not fully possessed by one who does not live it. To learn this love is to live by love and to say with St Paul: 'For me to live is Christ.'

St Benedict lays down the basic requirements which we must follow in order to learn the love of God. The monastery, he says, is a school of divine service in which nothing at all is to be preferred to the love of Jesus Christ. But the first sign of a soul that loves Christ is obedience without delay.

To seek God means to renounce your own will. It means giving up attachment to your own ideas in order to live by faith, and travel the narrow path of self-denial. These are not mere words. Faith is the central 'existential' reality of the monk's life. Faith is not just a matter of psychological experience. It puts the monk in contact with the theological bedrock without which his structure of charity is doomed to fall under the onslaught of the first storm.

Without faith and deep spiritual principles, without an entirely supernatural sense of obedience which sees the will of God in the Rule, in the will of the superiors, and in the 'common will' of the brethren, love will be nothing but shallow sentimentality of self-indulgent illusion.

Faith alone can provide sufficiently strong motives to make the sacrifices that love demands: for love is a matter of giving, not of getting. Love seeks its highest reward in its own gift of itself, and as long as it bends back upon itself to enjoy any other recompense, it tends to destroy its own being and return to nothingness.

Love is nourished by an inexhaustible source hidden in the mystery of God Himself—a source which we represent to ourselves in the dogma of the three divine persons in one nature. But faith alone can put our hearts in contact with this source of living waters. Faith alone can make the everlasting love of the triune God, one in three, transform the desert of our soul into a paradise of joy where wisdom dwells.

St Benedict, following the tradition of the monks of the East, proposed to his followers a life in which everything is nourished by faith and every action bears fruit in the growth of love. The first word of the Rule opens our ears to the inward promptings of the Holy Spirit: '*Ausculta!*—Listen, my son, to the precepts of the master!' Who is the master? The Gospels tell us: 'One is your master, Christ' and St Benedict himself adds, 'he that hath ears to hear, let him hear what the Spirit says to the Churches'. The whole Benedictine life is a life of faith in the word of God, received into the faithful heart like the seed in good ground, to bring forth fruit in patience.

Let us quote the closing words of St Benedict's prologue:

Therefore must we establish a school of the Lord's service; in founding which we hope to ordain nothing that is harsh and burdensome. But if, for good reason, for the amendment of evil habit or the preservation of charity, there be some strictness of discipline do not at once be dismayed and run away from the way of salvation, of which the entrance must needs be narrow. But as we progress in our monastic life and in faith, our hearts shall be enlarged and we shall run with unspeakable sweetness of love in the way of God's commandments; so that, never abandoning His rule but persevering in His teaching in the monastery until death, we shall share by patience the sufferings of Christ, that we may deserve to be partakers of His Kingdom, Amen.

St Bernard of Clairvaux expanded and implemented the thought of St Benedict when he called the monastery a school of charity. The main object of monastic discipline, according to St Bernard, was to restore man's nature created in the image and likeness of God, that is to say created for love and for self-surrender.

Readers who have been brought up on a more recent vintage of spirituality may be surprised at St Bernard's declaration that monastic discipline is in favour of human nature rather than against it. St Bernard never regards human nature as evil, or as the source of evil. On the contrary, what is made by God in His own image and likeness must necessarily be a great good, and the saint declares that it is a real evil for men to ignore the good that is in themselves. Indeed, this ignorance of the good that is within us leads us into every sin, makes us resemble the beasts rather than God.

Ignorance plunges us ultimately into despair. Our first task then is to know ourselves—to know the good that is in us, to know God's love for us, so that we may reply to Him with the love of our own hearts and love Him 'without measure'. But at the same time we must be realistic. The divine image in us has been disfigured and mutilated by sin. What is this divine image? Our liberty, that is to say the capacity to commit ourselves, to give ourselves, to surrender ourselves, to pay the supreme homage of our inmost being to what we have chosen as our good. One can see that in our liberty is hidden supreme power for good as well as for evil. We can dedicate our lives, in love, either to truth or to falsity, to good or to evil. We can give ourselves to God or to mammon His enemy. We can surrender to Him who is, or we can cast ourselves away with one who is not, who is only the shadow and the negation and the denial of what is.

However sober the Fathers of the Church may be in the presence of the tragic reality of sin, they are always optimistic. Christianity is, after all, a religion of hope. The great reality is not man's wickedness but the mercy and goodness of God. And God has stamped our very nature itself with the seal of His goodness. The divine image should always remind us that we were created by God to be His sons, and if we are far from the house of our Father, He remains our Father and He is awaiting our return. Indeed, He has given His own Son to be our 'way' back to our true home.

Man was created by God to love Him, and every one who is born into the world is born with a free will, capable of loving God. But because of original sin, this liberty is turned away from God and biased, from the beginning, in the direction of nothingness. We are born fully disposed to cast ourselves into the abyss, all the more so because the surface of the abyss is covered with a shimmering and attractive mirage in which we think we see all good things. This mirage, created by our sensuality, is the selfish love of creatures for their own sake.

Now the created world is not evil or illusory: all things that have come from the hand of God are good because they bear the stamp of His reality and of His love. It is our love for created things as ends in themselves that is evil and illusion. And if we follow the mirage of this deceptive love, we end in everlasting death: the death of a spirit that hungers for reality and has dedicated all its undying love to an unreal shadow!

For St Bernard, the function of the monastery is to liberate man's love from this disastrous illusion and reorientate it to the one true good, which is God Himself. The beginning of this reorientation and healing of our wounded nature is to be sought in ascetic discipline, in the fasts, labours, austerities and privations of the monastic life.

By means of these things we curb our sensuality. And unless our sensuality is brought under control, we can never master the insidious rebellions of our own will. Failure to control our own will means that we do not have possession of ourselves and therefore cannot give ourselves to God. If mortification of the senses is important in monastic discipline, far more important is the mortification of our own will by obedience. As St Benedict points out, it is quite possible to practise severe asceticism without any other result than a growth in pride. What really matters is not to starve our flesh but to starve our own self-will.

As St Bernard says: our self-will has led us so often into sin, that it would be tragic if we continued to follow it as our guide when we have entered the monastery. The monk, therefore, as an act of pure faith, surrenders his life into the hands of God, and lets God henceforth guide and direct him *through His human representatives*, so that he learns to seek not his own good but the good of others.

Monastic discipline gives the monk mastery over his own liberty, so that he is at last capable of a full and spontaneous self-surrender to his perfect good, which is charity.

In other terms, monastic discipline places our wills under the sign and the guidance of the Holy Spirit, so that we become able to love with the freedom of the sons of God.

Discipline however is only the beginning. The more crucial and more significant step in the conversion of a worldling into a saint, is on the level of '*natura*' where we learn to love others as we love ourselves, to identify ourselves and our interests with others, to become one with others, to become, in a word, co-members of Christ with our brethren.

When this level is perfectly attained, selfishness is transcended, the monk no longer considers his own private interests in opposition to those of others, for the interests of the monastic community have become his own, and his own are the interests of the community. Note that this is not the submersion of a personality in the social whole (St Bernard had nothing in common with modern totalitarians!) but the emancipation of the person through his full and mature participation in the common life by self-oblation.

At this point it is well to sound a note of warning. This transformation and elevation of the person in the community is neither easy nor automatic. The mere fact of living in a monastic community and keeping a monastic rule does not suffice of itself to bring about this change. There are other forces at work—forces of inertia and death which, due to the inevitable frailty of man and of his institutions, can work in the best of monasteries and in the best of souls.

Every member of the community, from the Abbot on down, is responsible for the vitality and dynamism of the Rule and the common life. In communities where the Rule is observed without comprehension and without spirit, even though the observance may be sufficiently exact, its very exactitude does harm to souls rather than good. The sense of integration is lost, and the community dispenses its efforts in a series of unrelated and futile pursuits that have very little spiritual value. There follows a general lassitude and disgust in many souls, the community is divided by petty hostilities, and the true spirit of charity evaporates. In such an atmosphere, a real spiritual life becomes difficult even for strong souls, and the weak are simply broken by the strain.

In order to be transformed and elevated by community life, one must have the strength of soul to rise consistently above mere automatism and routine. One cannot drift into spiritual perfection. The man who merely drifts, in a monastic community, becomes a passive misfit. One must apply himself with fervour and determination to the life of charity and prayer. One must accept frankly and fully the difficulties of common life. The monk who conceals real interior resentment of his brethren and superiors under a front of passive conformity runs a serious risk: he faces a conflict in which his own spirit may be utterly broken. And if, after this, he resigns himself to a kind of inert and despondent indifference, his life will have been practically ruined. He may survive and save his soul, but in the end he will be forced to admit that he would have been better off outside the monastery.

At the same time, the community life is impossible without struggle and without at least occasional bursts of strongly felt repugnance. Such things must be felt. There is a great difference between *feeling* them and *willing* them. There is no serious danger in an emotional repugnance that leads us to face the truth about ourselves, and shows us where sacrifice really needs to be made.

The man who 'fits in' without the slightest difficulty is probably incapable of a really deep transformation. In any case, it is hard to see how one can give himself to God in a strict monastic community without a salutary interior rending of heart which prepares the way for the healing work of the spirit of God.

Liberated by the final self-surrender, the soul of the monk comes to live by love alone, loving because love is its life and its joy. *Amo quia amo*, cried St Bernard: 'I love because I love,' and love itself is sufficient reason for loving. God wills to bring us to this purity of heart which consummates our union with Him because He knows that love itself is blessedness. It is the infinite beatitude which He Himself finds in His own divine nature.

Charity is not fully explained when it is defined as 'a virtue by which we love'. In the mystery of our friendship with God, charity is also a love by which we are loved. It is the fruit of God's dynamic action in our souls. It is the effect of His love for us. Whoever loves can say, without doubt that he is loved. And whoever desires to love, loves. And so he is loved. God only loves us in order to love in us—for it is by loving in us that He unites us to Himself. Hence the whole of life is our surrender to God's action which makes us love in union with His Spirit: 'the charity of God is poured forth in our hearts by His Spirit, who is given to us'.

Charity and grace are two aspects of the same thing: divine love. Grace is the love by which God causes us to love Him, and charity is the love which He causes in us. Both are the effect of His spiritual presence within us as the saviour and Sanctifier and lover of our souls.

In the writings of the Fathers of the Church no clear distinction is made between the virtue of charity and the entitative habit which we call sanctifying grace. The term 'charity' tends to cover both indiscriminately.

This great reality, which we can simply call 'love', is the whole life of the monk, as it is the whole life of every Christian. God in us, loving and sanctifying our hearts, uniting us to Himself and to our brethren by His own Holy Spirit of love, this is the 'spiritual life', the life of grace. And since the monk abandons all else in order to plunge into this life with God, it is necessary that we examine a little more closely the concepts of charity and grace which go to make up the one great reality of the monk's existence: his friendship with God.

We have said that the monk is important more for what he is than for what he does. The reader may have felt a vague irritation at the fact that we did not immediately define what the monk *is*. He is a friend of God, a man of God, one who lives in God and for God alone. By this we mean, he is one for whom charity is his whole life, and for whom every action is another step toward living in closer intimacy with the indwelling Spirit of God.

This is what we mean in this context, when we speak of loving 'God alone'. It should be quite clear that living for 'God alone' in this sense by no means excludes the love of other men. On the contrary, the quotation we took from St John the Evangelist above shows conclusively that if the monk does not love his brethren and all men, he is not 'living for God alone'.

The opposite extreme from the love of God alone, is the love of ourselves alone. In between there are varying degrees of love, in which our love extends to a few, to many, or to all, and gives itself to them with a more intensive and disinterested purity. The man who loves God alone loves all men in God and for God. He does not have to leave Him to find them in Him, and his love for them is no distraction from his love for God. Indeed, it is by loving them that he has ascended to the love of God alone, in which ascent he has not left them behind but brought them with him—and they, in their ascent, have brought him with them. For all have ascended together and St Augustine would see, in them, only 'one Christ loving Himself'.

The whole life of the monk is then to grow in grace and in the friendship of God. Now when we speak of 'growing in grace' and 'becoming perfect in charity' we must be careful not to be misled by the language of spiritual writers, and take too materialistic a view of 'grace'. We are so accustomed to talking about 'the state of grace' and 'degrees of grace' that we come to imagine that grace is some kind of 'thing' or commodity, like oxygen or gasoline.

We are almost in the habit of treating grace as something that fills up a tank in our soul and keeps us going like supernatural fuel. We even go so far as to imagine the possibility of measuring the 'amount' of this precious commodity we have stored up.

It is folly to think of grace in terms of 'supply', as if it were a material commodity that we could pile up and preserve for ourselves. It is of course correct to speak of different levels of merit—as long as we do not delude ourselves that we know precisely what we are talking about. Merit and grace are definitely not susceptible of real quantitative measurement, because they do not come in various 'amounts'. Grace is simply the intensity and vitality of our life in God. It is a special quality of soul resulting from the radiation of the divine life in us, and from the presence of God in us.

Now when God gives Himself initially, He gives Himself totally, and in that sense He does not become 'more present' later on. But our growth in grace is a growth in our own supernatural participation in His presence and life within us. It is a purer and more intimate union with Him, not psychological but mystical and spiritual. It has nothing essential to do with our feelings, nor even anything essential to do with our external works, still less with any external appearances.

The soul that is most closely united to God is the one to whom He has been pleased to give Himself the most, to make Himself the most present, to illuminate with His greatest love. No one really knows on earth who these souls are. There may indeed be certain external signs of growth in grace, but who can interpret these signs correctly? Many of the saints appeared to the men around them to be great sinners, and many deluded or even wicked men have been held for saints. Christ our Lord, the saint of saints, was criticized as a drunkard and glutton by the holy men of Israel and He was finally put to death by them as a blasphemer because He called Himself the Son of God. . . . And yet He was the 'only-begotton Son of the Father, full of grace and truth'.

What, then, can we finally say of the mystery of grace? It is simply the embrace by which God takes us to Himself, in His Holy Spirit. It is our divine sonship in Christ. All grace reaches us in and through Christ as head of the Church. To possess grace is to be possessed by God. *Habere est haberi.* Active charity is the response of our wills to this embrace of God, returning to Him the love in which He has given us Himself, surrendering ourselves to His Spirit who has surrendered Himself to us. Grace and charity are two aspects of the same reality: God living in us.

This is the 'existence' of the monk—this mystery of grace and love, of secret and mutual exchange between the invisible spirit of man and the transcendent Spirit of God. We must never forget that it is a mystery full of awe—*a mysterium tremendum*. A certain glib facility in the use of theological catchwords must never distract us from the unknown and unknowable reality which they so feebly strive to express. God cannot be contained in a concept, neither can His 'grace', and indeed our own soul remains a mystery to us.

This mystery of grace is the bright cloud with which God overshadows His tabernacle, which is the intimate centre of our own being. We must be careful not to desecrate the sanctuary by setting up our own idols—our own concepts and images—in the place of God. One of the main functions of the monastic life is to keep the inner temple of the soul clear of all idols, so that the mystery of God and His presence may ever be adored in the sacred silence in which alone He can be 'heard' by our spiritual senses.

The monastic life is so designed that everything in it contributes to the monk's growth in intimate friendship with God. That is why the monk is first of all a man of *prayer*.

Wherever there is grace, the soul inevitably responds at least from time to time with an obscure desire for awareness and communion. In the monastery, distractions are set aside, absorbing occupations are kept at a minimum, and the monk is left free to respond to God's call to intimate communion in the secrecy of his own soul.

The first essential of a true life of prayer is *freedom*. It is very important to remember this. The fact that the Rule marks out very precisely what is to be chanted in the divine office, and that the Church with her liturgical cycle prescribes every detail of the Mass and other sacred rites, does not detract from this great truth. This very exactness is a guarantee of liberty.

Anyone who has read the Encyclical *Mediator Dei* with insight, must have noted that it is a timely defence of liberty in the life of prayer. The Christian is in fact protected by the Church herself from all deviations and exaggerations which would ultimately take him into a blind alley. All those who condemn private and personal prayer, who encroach upon the liberty of the Christian to follow the Holy Spirit and pray in his own way, are themselves condemned by the Holy Father. The broad universal wisdom of the liturgy remains, however, to protect the individual from eccentricity and illusions of his own.

The liturgy is the Church's great school of prayer. This is not merely a matter of art, chant, and symbolism. There is much more. In the liturgy, Christ Himself, by His Holy Spirit, prays and offers sacrifice in His body, the Church. Active participation in the liturgy is, then, much more than mere rubrical exactitude and aesthetic appreciation, more even than the spiritual understanding and application of the great inspired texts. It is a mystical participation in the prayer and sacrifice of Jesus Christ, the incarnate word, the new Adam and the high priest of the new creation.

When we celebrate the holy liturgy, Christ prays in us, His Holy Spirit adores and loves in us. Light to understand what we sing and what we do is given to us supernaturally by the Holy Spirit Himself. His grace transforms us in Christ so that our inmost souls begin to take on the likeness of Christ and our hearts share in the love and self-surrender with which, on earth, He offered Himself to the Father for the sins of the world. Every time Holy Mass is offered, the great mystery of our redemption is accomplished in us and by us, in union with Jesus Christ. What was done once for all objectively and definitively on Calvary, is renewed by us, Christ being mystically present in the midst of us as priest and victim. By virtue of this renewal, we too are drawn, heart and soul, body and spirit, into the great mystery of Christ. In so doing we save our souls and give perfect glory to the Father.

In the words of the liturgy, at the end of the canon, we find ourselves 'instructed by sacred precepts and formed by the teaching of God Himself'—thus prepared we can go on to pray with all joy and spiritual freedom the sublime prayer of Christ Himself, the Our Father. This simplest and greatest of all prayers contains within itself the substance of every other prayer. The words are but the external species, as it were, of a great sacrament of prayer by which we plunge, if we so desire, into the ineffable liberty of the Spirit of Christ in His adoration of the Father.

Who then shall limit or determine the course of a prayer that is carried away by the Spirit of God? 'What is born of the flesh is flesh, and what is born of the Spirit is spirit. Do not be perplexed because I said to you, you must all of you be born anew. The breeze blows at will, and you can hear it sound; but you do not know where it comes from or whither it goes. Something like this takes place in everyone born of the Spirit.' 'Whoever are led by the Spirit of God, they are the sons of God. Now you have not received a spirit of bondage so that you are again in fear, but you have received a spirit of adoption in virtue of which we cry, "Abba, Father!" The Spirit Himself joins His testimony to that of our spirit that we are the children of God. . . . The Spirit also helps our weakness. For we do not know what we should pray for as we ought, but the Spirit Himself pleads for us with unutterable sighs. And He who searches the hearts knows what the Spirit desires and that He in accord with God's designs, pleads for the saints.'

If the monk is above all a man of prayer, then it is clear that his life of prayer does not confine itself to the liturgy. He comes to the monastery to 'pray without ceasing'. A frightening project, indeed, to one who does not quite grasp what it means. Actually, however, the life of prayer is not a life of uninterrupted and intense concentration. In the first place, concentration implies discursive thought and attention to clear concepts, and the monk's life of prayer is by no means a life of intense analytical thought. Thought is part of his life, indeed. But prayer is more than thought. Needless to say, it is also something more than words and formulas.

The uninitiated layman may tend to imagine that a life of continual prayer is a life of uninterrupted *prayers*. A southern newspaper, reporting on the foundation of a Cistercian monastery in the Bible belt of the United States, began its account of the monk's day with these words: 'The Trappists rise at two a.m. and from then until six they *say their prayers*'. The statement was doubtless true in its own way, but the choice of words betrayed complete incomprehension in the mind of the reporter.

Even when the primitive monastic tradition demanded that the monk recite the entire psalter each day, this occupation was not a strain, and did not demand an inhuman effort. The ones who spent their days reciting the psalter did, in fact, very little else, for they were generally hermits. Also, they knew the psalms by heart, and while they recited them they meditated on them. At the same time they engaged in simple and rather soothing manual work, such as the weaving of baskets or of rush mats. Prayer under such conditions is by no means exhausting, if it is approached in the right spirit. That is why manual work is one of the essentials of the contemplative life.

The modern monk does not spend all his free time reciting psalms. The monastic life however permits him to live in an *atmosphere of prayer*. But to live consciously in an atmosphere of prayer is in fact to pray constantly. Everything one does becomes a prayer, since it is intended as a prayer. Hence, 'constant prayer' or 'uninterrupted recollection' is not a negative and violent effort to exclude everything except one concept (the concept of God), or to negate every other activity than the recital of special formulas or the meditation of certain thoughts. Living in the atmosphere of prayer does not mean inhibiting the activity of all the faculties but one—the mind, or the heart. On the contrary, a negative approach to prayer, a 'nothing but' attitude, is what effectually prevents misguided souls from actually learning how to pray all the time. Constant prayer is not difficult when prayer is not just confined to the mind, or to the heart, but takes in man's whole being and all his activities.

The true life of prayer engages the whole man. It occupies not only his intelligence and will, but also his emotions and his senses, his bodily faculties, all that he has and all that he is. If anything good or vital in man is excluded from his prayer, he cannot live a life of prayer.

That is why it is important to understand the positive and dynamic character of recollection. Let us not think of recollection as the blackout of the senses which takes place, for instance, in a catatonic trance. On the contrary, recollection is more like the absorption of a child in his play. Recollection in the fullest sense implies not only an alert spirit, but also deep interest and love and wonder.

Recollection, to be properly understood, needs to be heightened by admiration. It includes, naturally, that holy 'fear' which is really a kind of religious awe, produced by the awareness of the reality and the presence of the all-Holy God. Recollection is the absorption of the spirit in mystery. If recollection is merely the exclusion of sensible objects regarded as essentially distracting, then it is of little worth. Such a narrow and negative concept of recollection will never help anyone to practise constant prayer. Of course, we have to be free from the appeals of sense in order to pray. But that does not necessarily mean *rejecting* every sensible object. On the contrary, it is often impossible to be recollected when one has shut his eyes and 'excluded' all sensible things. Yet it is quite easy to be recollected when, in tranquillity and peace, one gazes at some innocent and neutral thing—a tree, a picture, a flower, a ray of light, a landscape, a corner of the sky. The senses are occupied and kept quiet by something akin to themselves, and the spirit is free to engage in a simple intuitive communion with the invisible God.

Once again, we can see that the liturgy, which takes full account of man's natural make-up, as being of body and soul, offers one a perfect education for the life of prayer. The *opus Dei* divides up the monk's day of reading, work and prayer, with simple periods of formal public worship. These suffice to place the whole day and all its works under the sign of God, and the monk, interiorly occupied with the presence of God whether he works or reads or meditates, makes everything a prayer.

To succeed in this, one must have a fundamental *preference* for prayer and meditation over all other activities. Meditative reading and even a certain peaceful and tranquil occupation in study should be the monk's chief joy and recreation. The monk will normally be most himself and most 'occupied' when he is thus alone with his thoughts of God or rather with God Himself, known and loved, as it were, without the medium of precise thought.

The monastic life is designed above all for men with this type of vocation. Everything in the life is meant to favour this peaceful and interior union with God in mystery. Monastic silence is above all important for this very reason. The noise and turmoil of the world are generally unfavourable to prayer, and for that reason silence and solitude are absolutely essential in the monastic life. All the rest of the monk's asceticism serves the same purpose, of preserving an atmosphere in which the life of prayer can be lived without difficulty and, as it were, by instinct.

If the monk is a man of prayer, he is also a man of sacrifice. Prayer and sacrifice complement one another. In a well-integrated spiritual life they are simply two different aspects of the same reality. A life entirely given to prayer is made possible by the renunciation of those things which impede prayer, and such a life becomes, in its entirety, a sacrifice of praise to God. What better testimony could we give of the fact that we prefer God to everything else, than by leaving everything else aside in order to devote ourselves to Him?

This renunciation is not left altogether to free and subjective inspirations. To protect the individual monk against caprice, there is a basic objective standard of renunciation marked out by the monastic vows. The Church understands that without certain definite and universal sacrifices, one cannot truly follow Christ in the monastic state.

The first of these sacrifices is the renunciation of all private ownership by the *vow of poverty*. The monk has nothing of his own, and even gives up the power and the right to possess anything as his own, however insignificant its monetary value.

What is the idea of monastic poverty? Is its function to detach the monk from material possessions? Yes. The instinct to possess is deeply rooted in human nature. Besides that, fallen man has abandoned himself without reason to greed, and in doing so he has unjustly deprived others of what was due to them by right. Nothing is so common or so flagrant, in the world today, as injustice and greed. Indeed, we are so accustomed to hear politicians and business men rant about justice which they violate without scruple, that the world has become cynically indifferent to the very concept of justice.

Without doubt the most serious problem of our time is the problem of justice. The renunciation of the right of ownership on the part of the monk should, then, have a symbolic, or shall we say prophetic significance. It is a silent and implicit condemnation of the misuse of ownership. It is an eloquent affirmation of the fact that everything belongs to God, and that men have a right to be owners only in so far as they are also administrators of God's possessions, instruments of His providence in sharing with others what they themselves do not need.

But for the monk to fulfil this 'prophetic' function his poverty cannot be a mere sham. To enjoy all comforts, to have all his needs immediately cared for, to have all his desires satisfied every time he condescends to ask a routine permission: this is not poverty, it is pharisaism. Monastic poverty is not mere dependence on a superior, nor is it mere external simplicity. These are secondary aspects of the mystery of poverty.

To make the renunciation demanded by the monastic state, one must not only give up juridical ownership. He must generously and seriously face certain fundamental privations. These privations are not arbitrary: they are well defined. The monk is obliged, by his state, to share the privations of the poor in the region in which he lives. Poverty therefore has both a negative and a positive aspect. On one hand, the monk has to do without certain comforts and pleasures and advantages (not to mention luxuries). On the other he must earn his living by the labour of his own hands. Both these obligations are to be taken seriously, even though a casuist might only with difficulty define the point where their evasion would constitute a mortal sin.

This is not all. By his poverty, the monk places himself in a state of complete dependence not only on his superiors but above all on God. The monk becomes a poor man because God provides for the poor. The monk embraces a state of direct dependence on providence out of love for God, and for the poor. The secret joy of monastic poverty is the joy of faith that expects and receives everything from the hand of God. And then, too, there is another joy: the satisfaction of a conscience that is at peace because the monk knows that the surplus produced by the monastery is shared with Christ in the poor.

This, at least, is the mystique of religious poverty. Would that this ideal were always fully realized.

By his vow of poverty, the monk renounces possessions. He gives up what is exterior to himself. By *chastity*, he renounces his own body. He sacrifices and consecrates one of his most fundamental instincts to God. Here again, the sacrifice is not merely negative. If chastity were nothing more than the *refusal to give in* to sexual desires, then it would hardly recommend itself as part of a programme of spiritual perfection. It is true of course that the desire for sexual pleasure is exceedingly powerful, and at times it demands an all-out resistance which is almost entirely a matter of refusal. But in itself, chastity is positive and constructive. It is not merely a refusal, but a gift. The chaste mind, refusing to surrender to passion, at the same time cultivates an interior and fruitful purity, a freedom of spirit which offers itself to God in a higher and more spiritual love in which the lower instinct is sublimated. Without this interior sublimation, chastity could hardly consecrate our bodies to God.

In point of fact, chastity is a liberation of spiritual energies that would otherwise be held captive by animal passion, and these liberated energies are channelled into the creative and spiritual activities of the monk's life of prayer. The virtue of chastity does not merely stifle passion, but enlists the energies of our sensible nature in support of a higher love, the love of God. Chastity is therefore not sterile, but supremely creative and fruitful.

The chaste soul is 'wedded' to God in contemplation, and the love of the mystic for God is not without passion. But passion is here elevated to an entirely spiritual level, and the fire of love that burns in mystical prayer is no longer the red and smoky flame of bodily desire, but the white flame of the Spirit of God.

The monk, vowed to virginity, is by that very fact also consecrated to a life of praise. He is gifted with the power to sing a 'new canticle' which is unknown to others, and with this hymn on his lips he is free to travel in realms where no one else can enter. In the words of the Apocalypse, 'he follows the Lamb wherever He goes'. He has acquired complete liberty of spirit, and by that fact he lives in intimacy with God alone.

Christ Himself made clear in the Gospel that some men were called to become 'eunuchs for the kingdom of heaven' but He added that this was not for all. 'He that can take it, let him take it.'

The Benedictine monk makes no explicit vows of poverty and chastity, for they are contained implicitly in the vow of 'conversion of manners' which covers all the peculiar means by which the monk seeks God in the monastery.

The greatest of the vows is *obedience* by which the monk renounces not his possessions, nor his body, but the inmost sanctuary of his spirit. The right to run our own life, to exercise our freedom as we please, is what is most intimate and personal to every one of us. This inner sanctum of the personality is something that can never be violated from outside unless we ourselves admit the intruder. No matter what pressures may be brought to bear on the human spirit from the exterior, it is impossible to force a man to will something. The will acts freely, or not at all.

It is true that certain techniques used unscrupulously by totalitarian police may interfere radically with man's psychological balance. But these techniques never reach the inner sanctuary of the will. When the victim of such pressures is made subject to compulsion from the outside, it is because his will has been put out of contact with the outside and he has been reduced to helpless dependence on psychic mechanisms which respond automatically to external stimuli. In a sense, the will that is made prisoner is no longer 'free' because it can no longer command its faculties to carry out its decisions. In the same way, when the body is imprisoned, man is said to have lost his freedom, because he cannot go wherever he likes. Nevertheless, his will remains fundamentally master *of itself*, even though it may not have command over the other faculties. All man's other faculties can be enslaved from the outside, but not his intelligence and his will.

Consequently, to surrender our own will and judgement to another is to surrender that which is most personal and inviolable in ourselves.

Of all the vows, that of obedience is perhaps the most easily misunderstood.

First of all, in obeying his superior, the monk does not really surrender his will to the superior *but to God*. No mere man can ever claim the gift of another man's will to himself for his own sake, but only for the sake of an authority which makes him the representative of God. Secondly, however, mere external obedience is not a real surrender of the will. Religious superiors have dominative power over the wills of their subjects by virtue of the vows of their subjects. That is to say the superior can demand not merely that the subject *do* what is commanded, but that he interiorly *will* what is willed by the superior. Hence, although an unwilling exterior fulfilment of a command, with interior rebellion may exteriorly satisfy an obligation, it does not constitute real obedience.

It is true that speculative disagreement with the superior is always permissible. Practical disagreement is not permitted, unless the superior is obviously beyond the limits of his authority. (No superior, for instance, would be allowed to command a subject to do something forbidden by the law of nature, or of the Church, or of God.)

In practice, then, when a monk is commanded to do something by a superior, he must respond as if he were commanded by God Himself. In this way, he puts his whole life under the sign of perfect faith. He liberates himself from the necessity of running his life according to his own caprice. But note that he does not completely abdicate all control over his own life. That would not be a means of attaining spiritual perfection, for perfection consists precisely in supreme spiritual autonomy under God, that is, in the freedom of perfect charity. Hence, the monk by no means ceases to be the master of his own fate. He is definitely responsible for running his own life, but he runs it according to the views and commands of another seen as the representative of God. The obedient man does not renounce his freedom of choice, but rather exercises his freedom in choosing to obey.

Now the superior is not a kind of fetish. If he is a 'representative of God' it is not because he is superstitiously feared as a 'father figure' or something of the sort, but because he is the head of the religious community and as such defines the interests and guides the destinies of that community. Obedience to a religious superior is then something quite different from compulsive submission and abdication of responsibility. It is a voluntary assumption of responsibility, a clear-sighted renunciation of private and limited interests in favour of the general good of the community. Hence monastic obedience should be a full and mature act of self-oblation to the community, to the interests of all those with whom we live, and, by that very fact, to our own higher spiritual interests. Only such obedience as this gives glory to God.

The real value of monastic obedience does not lie, however, merely in the fact that it is mature and generous. These are psychological prerequisites for perfect religious obedience, but they do not of themselves constitute such obedience. The whole monastic consecration derives its theological value not from the subjective disposition of the monk himself but from the fact of his objective incorporation in the mystery of Christ.

In making his monastic vows, the monk unites himself completely to the sacrifice of Christ on the cross, which was a sacrifice of obedience. The obedience of Jesus Christ was necessary not merely to satisfy the justice of the Father, but also to restore to mankind that unity in charity which had been lost by Adam's disobedience.

The obedience of Christ should not be regarded merely as paying a debt for us. It enters far more intimately into the very structure of our supernatural life. We who had lost our divine sonship by the sin of Adam, and thereby lost our contact with truth and our liberty to love without error and without obstacle, recovered in the obedience of Christ the power to love God as sons, instead of serving Him as slaves. In Christ we have been restored to the light of that truth which makes us free. And this was made possible by the fact that Christ, who was without sin, and therefore was under no obligation to suffer or to die, willingly took upon himself the burden of obedience which was proper to sinful man, willingly underwent suffering and death in His flesh, so that by the death of an innocent one we might all be restored to everlasting life, and by the servitude of the free one we might regain our liberty.

The monk therefore obeys not only because the discipline of obedience has a special psychological and ascetic value, but rather he obeys above all out of love for Christ, in imitation of Christ, in union with the sufferings and the death of Christ, in order to share with Christ the great work of restoring liberty to mankind and of renewing all things in the power and sanctity of the Spirit of God.

The monk obeys not just to make himself ethically perfect, but in order to enter most fully into the mystery of Christ, which is the restoration of the world to God in Christ. The ascetic elements of monastic obedience do not make sense unless they are seen in the light of this mystique of obedience in union with Christ the saviour. The monk studies, with St Paul, to have in himself 'this mind which was in Christ Jesus, who though He was by nature God did not consider being equal to God a thing to be clung to, but emptied himself, taking the nature of a slave and being made like unto men. And appearing in the form of a man, he humbled Himself becoming obedient unto death even to death on a cross.'

Although it is not likely that St Benedict invented monastic vows themselves it is certain that the vow of *stability* was one of his original contributions to monasticism. At a time when the monastic Order was threatened with decadence because of the lax discipline of so many wandering monks who were not subject to a regular superior or attached to any particular community, St Benedict realized the vital importance of a permanent and lifelong attachment to the monastery of one's profession. This vow is one of the most important factors in the Benedictine life, and it is one of the foundation stones on which St Benedict raised his edifice of monastic peace.

Here, too, the vow must not be seen merely in its negative aspect. There is more in it than the obligation not to travel from one monastery to another, or not to wander about freely outside the monastic enclosure. By the vow of stability the life of the monk is rooted in peace. He is protected against his natural restlessness. He is reminded that he does not need to travel across the face of the earth to find God. He is reassured of the fact that he no longer lives a life that can be contained within the limits of measured space. His journeys are no longer spatial but spiritual, and his ascent to God is, in fact, a descent into the depths of his own humility.

At the same time, stability is not so absolute that the monk cannot be sent, under obedience, from one community to another. Nor does it imply that he cannot leave the monastery for a serious reason. But if he travels, it must not be out of caprice. His body and soul belong to God and their movements must therefore serve not the monk's own fancy but the needs of the Kingdom of God. And these needs are determined by his monastic superiors. The monk himself remains indifferent to place and space. Wherever he is, he dwells in God.

In a sense it is correct to say that the vow of stability makes attachment to one's monastery a virtue rather than a vice. But the fact remains that the monk is detached from everything, even from his own monastery. It is his home on earth, but only in so far as it is the image of his only true home, which is heaven. Even with his vow of stability, the monk remains a disciple of Him who said: 'The foxes have holes and the birds of the air have nests, but the Son of Man hath nowhere to rest His head'.

As a matter of fact, stability attaches the monk not so much to his monastery as to his monastic family. In the event that the community would be dispersed, or exiled, the monk would be bound by his vow to rejoin the other monks wherever they might unite to form a new settlement. He would then have no further obligation to return to the former monastery. It is clear that the monk's 'stability' is not made in an earthly place so much as in a spiritual family. Hence the roots which it gives to the monk are spiritual and mystical, not physical. They do not establish him in time and space, they situate him forever in the heavenly Jerusalem, they give him his place in the paradise of Christ.

But since St Benedict is always concrete, the monastery itself is a 'sacrament' of the future home to which the whole monastic family is tending with all its efforts. Love of the spiritual monastic community by no means excludes love for one's monastery and its surroundings. On the contrary, one would not be a true monk of St Benedict if he did not have a deep affective attachment to the place singled out by providence for his soul's salvation.

The real secret of monastic stability is, then, the total acceptance of God's plan by which the monk realizes himself to be inserted into the mystery of Christ *through this particular family and no other*. It is the definitive acceptance of his communion, in time and eternity, with these particular brothers chosen for him by God to share his sorrows and his joys, his difficulties and his achievements, his problems and their solutions. It means the glad realization of the fact that all who are thus called together will work out their salvation in common, will help one another to find God more easily, and indeed that we have been destined from all eternity to bring one another closer to Him by our love, our patience, our forbearance and our efforts at mutual understanding.

The vow of stability clearly reveals itself to be essential to monastic peace when it is seen in the full light of the charity of Christ.

The Vision of Peace

When the Holy Spirit descended upon the disciples of our Lord in the Cenacle on the first Pentecost, He made Himself visible in His Church, and He has continued so ever since that time. The Church is the great manifestation, on earth, of the glory, the mystery, and the love of God. Jesus Himself teaches us this, in his discourse at the last supper. In witnessing the unity of the faithful, the world can see that God has sent the son, and has loved the members of the Church as He has loved His own son, because they are one in Him, and in the son they have received the 'glory' which He had from the beginning.

The monk does not enter the monastery merely to find psychological peace by retirement from the confusion of the world. He comes, as we have suggested in the first chapter, to become a peacemaker, to possess peace by 'making' peace, and to make peace by building his monastic community into a unified Church, a little body of Christ, united in the Holy Spirit, and thus giving glory to God.

The monk does indeed seek solitude and contemplation and union with God alone. But he goes far beyond the limits of mere 'exterior things' in order to descend within himself and there be 'alone with the Alone'. Such an intellectual and psychological ascent to contemplation is pagan rather than Christian, and it does not form part of the true monastic ideal because it is clearly insufficient.

The monk does indeed seek solitude and contemplation and union with God alone. But he goes far beyond the limits of mere interiorization. St Augustine, who was thoroughly imbued with the ideals and principles of Neoplatonism, himself goes beyond Plotinus when he shows not only that we must enter within ourselves, and find God above and beyond ourselves, but also that the way to do so is to find Him in His 'house', which is the Church, and to find Him by entering into the glad festivity of His love. It is in the great banquet of charity—a banquet which is celebrated both on earth and in heaven, though on earth its glory is not seen—that the monk passes beyond the apparent conflict between solitude and communion, and finds both together in God. For the more he loves his brethren and surrenders his will to the 'common will' the more he is at liberty to be alone with God in Himself, since he rises above himself to find both himself and others in God. In the mystery of God there is both solitude and community, for God is three persons in one nature. Great and sacred indeed is the mystery of our vocation to share with Him His solitude and His community, for in Him we are so closely united to one another as to form but 'one man', and that one man is Christ.

In Christ there is no conflict and no anguish, no dissension and no shadow of division, no change, no sorrow, no need and no poverty. In Him we find both liberty and security together because we are no longer divided from one another but are perfectly united in Him who is all in all, and in Him we are one with God our Father.

Our vocation to peace is then a vocation to become so perfectly one in Christ that we are immersed in His infinite peace, the peace which is His life, His substance, and His person. *Ipse est pax nostra.*

But the peace of Christ is not tasted perfectly on earth. There are moments when the spirit is indeed so lost in Him that it does taste something of the mysterious joy and tranquillity of that other world in which there is no division, and in which we are all one in Him who is one with the Father. Yet most of the time we are left with an acute awareness of the divisions which separate us from one another, and even, more tragic still, of the division within our own self.

The paradox of monastic peace is precisely that it does *not* seek to put an end to all division on earth to solve all conflicts, and to pacify all anguish. The life of the monk generally begins, indeed, in great consolation. The novice receives some taste of the life of heaven, and knows by experience that God is close, that He dwells in our hearts, and makes the monastic community His tabernacle. This joy is necessary to wean the heart of the young monk away from other and baser joys which belong to the life of 'the world'.

But let him not think that all conflict is at an end. Indeed, he may soon discover that the battle has not even begun. When it begins, it may take the form of an acutely felt lack of harmony, in spirit and in thought, with the other monks, or with some of them, or with 'the community' or perhaps with a particular superior. This conflict may in some cases be the sign that one has no vocation. In others it is the beginning of a salutary and purifying struggle, a *'disciplina'*—a providential education of soul, in which he is first taught how little he can love, and then led, almost in spite of himself, to learn to love with true charity and not out of mere natural attraction. The only solution to this problem is the sacrifice of views and even of ideals that are insufficient because they are too particular, too narrow, too personal, and too small.

If we are to live as members of Christ, we are forced, by the very nature of our vocation and by the insistent demands of the Spirit of Christ, to rise above ourselves, to burst out of our own limits, and stretch out to attain something of the stature of Christ. But one who remains narrow and petty and self-centred cannot expand to embrace the whole world without feeling some strain and suffering in the process. In order to become big we must sacrifice our smallness. In order to reach out to many, we must abandon our miserable concentration upon our self, with its little needs, its demands, its whims and its illusions.

Paradoxically, the first thing we must sacrifice, in order to become great, is our own idea of greatness. That is why St Benedict insists that the only way to perfection is humility. Our human notions of what is 'great' and 'big' and 'noble' are all in fact corrupted by egoism. We find it difficult to realize that one who would be truly great must totally disappear. If our light is to shine before the world, and give glory to God, it must first of all be extinguished, then re-enkindled with the flame of the Holy Spirit. Otherwise it will be only another smoky reflection of the light kindled by the Pharisees in their own honour.

Again, if we are to find true peace, we must sacrifice our own imperfect notion of peace. It was for this reason that Jesus said He would bring not peace but the sword. Of ourselves we know no peace but that which the world gives, and this is not true peace. Jesus brings to us the peace which the world cannot give, and the way to this peace is spiritual war.

Hence we cannot evade the conflict which is in us, and the monastery will not enable us to escape it. On the contrary, we have come to the monastery to face that conflict and fight it out to the finish. The basic conflict in the soul of the monk is not lessened by his monastic vocation, but intensified . . . until at last the problem is solved and true peace is received in mystery, not as the prize of conquest but as a gift of the divine mercy.

What is it that makes every man struggle with himself? It is the deep, persistent voice of his own discontent with himself. Fallen man cannot abide to live with himself. Now the apparent peace which the world gives is bought with the price of continual distraction. Distraction merely drowns out the inner voice, it does not answer any questions, or solve any problems, it merely postpones their solution. And behind the smokescreen of amusements and projects, the inner dissatisfaction marshals all its forces for a more terrible assault when the distraction shall have been taken away. At last, the spirit that has fled from itself all its life, is stripped of its distractions at death and finds itself face to face with what can no longer be avoided: there is nothing now to prevent it from hating itself utterly, and totally, and for ever.

The peace which Christ brings is the outcome of this war faced and fought on earth: man's war with himself, in which (by God's grace) he overcomes himself, conquers himself, pacifies himself, and can at last live with himself because he no longer hates himself. But this conquest of himself can never be definitive unless it is a surrender to another: to Christ, and to our brother in Christ. For our destiny is to be one in Christ, and in order to love others as ourselves, we must first love ourselves. But in order to love ourselves we must find something in ourselves to love. This is impossible unless we find, both in ourselves and in others, the likeness of Christ.

Once again, in order to find Christ we must give up our own limited idea of Christ. He is not what we think He is.

He is not, and cannot be, merely our own idealized image of ourselves.

The Christ we find in ourselves is not identified with what we vainly seek to admire and idolize in ourselves—on the contrary, He has identified Himself with what we resent in ourselves, for He has taken upon Himself our wretchedness and our misery, our poverty and our sins. We cannot find peace in ourselves if, in rejecting our misery and thrusting it away from us, we thrust away Christ Who loves in us not our human glory but our ignobility.

Hence the first step to monastic peace is the acceptance of our own spiritual indigence. We cannot attain to purity of heart unless first of all we accept the fact that our hearts are not pure and that there is in us no way of making them pure. On the contrary, we must contemplate in ourselves Christ crucified for our sins. We must see in our own poverty not the abject image of our failure, but the victory of Christ on the cross when He took upon Himself our failures and transfigured them.

We must learn to listen to what goes on in our heart and interpret it correctly. We will never find peace if we listen to the voice of our own fatuous self-deception that tells us the conflict has ceased to exist. We will find peace when we can listen to the 'deathdance in our blood' not only with equanimity but with exultation because we hear within it the echoes of the victory of the risen saviour.

Only in this proper understanding of ourselves can we come to that true compunction which is the very heart of monastic prayer. How shall we sing *Lord have mercy* if our eyes have never been opened to our need for mercy? But what will be the rending of our heart when we recognize that it is Christ Himself, in us, who cries out for mercy—and that He cries not only to the Father, but to us. Yes, it is Christ Himself who has identified Himself with us and begs us to begin by having mercy on ourselves, not now for our own sake but for His! Such is the love of God for us, so great is its mystery, and so far beyond the capacity of our hearts to comprehend! He who could have punished us, instead forgives us. But His is a strange way of forgiveness: He identifies Himself with us and asks us, as it were, to begin by forgiving our-selves. In doing this for Him, we are, as it were, forgiving Him. If we forgive Him, He forgives us. Then He gives us peace with ourselves—because we are at peace with Him.

This mystery, which begins in ourselves, goes on in our relations with others. For we look about us and see Him ev-erywhere, asking our forgiveness in others. On all sides the God of glory, whose glory we have rejected, confronts us in human weakness and poverty that we may receive Him again by—forgiving Him! It is as if He had sinned, and not we. It is as if we were not the ones who needed forgiveness. But this is only apparent. For ours is and can be no mere juridical salva-tion. If we are to know forgiveness, we must experience the full reality of forgiveness: we must not only know what it is to be forgiven, but we must know before all else what it means to forgive. In forgiving and in being forgiven we are one with the God who took upon Himself both our flesh and our sins, in order that in us and for us He might both forgive and be forgiven.

The secret of monastic peace is therefore not to be sought on the shallow level of psychological tranquillity, but in the infinitely deep abyss which men call the divine mercy.

Karl Marx believed that religion had its roots in man's inner conflict with himself—the basic disproportion between man's idea of himself and his concrete reality, the contra-diction of the ideal and the real in man's society. Since Marx diagnosed the cause of this disproportion as an economic one, he also prescribed an economic cure. In a word, Marx believed that all man's religious problems were merely a smokescreen veiling practical problems which he evaded or could not solve. Seeing all around him the hypocrisy and the fake humanism of the early nineteenth century bourgeoisie, Marx believed that the problems which confronted all reli-gious people were simply the indication that they had manœuvred themselves, by their own spiritual dishonesty and incompetency, into an intellectual blind alley, where there was nothing left but to give their hopelessness a tran-scendental justification. The society which they had made for themselves by their own greed was indeed unjust: but what could be done about it? It was the 'will of God'.

Marx's solution was dictated by what he believed to be his own superior honesty and acumen; solve your problems, he said, by transforming your world. Or, to be more accurate (since he believed that the world could not be transformed by the bourgeoisie), the inexorable logic of history would eventually bring about a sweeping and perfect change from below. While the bourgeoisie was immersed in these abstractions which enable it to evade the logic of the class-struggle, the proletariat, apparently immune to theorizing, free from all illusions and endowed with a marvellous infallibility, would settle the question once for all, liquidate the economic injustices of the capitalistic world, and from then on there would be no more conflict, either in man's society or in his own soul. Religion would then quite naturally disappear.

It is important that we glance for a moment at this symptomatic doctrine, and at its consequences. Marx after all was a genius, and the impact of his thought upon the world has been too tremendous to be ignored. Unfortunately he was also evidently a neurotic, and it is quite possible that his own illusions about himself and his myth of the all-perfect proletariat, the salvation of the world, flowed from hidden springs of guilt in the depths of what was essentially a bourgeois and Jewish conscience. The deep contradictions in Marx's own character and in his thought worked themselves out in his doctrine of revolution, and this doctrine was his 'solution' to his own inner conflict. It is indeed terrible when a genius reaches a wrong solution for his own personal problem, and the whole world has to pay the enormous price of his error. Because Marx raged at himself and everyone else and wore out a path in his carpet walking up and down the room cursing his boils, there are now twenty million persons in Soviet forced labour camps. . . .

Subsequent history, and the ideological 'development' of what claims today to be Marxism, has shown how laughable after all was Marx's claim that the 'intellectual honesty' of the Communist saviours would effectually liquidate all man's inner conflicts at their source. Dialectical materialism has finally erected the most monumental edifice of lies and hypocrisy that the world has ever seen, and in its efforts to replace God it has multiplied the miseries of man and intensified his despair beyond belief. Marx, Lenin and Stalin always appealed with reverent assurance to the verdict of history which would, they believed, reveal the precise value and import of their doctrine. History has not disappointed anyone's expectations in this matter. It has been giving clear and decisive answers—not the least eloquent being the treatment of Hungary by Soviet Russia in 1956.

These lines are not a digression. The monk is immersed in history, and forms just as much a part of it as the Communist. His role in history, though more hidden, is just as decisive. The fate of man is in the balance, and the monk has just as much to say as anyone else, perhaps more, as to how the question is to be weighed.

The question itself is basic: how shall we face the contradiction between the ideal and the real in our society, the ideal and the concrete in ourselves?

First of all, this is not merely a problem of the individual, or of the person. Nineteenth century individualism led finally to a moral and spiritual disintegration of man, the effects of which are evident everywhere in the hopeless atomized disjointedness of modern society with all its discontents. This wound cannot be healed merely by solving each individual conflict, one at a time. The problem has to be solved by society itself, and it is not at all evident that society is ready with a solution. We can hope, with Marx, that history has a solution (though we need not believe that history's solution will follow the lines laid down for it by Marx). We can also hope that it is possible for man to guide history towards this hidden solution. Such a belief is not only compatible with Christianity but essential to it.

The Christian religion is eschatalogical, and the vocation of the individual Christian is to help prepare the final victory of Christ in the world, and the salvation of mankind. The very substance of man's history is involved in what St Paul calls 'the mystery of Christ' and all events have their ultimate meaning in the 'reintegration of all things in Christ' which is the heart of the 'mystery'. Now when Christ said He came to bring not peace but a sword, He meant that He came not to solve man's basic inner conflicts in this world, but to help man to face his conflict so that, by his purifying struggle, he might first come to know himself, then to know other men, and to consecrate himself to the salvation and to the happiness of others as well as of himself.

The bourgeois paternalism, the flaccid humanitarianism which aroused the contempt not only of Marx but of every truly Christian thinker of every age, is no way of confronting this challenge. It is an evasion. And the great duty of every Christian is to see that he meets the challenge squarely, and does not try to delude himself and the world by merely 'going through the motions'.

This requires heroic honesty and almost unbelievable courage, and in fact it is not a work that man can accomplish by himself, without the grace of God. The monk's withdrawal from the world is indeed a recognition of the difficulty of the problem. That is the first thing we must do: admit that it is not easy, and then take the necessary means to do something effective about it. The monastic life is designed, among other things, to enable a man to become honest with himself and it shows him, if he is true to his vocation and to himself, how to become sincere. Real sincerity has never been easy, although of course *ersatz* sincerity has abounded in all ages. In our day, the *ersatz* is so commonly accepted that the reality is almost forgotten.

Real sincerity with ourselves is sometimes brutally discouraging. Even though we may really want to be sincere, we have an almost infinite resourcefulness in lying to ourselves.

The effort to be sincere keeps us face to face with our own inner contradictions. It makes it impossible for us to escape the conflict, the division within us. And this division keeps us in a state of constant anguish. The paradox that one must face, if he really takes the truth seriously, is the pragmatic fact that sincerity means insecurity. If we recognize how basic is the conflict within our hearts, we cannot settle down and take roots and become 'installed' on this earth. We will know the meaning of deep, bitter and even anguished insecurity.

But we will also come to know the value of this insecurity: it is, in fact, the guarantee of our sincerity. It is, paradoxically, the sign that we are on the right road. It tells us that we are moving forward in the only direction possible for a Christian, and that we are in contact with reality.

Only when we have become able to accept the basic contradictions in our own self, can we have the humility to understand the contradictions in others and in society. For even in the Church herself, the perfect society, there are contradictions—the everlasting distinction between wheat and cockle, with its attendant insecurity for all. No man among us can declare with assurance that he is wheat rather than cockle, and not one of us can assert that he, as opposed to 'those others' represents the Church in all her purity.

In the monastic school of charity, we learn to bear one another's burdens, and precisely the greatest burden of all is this burden of insecurity and interior conflict. The first thing of all that we must face is the obligation to bear this burden and to bear it in common, but in such a way that no one is able to abdicate his own liberty and responsibility.

A school of charity, if it is a school of true charity, is also a school of freedom. It is for mature and responsible men, and not for children who have decided to leave their burden of responsibilities on the shoulders of another. A monastery is then (or at least should be) a place where man learns to bear the weight of his own freedom, and to enable others to stand up under the burden of their freedom also. Freedom is, after all, heavy to us until we become strong enough to bear it.

The Marxian approach to this problem has been to take away all freedom from the individual, and place all responsibility in the hands of a few who remain themselves accountable to mysterious laws of history—laws whose action they themselves think they can determine. There exists for the monk a temptation remarkably like the Marxian solution: the temptation to *renounce his freedom,* to remain inert and apathetic in the hands of others who themselves pass on the responsibility to higher superiors and—to divine providence. But that is not the true solution. The 'renunciation' of freedom made by the monk is a sacrifice of a lower and more material kind of autonomy in order to attain to a higher and more spiritual autonomy—the autonomy of one who is so closely united to the Holy Spirit that the Spirit of God moves him as his own spirit. 'For He that is joined to the Lord is one Spirit . . . I live, now not I, but Christ liveth in Me.'

Such a one must dare to understand the frightening dictum of St Augustine: 'Love, and do what you will'. Great is the risk involved, but it is the risk involved in true perfection—the risk that has to be faced by one who is determined in all things to be moved by nothing but the love of God.

It is quite evident that if one were to misapply this principle, if one were to be led by illusion instead of by love, the error would be disastrous. That is probably why some monks are incapable of surrendering themselves to the Spirit of God. They prefer to restrain the dangerous impulse of a freedom which they do not *know with certainty* to be pure love. And because of this they fail in hope.

This fear of insecurity, this dread of error, accounts for the rigidity of modern monastic legislation. The constantly recurrent need for monastic reform has convinced the Church that men cannot easily be trusted with freedom because they are not always as interested in love as they pretend to be. Both love and freedom have been called upon to justify decadence and moral laxity. The fact remains that too much juridical rigidity risks, in the end, grieving the Spirit of God and imprisoning grown men within the narrow limits of spiritual infantilism.

This much must be well understood: interior growth is essential to the monastic and spiritual life, and indeed the purpose of the vows is to foster this growth. But to grow interiorly, one must grow in maturity and freedom, in the ability to govern one's own life from within, and not merely to conform to exterior standards. Interior self-government must of course follow the lines laid down by the exterior norm, but it goes far beyond that norm in spontaneity and perfection.

This problem is as old as Christianity itself. It was one of the great challenges that was met by St Paul: the conflict between 'law' and 'grace'. His answer still holds. Law is still nothing more than a pedagogue, and mere fidelity to law, with nothing more, will never constitute true perfection.

The monastery, in any case, should be a school of freedom: a place where we can come to understand our liberty, our fear of liberty, and our brother's fear of liberty. Here we can educate one another in liberty by patiently bearing with one another's misuse of it, and our own incapacity to bear it. We are not here to provide one another with a shallow sympathy that is a refuge from responsibility, nor with stern incitations to toe the party line. Neither *laissez faire* nor authoritarianism can be of any real use in educating man's freedom.

Love is learned by loving, and we have come to the monastery to strengthen one another in love in order that we may become strong enough to face the truth and noble enough to use the freedom implanted in our nature when it was created in the image of God.

The stronger our love, the greater will be our ability to bear responsibility not only for ourselves but for others. In proportion as we grow in the likeness of Christ by charity, we become able, as He did, to take upon ourselves the sorrows of other men without complacency and without patronage, but with a strength that really lifts the burden from their shoulders, and really helps them carry it.

This is the true meaning of Christian penance which destroys sin. Penance is more than a matter of 'doing penances'. It is a *metanoia*, a complete change of heart which fills our soul with a love *strong enough to consume sin* and pure enough to go out and heal the wounds in the soul of the sinner. Such love is given only by the Spirit of Christ, the sanctifier of the Church, and the hidden God who dwells in each soul as in His temple.

The Church is holy because of the mercy of God that is in her, and not merely because of the absence of sins. This mercy, the dynamic action of the Spirit of Love constantly going to and fro and healing the wounds of sin by forgiveness, must obviously be exercised in the midst of weaknesses and of sins. The true freedom of the sons of God is therefore a freedom from preoccupation and fear, a freedom from resentments and hostilities, a freedom from pride and contempt, a freedom which can avoid sin without hating or repelling the sinner, a freedom which, while refusing to offend God in any way, nevertheless gladly takes upon itself the burden and the responsibility for the sins of the world, *destroying them by charity, and, wherever occasion presents itself, by forgiveness.*

Only where the infinite truth, pity and freedom of God live in the heart of man can there be any effective social co-operation in striving for justice and truth on earth. The monk, who abandons himself to the love of God, who takes upon himself responsibility for the sins of all and holds himself responsible to all, by that very fact places himself below all, recognizes himself as worse than all, and spiritually 'washes the feet' of everyone in the world—principally of those with whom he lives. In the soul of such a one there is such great meekness, such humility, such mercy, such self-effacement, such power of love, such freedom and such joy in God that his very presence brings the Holy Spirit to the hearts of men, and delivers them from sin, and shows them the way to repentance and joy in a change of heart.

Christ alone is able to bring true peace to the hearts of men, and it is through the hearts of other men that He brings it. We are all mediators for one another with Christ by our charity, by our sharing in His cross, by our love and humility in taking upon ourselves the sins of the world without condemning sinners, placing ourselves below others and forgiving all. By our humility and charity Christ lives in the world, and prepares the consummation of His kingdom, inviting men to be merciful to one another, to be just, to give every man the good that is owing to him and more besides—to repay evil with good. If all men will not hear His invitation, there must still be some in the world who will bear the sins and injustices of all, and repair them by their love. If God's justice is not visible in civil society, at least it must appear in His Church, and in His monasteries, and woe to the monastery whose monks are not felt, by the disinherited, to be their brothers.

Staretz Zossima, the saintly monk described by Dostoievski

in a portrait based on reality, summed up Christian perfection in these beautiful words:

Love one another, Fathers. . . . Love God's people. Because we have come here and shut ourselves within these walls, we are no holier than those that are outside, but on the contrary, from the very fact of coming here, each of us has confessed to himself that he is worse than the others, than all men on earth. . . . And the longer the monk lives in his seclusion, the more keenly he must recognize that. Else he would have had no reason to come here. When he realizes that he is not only worse than others but that he is responsible to all men for all and everything, for all human sins, national and individual, only then the aim of our seclusion is attained. For know, dear ones, that every one of us is undoubtedly responsible for all men and everything on earth, not merely through the general sinfulness of creation, but each one personally for all mankind and for each individual man. This knowledge is the crown of life for the monk and for every man. For monks are not a special sort of man but only what all men ought to be. Only through that knowledge our heart grows soft with infinite, universal, inexhaustible love. Then every one of you will have the power to win over the whole world by love and to wash away the sins of the world with your tears. . . . Each of you keep watch over your heart and confess your sins to yourself unceasingly. Be not afraid of your sins, even when perceiving them, if only there be penitence, but make no conditions with God. . . . Love God's people. Let not strangers draw away the flock, for if you slumber in slothfulness and disdainful pride, or worse still in covetousness, they will come from all sides and draw away your flock. . . . Pray thus: Save O Lord all those who have none to pray for them, save too all those who will not pray, and add: it is not in pride that I make this prayer, O Lord, for I am lower than all men.

'I Have Chosen You'

To have a vocation is something quite different from following a career. Religious vocations are the work not of man, but of God. It is not sufficient that one should feel a certain interest in the monastic life, or an attraction to it. This alone does not constitute a 'vocation'. It is not sufficient for one to have certain aptitudes which fit him for life in a monastery. Nor is it enough that the superiors should desire one to enter the monastery, in the belief that he would make a good monk. All these elements together may unite to give us a sign of a probable vocation, but unless the one called believes himself called and is willing to respond to the call, we cannot presume to say that he has a vocation. God's call makes itself heard in the depths of the heart. External signs are only indications of an interior vocation.

If, however, a mature Catholic man, who is not prevented by a canonical impediment from entering the monastery, has the aptitude for the monastic life and believes that he could please God by embracing that life, and if the superiors who have carefully studied his case agree that he should make a trial of the monastic life, then that person should consider himself invited by God Himself to embrace the life of a monk. He should set aside everything else in order to respond, with gratitude and humility, to this divine invitation.

Our Christian faith tells us that the whole purpose of life is to love God and know Him and serve Him in this world in order to find our eternal rest in union with Him thereafter. For He who is the creator of all is also the last end of all. Only in Him from whom all things have come, can we find the ultimate meaning and purpose of all things. Until we have come to the vision of God in the divinizing embrace of His 'admirable light', our life still falls short of full reality and our existence lacks its total coherence and meaning. Furthermore, we know that only God can bring us to the end of our journey: for since we have no natural end, the means to our supernatural end must themselves be supernatural. And

God, who loves all men and desires that all should be saved, has provided all with sufficient means to be saved. But to some He has given special light and more particular graces to reach their goal. This He does not for their sake alone, but for the sake of hundreds and thousands of other souls whose salvation is intimately involved in God's plan for these chosen ones.

So, when a Christian begins dimly to realize that he is called by divine grace to a life of prayer and sacrifice, he should try at all costs to appreciate the meaning of so great a favour. Without any special merit on man's part, the Father and Creator of the world sends forth His Spirit and 'chooses' special ones who will henceforth exercise a particularly important function in the mystery of Christ, in the manifestation of God's love to the world in His Church, the mystical body of His Son. Such chosen ones should never forget the words which Jesus spoke to His disciples at the Last Supper: 'you have not chosen me, but I have chosen you: and have appointed you that you should go and bring forth fruit; and your fruit should remain: that whatsoever you may ask the Father in my name, He may give it to you.'

A vocation to the priesthood or to the monastic life is then a pledge of very special love on the part of Christ, and one who is faithful to his vocation can be certain beyond doubt that he will safely reach the end of his journey and save not only his own soul but countless others as well. How can such grace be taken lightly? How can any other person dare to interfere with the designs of God for this soul who is especially loved by Him? The possibility that one has a monastic vocation demands the greatest fidelity and the most fervent cooperation on the part of the one who is called. Like a spiritual seedling, the nascent vocation must be tended with the greatest care by those whose business it is to help the chosen one grow in the Lord.

At the same time, since a vocation is such a mysterious and important gift from God, those who are appointed by the Church to guide and select future religious must exercise the greatest prudence in their work. After all, when there is question of spiritual gifts, subjective illusion and self-deception are always possible. Sometimes men think themselves to be 'called' by God when they are in fact only misled by their own emotions. Others, on the contrary, may be deceived by a certain natural distaste for the religious state or a fear of its obligations, and imagine that because they do not feel a strong sensible attraction to the monastery they are therefore not 'called'. In all such cases, the greatest attention is to be paid to the opinion of prudent spiritual guides, while the final verdict, of acceptance or rejection in the external forum, rests with the religious superior. The one 'called' must himself respond to his vocation by his own, free and deliberate choice.

St Benedict, with his usual simplicity, sets down in the Rule the four main signs of aptitude for the monastic life.

First of all the novice must *truly seek God*. This does not mean that he seeks merely the satisfaction of certain obscure religious emotions, but that he is guided by a spirit of deep supernatural faith to devote his whole life to the service of God, in order to fulfil the whole purpose of his creation and arrive at union with Him. Hence there can be no other valid reason for entering a monastery than this search for God, the Living God—*summi Dei, veri Dei*. A vocation to the monastic life can never be constituted by a search for some kind of psychological fetish, some interior idol. One does not enter a monastery to fulfil a personal ambition, to carve out a career for himself, to become a learned man, or a teacher, or a writer, or a singer, or an artist. One does not enter a monastery in order to practise a trade or to go in for 'scientific farming'. All these things may be fitted into the monastic life in so far as they can become part of man's search for God: for the monk seeks God not in a vacuum, but in his daily work and his daily life. The reality of a monastic vocation depends precisely on this ability to combine the simple, every day work of the monastery with the interior search for God and His devoted and constant service. In order to have a monastic vocation, one must be able not only to keep on seeking God in the monastery, but also *to find Him* in the monastery. What this means in practice is the interior realization that to seek Him with all sincerity is, indeed, to find Him in an inchoate and mysterious way: for as St Bernard said, we could not seek Him at all unless we had already found Him.

Next the novice must be obedient. The very essence of monastic asceticism lies in the surrender of our own judgement and our own will, in order to be guided and governed by the 'common will' (*voluntas communis*) of the monastery, which is ordinarily determined by the Rule and the Abbot. Obedience is essential, not only from the point of view of discipline, but above all because union with the *voluntas communis* is true charity, and one who resists the 'common will' thereby excommunicates himself spiritually and cuts himself off from the life-giving flow of grace which circulates in the monastery under the impulsion of the Holy Spirit, who is the 'soul' of the monastic community as He is the soul of the Church herself.

In order to be called to the Benedictine life, the novice must realize that his whole ascetic purification is to be governed by the great Benedictine principle that 'everyone who exalts himself shall be humbled and he who humbles himself shall be exalted', and that 'no one in the monastery shall presume to follow his own will'. Hence even in the holiest and most spiritual things, in the choice of means and methods of asceticism and of prayer, the true monk remains docile and subject to the guidance of the Rule and of his superiors. Those who are unable to renounce a persistent attachment to this or that spiritual method, this or that practice of penance or of prayer, in order to embrace the higher good of humble obedience, must recognize that they do not have the true monastic spirit. Such lack of flexibility is usually the sign that one does not have a Benedictine or Cistercian vocation.

The third sign of a true vocation is that one is a *man of prayer*. The Benedictine life of prayer is built on the *Opus Dei*, the divine office chanted in choir, and on *lectio divina* or meditative reading. Note that the monk's prayer life is not exclusively a life of public prayer. Indeed, if one were to have an appreciation of the divine office *only* and no inclination to private meditative prayer and holy reading, this lack would indicate a deficiency in one's vocation. The monk of St

Benedict is not merely called to sing the office, but to consecrate himself to God entirely in a whole *life of prayer*. If we
do not read, meditate and pray outside choir; if we do not
love to speak to God and contemplate Him in the silence of
our own hearts; if we do not relish the silent, humble work
which gives us opportunities for simple prayer in the woods
and fields, then we will not really be men of prayer in choir.

Finally, to have a true monastic vocation, one must appreciate the value of humiliation and spiritual poverty. That is
to say, one must understand the necessity of everything that
lessens our preoccupation with self and makes us small and
worthless in our own estimation. The monk is dedicated to a
greater humility than all other religious in the sense that he
must pass through the purifying darkness of interior trial by
which he comes to know the greatness and holiness of God,
the heinousness of sin, and man's utter need for the divine
mercy. The monk is called to experience these great realities
in all their depth, and he cannot fulfil this important aspect
of his vocation if he resists humiliation. He must on the contrary love the cross which kills his self-love at the very roots
and establishes him firmly and totally in the heart of Jesus
Christ.

It should not be necessary to add that the monastic life
requires normal physical and mental health. The monastery is
no place for one who is especially nervous or hypersensitive,
who is easily offended and 'cannot get along' with other men.
Hypercritical and scrupulous persons will tend to pervert the
whole monastic life to their own ruin. To be a monk one
must have plenty of common sense, as well as a sense of
humour, and a normal sympathy and toleration of the
weaknesses of other human beings. These are a few of the
natural qualities on which grace must build the structure of
supernatural sanctity. It stands to reason that the 'common
life' is no place for one who is anti-social. But at the same
time, the plainness, simplicity and hiddenness of the monastic life of silence will be particularly difficult for men in need
of exterior activity. The monastic life is certainly busy, and
no one can become a monk by inertia and thumb-twiddling.
Nevertheless the constant silence, the lack of exterior con-

tacts, the solitude, the simplicity of manual work, all these generally fail to satisfy the need for extraversion which is a healthy characteristic of souls called to the active life of teaching, preaching or administration. In the monastery, one must be able to maintain a healthy balance between active work and silent prayer. The Benedictine, cenobitic life, is not a hermit life, and it is not devoted to uninterrupted deep recollection. Those who seek total physical silence and solitude must go elsewhere.

When all these things have been noted, we must recognize that there is no such thing as a person 'perfectly adapted' to the monastic life or to any other life. It would be folly to expect any man to fit in so completely to the Benedictine pattern that he would never have any trouble, never feel out of place, never have to make a serious effort to adapt himself, and never feel the pain of frustration and failure. On the contrary, the sign of true adaptability is not the total lack of problems, but the ability to accept the normal problems of the religious life in a spirit of realism, self-sacrifice, and generous faith.

If any man finds in himself a desire to give himself to God in this hidden life, and sincerely means to seek God alone in the monastery, trusting in the Holy Spirit to help him accomplish what is not possible to man alone, then let him pray earnestly for the gift of a monastic vocation. For no man is called to the life of prayer unless he has first prayed earnestly for the gift of so great a calling. The mere desire to pray for a vocation may be a sign that God has already decreed a favourable answer to your prayer.

PART TWO

Monastic Themes

THE HUMANITY OF CHRIST
IN MONASTIC PRAYER

A Modern Problem

Readers of St Teresa are familiar with a problem (or pseudo-problem) that was raised by illuminism and quietism in the sixteenth and seventeenth centuries. Mental prayer grows progressively simpler until it becomes 'contemplation' in which there are few ideas or even none at all, and in which images play little or no part. But Christian prayer is obviously centred on the Person of Jesus Christ. Should contemplative prayer be understood as directed only to Christ as God, not as man? In other words, is there a time when the humanity of Christ no longer has any place in mental prayer? Or is there even a time when it becomes right and proper to deliberately *exclude* Christ the man from prayer, in order to be able to lose oneself entirely in His divinity? St Teresa, with a healthy Catholic instinct, rejected the idea that the 'one mediator' between God and men, the Man-God, should somehow become an obstacle instead of a mediator. She doubtless sensed the inner confusions and contradictions inherent in this abstract and arbitrary separation between the humanity and divinity of Christ. Let us recall briefly what she tells us of the 'problem' as she experienced it.[1]

First she refers to writers 'who advise us earnestly to put aside all corporeal imagination and to approach the contemplation of the divinity. For they say that anything else, even Christ's humanity, will hinder or impede those who have arrived so far from attaining to the most perfect contemplation. They quote the words of the Lord on this subject to the Apostles with regard to the coming of the Holy Spirit. . . .'[2]

Then she admits that she herself 'when I began to gain some experience of supernatural prayer—I mean the prayer of quiet—I tried to put aside everything corporeal . . . I thought

I was experiencing the presence of God, as proved to be true, and I contrived to remain with Him in a state of recollection'. She found this so profitable that 'no one could have made me return to meditation on the humanity', but afterwards she reproached herself for this as for 'an act of high treason'. She addresses Christ, saying: 'Is it possible, my Lord, that for so much as an hour I should have entertained the thought that Thou couldst hinder my greatest good?' And she surmised, quite rightly, that there is a kind of pride and human self-conceit in wanting by deliberate effort and technique to attain to an 'experience' of the 'divine essence' while by-passing the Person of the Man-God as though He were an obstacle.

The problem, if it is really to be seen as a problem, arises when the *Person* of the God-Man is conceived as being an obstacle to 'contemplation of the divine essence'. So, in reality, what St Teresa saw was that for a Christian there could be no contemplative experience of the divine essence except in and through the Person of Christ, the God-Man. However, she distinguished quite rightly between the state in which Christ lived and acted before His resurrection, and the glorified life in which He lives now after His resurrection and will live forever. Thus she says:

> I cannot bear the idea that we might withdraw ourselves entirely from Christ and *treat that divine Body of His as though it were on a level with our miseries*. . . . It may be that our temperament or some indisposition will not allow us always to think of His passion. . . . *But what can prevent us from being with Him and His resurrection body* since we have Him so near us in the sacrament, *where He is already glorified?*

Here we see that St Teresa was in full accord with patristic and monastic tradition. A study of that tradition will enable us to appreciate more fully the real place of the humanity of Christ in monastic prayer.

What was the extreme and erroneous position against which St Teresa reacted? Cardinal Casanata, preparing the condemnation of quietism by the Holy Office in 1687, summed up the error in these words: 'True and perfect contemplation must fix itself upon the *pure essence of God, stripped of Person and of attributes.*' 'There can be no perfect contemplation *save only of the Divinity.*'[3] The Bull of 20 November 1687, condemning Molinos, listed this as the thirty-fifth condemned proposition: 'Souls in the interior way must not elicit acts of love toward the Blessed Virgin, the saints, *or the humanity of Christ* because, since these are sensible objects, love for them is also sensible'.[4] Without going into a detailed theological analysis of these statements, we can easily see what confusions they led to in 'spirituality' and in 'prayer', whether orthodox or otherwise. To begin with, the terminology in which the controversy was sometimes carried on created an impression that one could make an absolute and quasi-Nestorian separation between the 'humanity' and the 'divinity' of Christ. Forgetting or ignoring the concrete unity of the two natures in one Person, and forgetting that the object of all Christian prayer is union with the Father, through the *Person* of the Son, by the Holy Spirit, writers discussed the extent to which the 'human nature of Christ', considered almost as if it were a self-subsisting entity, entered into pure contemplative prayer.

Sometimes, it is true, theologians who were more perspicacious referred not so much to 'the humanity of Christ' as to 'the *mysteries of the life of Christ*'. For instance in drawing up the articles of Issy, Fenelon and Bossuet with their associates agreed that: 'It is a dangerous error to exclude from the state of contemplation the attributes, the three divine Persons, the *mysteries of the incarnate Son of God*, especially that of the cross and that of the resurrection.'[5]

For early monastic tradition there was no problem concerning the humanity and divinity of Christ in prayer, at least when that tradition was orthodox. It is true that some of the uneducated Coptic monks in Egypt were tempted to the heresy of anthropomorphism, as Cassian tells us. It is true also that the Fathers frequently quote and expound such texts as: 'If we have known Christ according to the flesh we know Him so no longer' (2 Cor. 5.16) and 'it is good for you that I go, for if I do not go away the Paraclete will not come to you' (John 16.7). But since the Fathers used these texts in the light of their context, and not torn out of context and applied more or less arbitrarily as 'arguments', they did not miss the real and profound meaning of the biblical revelation concerning the Person of the incarnate word, and His promise: 'Behold I am with you all days, even to the consummation of the world' (Matt. 28.20).

The purpose of this essay is to discuss some typical texts from early monastic tradition on this point, with a view to deepening and clarifying our theology of monastic and contemplative prayer.

John Cassian

Cassian is perhaps the most important and influential writer in Western monasticism. It was he who, in the early fifth century, transmitted to the West the Origenist and Evagrian doctrines on monastic life and prayer which were, and remained, dominant in Hellenistic monachism. The ninth and tenth *Conferences* of Cassian represent not only what was probably the accepted doctrine on prayer in the monastic centres of lower Egypt, but also his own synthesis of the monastic ideology of Southern Gaul in the early fifth century. In any case, this teaching of Cassian on prayer, disseminated by the monastic Fathers of the West and by generations of Western monks, had a decisive influence on the whole of monastic theology, particularly that of the Cistercians. In these conferences on prayer we find a kind of early synthesis between the twin traditions of Eastern and Western monachism which later, after the tragic schism of 1064, split apart and developed separately. By returning to Cassian we are able to transcend some of the problems, or false problems, that developed in the later history of Western spirituality, and we are also able to obtain a vantage point from which to get a more intelligent and sympathetic view of Oriental monastic theology on prayer, including such movements as that of the Hesychasts of Sinai and Athos.

The whole monastic doctrine of Cassian is summed up in the equation: *perfecta caritas=puritas cordis=pura oratio.*

The monk has left the world to seek the Kingdom of heaven, which is union with God in contemplation. While Evagrius distinguishes the 'Kingdom of God' and the 'Kingdom of Christ', Cassian makes no such division. The monk fully enters the Kingdom of God when, through purity of heart, he receives the illumination of the Holy Spirit, the Spirit of Christ. His proximate end, as a monk, is to purify his heart by asceticism, thus attaining to a state of tranquillity, or *puritas cordis*, in which his spirit recovers a natural 'lightness' or freedom from material ties, and, like a dry feather in a light breeze, can be carried towards heaven by love. He is no longer weighed down by the cares and desires of a sinful or passionate existence. He is no longer distracted and dominated by earthly concerns, and hence he is able to pray without ceasing, thus fulfilling the Apostle's command in the most perfect manner (1 Thess. 5.17). It is for this end that men become monks.

Of course there are degrees in monastic prayer, and since the monastic ideal of Nitria and Scete was, as opposed to Pachomian cenobitism, explicitly contemplative and mystical, rather than merely ascetic, Cassian takes pains to make clear the nature of the highest kinds of contemplative prayer. In the first *Conference*[6] Cassian describes the many different kinds of contemplation of God. Contemplation assumes a variety of forms. For, he says, 'God is not known *only in the wondering contemplation of His incomprehensible substance* which is *still hidden in the hope of the promise given to us*', but He is also contemplated in His creation, in His providential government of the world, in history, in our own life and vocation, and finally He is contemplated in the 'dispensation of His incarnation for our salvation'. As we see, the contemplation of the 'incomprehensible substance' is reserved for heaven, and we know from the Evagrian background that this contemplation means not merely the contemplation of the essence of God in unity, but above all the trinity of Persons. All the other objects of contemplation—providence, incarnation, etc.—'arise in our minds according to the quality of our life and the purity of our heart, and in these forms of contemplation *God is seen with pure vision or else is pos-*

sessed (i.e. by love)'. The importance of this text is that it shows how the essence of God and the Trinity of Persons will be contemplated in heaven, while on earth we come, through meditation on the incarnation and redemption, to a contemplative experience of God that is not, however, a vision of His essence. It also reminds us that for Cassian the way to contemplation is through meditative reading of the Bible. However, these higher contemplations are described as intuitions of God alone: *solius Dei intuitus*, and *contemplatio solius Die*.[7] Here there are no more words to utter, as the spirit is carried away beyond words and indeed beyond understanding into that *oratio ignita*, 'burning prayer' or 'prayer of fire', in which flame-like movements of love burst out from within the depths of the monk's being under the direct action of the Holy Spirit. This powerful surge of inner spiritual life and love is the pure gift of God, expressed in prayer of 'most pure energy uttered within us by the Holy Spirit interceding *without our knowledge*'.[8]

Finally, Cassian quotes the celebrated statement attributed to St Antony, in which the Father of Monasticism declared that the purest prayer was one in which the monk no longer knew that he was praying and was, indeed, no longer even aware of his own existence.[9]

The highest form of prayer is, then, a prayer 'without forms', a pure prayer in which there are no longer any images or ideas, and in which the spirit does not take any initiative of its own, for all activity of the human mind and senses is here completely surpassed.

In a very important text,[10] which has rich implications for both Eastern and Western monastic theology, Cassian discusses the place of Christ in this pure prayer. And we must say at once Christ is, as we might obviously suppose, *at the very centre* of this prayer, since all Christian prayer develops and becomes perfect by penetrating deeply, in the spirit, into the hidden mystery of Christ. How does Cassian explain this? By comparing it with the experience of the apostles who witnessed the Transfiguration of Christ on Tabor.

Now it is quite true that in this passage, Cassian says explicitly that the mature contemplative 'with most pure eyes gazes UPON THE DIVINITY' of Christ: *illi soli purissimis oculis divinitatem ipsius speculantur.* . . . But he immediately adds an important qualification: the contemplative gazes upon the divinity of Christ only if he ascends, with Christ, the 'high mountain of solitude': *qui cum illo secedunt in excelso solitudinis monte.*[11]

Here, of course, Cassian is expounding his characteristic doctrine: the pure contemplative life is that of the hermit who, having finished his active life of ascetic purification, departs into solitude with Christ. But note that the solitude is *with Christ*. To embrace the eremitical life is to ascend 'the high mountain of solitude *with Christ*'. And to do this is to obey most perfectly Christ's monastic call to prayer. Indeed, it is to follow His example, for He Himself withdrew to pray on the mountain by night in order to give Christians an example of solitary prayer. Cassian says:

> He instructed us by the example of His withdrawal into solitude, showing that if we also wished to call upon God with a pure and complete love of our hearts (*puro et integro cordis affectu*) we too ought to go away from all the unquiet and confusion of the crowd.[12]

Hence, to ascend the mountain of solitude is to do what Christ asks of those who would be most perfect and uncompromising in following their monastic vocation to prayer. And the life of prayer which the monk will lead 'on the mountain' will be the same kind of prayer that was Christ's own when He was on earth: a prayer free from images and concepts, free from distraction and care.

Not only that, but it is Christ Himself who purifies our prayer. That is to say, He purifies our hearts, making them tranquil and perfect in love, so that we may pray as He did on earth *qui universa polluta emundat atque sanctificat.*[13]

It is clear that Cassian, who, at St Leo's request, wrote against Nestorianism[14] was not going to fall into the error of treating the two natures in Christ in practice as if they were two separately subsisting persons. There is no question whatever of the slightest division in the unity of Christ, and no

hint that the humanity of Christ might somehow get in the
way of His divinity. On the contrary, all the emphasis is, as it
should be, upon the Person of Christ, the God-Man, who is
the utterly pure source of all holiness, *ipse fons inviolabilis
sanctitatis*.[15]

However, it is quite true that in purifying our hearts,
Christ does raise them above all bodily images in prayer. And
it might even seem that in some sense Christ, as God, makes
us forget Him as man. Indeed, Cassian seems at one point to
be saying that this is so. He declares:

> They will not be able to see Jesus coming in His Kingdom,
> who still are held prisoners by a kind of Jewish infirmity
> and are unable to say with the Apostle: 'even though we
> once knew Christ according to the flesh, we know Him so
> no longer'.[16]

However, even the most casual glance at this text tells us
there is all the difference in the world between Cassian and
Molinos. It is not a question of 'refusing to make acts of love
for the humanity of Christ' or a captious division between
His humanity and His divinity. There is certainly no equiva-
lence between 'Christ in the flesh' and the 'humanity of
Christ'. It is, on the contrary, a much more fundamentally
Christian distinction: that between Christ, God and Man, as
He was *before His passion and resurrection*, and Christ, God
and Man, *as He now is in the glory of the Father*. In one
case, 'Christ according to the flesh' or the incarnate word
who no longer lives in that *forma servi* which marked His
kenotic and hidden state before the resurrection. In the
other, the Christ of glory, who reigns now in heaven, who is
what He will always be, the supreme reality, the 'pure source
of all holiness' ever present to His faithful, acting upon their
spirit through His spirit, and guiding their destinies toward
that day in which He will appear manifestly before all men
in glory to take to Himself those who have purified their
hearts by love, in anticipation of His coming.

According to Cassian, then, the expressions *solius Dei intuitus* (the sight of God alone) and 'contemplating the divinity of Christ' refer to the contemplation of the *glory of the*

risen God-Man. This does not mean representing to ourselves, by an effort of imagination, what Christ must have looked like on Tabor, or trying to picture Him as He will come in judgement. The contemplative, in the highest form of prayer, the *oratio ignita* or prayer of fire, perceives in an ineffable and mystical fashion something of the light of divinity which has taken complete possession of the glorified humanity of Christ. Cassian comes near, then, to the Athonite theologians who taught that the light of contemplation was the same kind of light as that which shone in the humanity of Christ on Tabor. Experience of this light is, of course, a purely spiritual and mystical gift. There is no question whatever of 'excluding' the humanity of Christ from contemplative prayer, in order to contemplate His divinity! On the contrary, humanity and divinity are contemplated in inseparable unity in the Person of the glorified Son of God.

Patristic Theology:
St Leo, St Gregory, St Bede

In order to understand this doctrine of Cassian on the humanity of Christ in prayer, let us consider for a moment the dogmatic teaching of three Western Fathers, St Leo the Great, St Gregory and St Bede. We do not find these doctors of the Church concerned with a purely abstract division between the humanity and divinity of the Incarnate Word. Still less can we find anything that suggests a conflict or opposition between the Person of Christ and the divine essence 'competing', as it were, for the attention of the monk at prayer.

Christian prayer goes to the Person of Christ and through Him to the Father. The monk does not contemplate abstract ideas of Christ, or form purely subjective images of Christ 'in His humanity'. Nor does the prayer of the monk lose itself in 'the divine essence' without regard for the divine Persons. Monastic prayer is fully objective, at least in the sense that it goes to the Person of Christ as He now is, seated at the right hand of the Father in glory, though this does not necessarily imply *imagining* Him in glory. Nor does it necessarily imply a subject-object relationship in our prayer. St Leo, in speaking of the human nature of Christ, emphasizes the fact that this human nature is really and concretely glorified and enthroned with the Father. Christ, he says, showed the disciples His wounds after the resurrection, that they might believe 'that same nature which had lain in the sepulchre was to be enthroned together with the Father'.[17]

At the ascension, in the sight of the disciples, 'the nature of humankind soared above the dignity of all the creatures of heaven [the angels]' and 'there was to be no limit to the advancement [of Christ's humanity] until, seated together with the eternal Father, it might share enthroned the glory of Him whose nature it shared in the Son: *illius gloriae sociaretur in throno cujus naturae copulabatur in Filio*'.[18] And, of course, the Fathers never ceased to remind their hearers that this same manhood of Christ which was enthroned with the Father in the divine glory, was to return and judge the world. 'He set a limit to His bodily presence, and would remain at the right hand of the Father until He should return in the same flesh in which He had ascended.'[19] Monastic prayer is eschatalogical and is centred on the expectation of the Parousia, the advent of the 'immortal and invisible King of ages' who is both 'God alone' and the Christ, our redeemer and liberator.

In the meantime it is *our nature* which is enthroned in heaven with Christ. It is our nature which shares the divinity of Christ and of the Father. Hence St Leo puts these words into the mouth of the glorious redeemer: 'I have united you to myself and *I became the son of man that you might become sons of God.*'[20] St Gregory adds that Christ has made us sons of God by taking us to heaven with Him: 'He has led captivity because *he has swallowed up our corruption in the power of His incorruption.*'[21] St Leo says that with Christ's ascension into heaven we have recovered possession of paradise, and not only that, 'we have even penetrated, in Christ, into the height of heaven',[22] we have been enthroned with Him because we are 'one body' with Him: *sibi concorporatos Dei Filius ad dexteram Patris collocavit.*[23] This is the reason why we should rejoice at His going to the Father: 'above all the heavens, your lowliness is raised, in Me, to be placed at the right hand of the Father'.[24] He is not separated from us unless we choose to remain bound to the earth by our passions. In contemplation we experience, at least obscurely, something of this mystery of our union with Him *now* in heaven.

This has important implications for the life of prayer. The life of the monk, being that of a perfect Christian, is a *conversatio in coelis*. While living bodily in exile and in his earthly pilgrimage, the monk is already spiritually in paradise and in heaven where he has ascended with Christ. That is to say, although he is not physically present in heaven, he is free to come and go there as he pleases, in spirit, in prayer, in faith, in thanksgiving, praise and love, because he already 'is' there mystically in Christ. 'Let us therefore, my beloved, exult with a worthy and spiritual joy, happy before God in thanksgiving, and let us lift up the free eyes of our heart (*liberos oculos cordis*) to that height where Christ is.'[25]

The Lord has already 'made known to us all that He has heard from His Father' (John 15.15). St Gregory, commenting on this line, says that Christ has made us His friends by making known to us 'the joys of interior charity and *the festival of the heavenly country which He daily makes present in our minds by the desire of love*'. And St Gregory explains that this loving knowledge of heavenly things is very real indeed, no mere fancy: 'For when, hearing of heavenly things, we love them, we already know the things we love, for our love itself is a way of knowing—*amor ipse notitia est*.'[26] It is by the charity of Christ in our hearts that we 'are in heaven' and know the things of heaven.

The source of our freedom and the power that raises our prayer to the height of heaven is the Holy Spirit Himself, sent by Christ and the Father after the God-Man ascended into heaven. And faith in Christ's presence in heaven *as man* merits for us the grace of the Holy Spirit.[27] The angels, says St Gregory, already rejoice to have us as their companions, while they adore the humanity of the God-Man: *nec habere dedignantur hominem socium qui super se adorant hominem Deum.*[28]

While the Fathers do not draw a sharp contrast between the two abstract natures in Christ, still less between the Person of Christ and the divine essence, they are very aware of a contrast between the state of the God-Man before His passion and resurrection, and after His triumph over death. Before the passion, Christ was living 'kenotically' in what St Leo calls the *dispensatio humilitatis.* Here He worked miracles which were 'signs of the divinity in the form of the servant'.[29] But St Leo adds: 'After the passion, the chains of death having been broken . . . weakness passed over into power, death into eternity, and humiliation into glory'.[30] Note here the 'paschal' implications of the idea of 'passing over', or *transitus.* This is very important for the primitive teaching on monastic prayer, which is essentially centred in the Paschal Mystery.

The Word of God descended into the world, veiling His light in our frail human nature,[31] to 'pass through' our mortal life, to die and rise from the dead and thus, having 'taken captivity captive', to raise us with Him into heaven. Meditation on the life of Christ and on His passion belongs, then, to our participation in the Paschal Mystery and is necessary for our realization of the true objective of our monastic life and prayer. Dom Leclercq, summing up the doctrine of St Gregory on this point, says: 'In Christ, in this passage from a carnal condition to spiritual glory, was accomplished that which is the very aim of contemplation in man, the passage from the visible to the invisible, from the exterior to the interior, from faith to understanding, from humanity to divinity.'[32] Meditation on the mysteries of the life and death of Christ is, then, to be seen as part of the *transitus* or *pascha* by which we 'pass over' to contemplation of the invisible light shed in our hearts, through the Holy Spirit, by Christ in glory. In this *transitus* we ourselves pass from a human to a divine life, in Christ.

Here we must admit that we can find in St Gregory some suggestion of the separation which was later to develop into a real split between the divinity and humanity of Christ. More precisely, we find St Gregory saying that while the *more perfect* are able to contemplate the divinity, ordinary Christians are perhaps in some sense limited to the consideration of Christ in His humanity. But let us pay attention to the context. Actually, St Gregory is speaking of St Paul who has ascended to the 'third heaven' and seen things which the tongue of man cannot repeat. Now this is something more than what is traditionally meant by 'contemplation of the divinity of Christ'. It was accepted by all the Fathers as a most extraordinary experience of divine vision, such as was granted perhaps to no one else except Moses. Obviously, then, this was not something that Paul could communicate to ordinary Christians. St Gregory then comments that since the apostle could not convey to his hearers the glory of the divine majesty, he preached to them Christ crucified, and indeed himself boasted of knowing nothing among them but Christ, and Him crucified.[33]

It is clear, then, that later medieval writers could find in St Gregory a basis for their distinction between the contemplation of the humanity of Christ, which is for the humble and ignorant, and the contemplation of His divinity, which is reserved for great and mighty spirits. From this it was necessary to take only one more step, with St Peter Damian, who exclaimed: 'Let others have the majesty of the divinity; let us be content with the Cross alone'.[34] We must not, however, exaggerate the import of this statement. It is a rhetorical trope rather than a firm declaration of theological principle.

It would certainly be anachronistic to imagine so strong a contrast in the early Fathers, or in St Gregory. With the Benedictine pope, the allusion is only a passing remark, and it implies, as always, that the *memoria passionis*, or devout reflection on the life, suffering and death of Christ is a normal and natural preliminary to the knowledge (through contemplative faith) of His presence in mystery, as our glorified redeemer here and now. There is in St Gregory no question of *preferring* the thought of the suffering Christ to that of the glorified Christ. In the paragraph immediately after the one we have just cited, he turns to Christ in glory, and, applying to His glorified humanity the text 'where the body is, eagles will gather' (Matt. 24.28), St Gregory puts these words on the lips of the risen Lord: 'I, your incarnate redeemer, who sit in majesty upon the heavenly throne, will raise up the souls of the elect to heaven when I shall have delivered them from their flesh'.[35] St Gregory is always aware of Christ as a living and glorious presence, the source of holiness and divine life here and now, whereas the passion for him is a *memoria*, a past event whose sanctifying effect is mediated by the light of the risen and victorious saviour.

It might, therefore, be closer to the spirit of the early Fathers to suggest that Christ in His earthly life and in His passion is the object of *meditatio* or *consideratio*, while Christ in glory is more than 'the object' of *contemplatio*, since the contemplative experience is an ineffable sharing in the light that radiates spiritually from the glorified humanity of the saviour. The Fathers meditated on the Passion as a past event, in order to come to contemplation of Christ in His present glory. Hence monastic contemplation, according to the Fathers, is more than an effective and simple consideration, however loving and however intuitive, of an idea, thought or image of Christ as He was before His victory. Meditative consideration of the life of Christ exercises our minds in faith and love, until we receive a special power to penetrate beyond ideas of the visible and to rest in love where the eye and even the intelligence cannot penetrate. 'This is the strength of great minds,' says St Leo, 'this is the light of truly faithful souls: to believe unhesitatingly what cannot be seen with the bodily eyes and to fix their desires where vision does not penetrate.'[36] This 'greatness' is not an elevation or assertion of the self to be feared and shunned. It is the power of faith, which is proportionate to humility. Contemplation of the glorified redeemer is for the humble who, loving His cross, have emptied themselves in order to be one with Him.

Thus the resurrection was the end of what St Bede, following St Gregory, calls the *dispensatio adsumptae mortalitatis*, and the ascension marks the triumphant return of the Man-God to the Father.[37] Our faith and our prayer follow Him in His journey and ascend with Him into heaven. We obviously cannot forget or ignore Christ in His *mortalitas* or in His *in-*

carnationis sacramentum. We do not neglect His passion in order to concentrate only on His glory. But the earthly life and the death of Christ have to be seen in their proper perspective in the *pascha* or passage out of this world to the Father. St Bede, with his usual simplicity, speaks clearly and realistically of the part played in the monk's prayer by the thought of Christ's life on earth and of His passion. It is by trying to imitate the life of Christ and by sharing in His death that we pass with Him into the glory of heaven. Hence we meditate on His life and passion. The constant thought of the life, suffering and death of Christ inspires and forms us in our active life of asceticism and virtue. The joy of His resurrection and of His life enthroned with the Father communicates itself to us in the light of contemplation. Note that St Bede sees the liturgical mysteries as the point of contact where all these different aspects of Christ are brought into focus by His living presence among us in the celebration of the holy sacrifice. He also says that contemplatives see the light of the majesty of Christ in the *lectio divina* of Scripture. The *majestas Domini* is communicated to us in the *majestas Scripturae*. 'Soli qui mente superna petierint, maiestatem sacrae Scripturae quae in Domino est adimpleta perspicient.'

St Bede says we

come early to the sepulchre of the Lord, bearing spices, when, being mindful of His passion and of the death He underwent for us, we show to others the light of good works exteriorly, and interiorly we burn in our hearts with the sweetness of pure compunction [note the reminiscence of Cassian and St Gregory]. This we should do at all times, but above all when we enter the church to pray, or when we approach the altar to partake in the mystery of the Lord's body and blood.[38]

However, St Bede goes on to add a characteristic note: If the holy women showed such reverence for the (dead) Body of Christ, 'how much more is it right that we who believe that He has risen from the dead, that He has ascended into heaven, we who have known the power of the divine majesty present everywhere, should stand in His presence with all reverence and celebrate His mystery'.[39] Here, as always, there is emphasis on the realization by faith and love of the victorious saviour as a living and infinitely life-giving presence, in the glory of the Father.

For St Bede says that by our faith in the resurrection, we enter the sepulchre and find it empty. 'With attentive hearts, going over the series of events in the incarnation and passion *we find that He has risen from the dead and is never to be seen again in His mortal flesh.*'[40] The 'sacrament' of Christ's mortal life has reached a new dimension. It has passed over into the glory of the resurrection in order to pour itself out on us in grace and life.

In other words, the Fathers reflected on the life of Christ much as they reflected on the Old Testament: that is to say, as on something which has been radically changed in achieving its final fulfilment and perfection. So St Bede says: 'We must remember continually that we cannot find the body of our Lord on earth, and we must be all the more humbled as we see our need to cry out from the depths, to Him who dwells in heaven; we must be all the more saddened as we see that we are on pilgrimage, far away from Him in whose presence alone we can live happily'.[41] However, this is to our advantage. 'It was fitting that the form of the servant was taken away from us that the love of the divinity might be more firmly established in our minds.'[42] To love 'the divinity' means, here, simply to love the God-Man as He is now and will be forever, and to follow Him with all our desire, so as to be where He now is and thus share in His divine life.[43] We shall never see Him in mortal flesh, *mortali et carne corruptibili circumdatum*, but all must behold Him in majesty, coming to judge the world.[44]

According to St Leo, when Christ told Mary Magdalen not to touch Him, on the morning of the resurrection, He was saying to the Church:

I do not want you to come to me in a bodily manner, or to know me with the senses of your flesh. I am making you wait for much higher realities and am preparing you for

better things. WHEN I SHALL HAVE ASCENDED TO MY FA-
THER, THEN YOU WILL TOUCH ME IN A MUCH MORE PER-
FECT, MUCH MORE REAL MANNER. YOU WILL APPREHEND
WHAT YOU CANNOT TOUCH AND YOU WILL BELIEVE WHAT
YOU DO NOT SEE.[45]

In losing the *mortalitas* of Christ we have in reality lost
nothing and gained everything. In passing over into a glorious
state in which He cannot be seen, He is in reality not with-
drawing Himself from us but giving Himself more perfectly
both as God and as Man by mystically illuminating our
hearts with the *lumen incircumscriptum.* 'Then indeed, beloved, THE SON OF GOD, THE SON OF MAN, MAKES HIMSELF
KNOWN IN A MORE EXCELLENT AND A MORE SACRED MANNER
when He returns into the glory of the Father's majesty; and
IN AN INEFFABLE WAY HE BEGAN TO BE MORE PRESENT IN HIS
DIVINITY when He was more remote in His humanity.'[46]

The Unlimited Light

It is clear, then, that the meaning of the presence of
Christ in prayer, as it was believed and understood by the
early monastic tradition, cannot be grasped unless we are
clear about the 'more excellent and more sacred manner' in
which the God-Man makes Himself known, now that He
dwells in the glory of the Father. Note that in the last and
most important text we have quoted from St Leo, it is quite
clear that Christ *both as man and as God* is now more intimately known since He has become 'in an ineffable way more
present'. The fact that this more perfect presence is a presence 'in His divinity' does not exclude the fact that in it He
is also more perfectly present *as man*, though not according
to the mode of presence which He had when He was on
earth in His mortal flesh. It is clear, then, that the monastic
Fathers are not merely setting aside the Person of the Incarnate Word and substituting the presence of the divine essence considered as 'more perfect' and 'more intimate' for
this would be nothing but the substitution of the 'God of the
philosophers' for the 'God of Abraham, Isaac and Jacob'—an

essence for a *Person*. The Fathers were not men who could be satisfied with prayer centred on an abstract essence.

According to St Gregory, what we contemplate and love in the Person of the Word is not purely and simply the divine essence as such, but rather the 'unlimited light', the *lumen incircumscriptum* which is His personal prerogative as Man-God, the 'glory' which He has received from the Father and which He communicates to us 'in the Spirit' (cf. 2 Cor. 3.17–18 and John 17.1–10). This is the light of contemplation that is poured out into our hearts by the Spirit of Christ, and which gives us an ineffable knowledge of God in the union of the two natures in the Person of Christ. The *lumen incircumscriptum* is none other than the *lumen Christi*, the light of the glorious and risen Christ, the light of which the Church sings exultantly in the Easter liturgy. It is the light of the divine, transcendent and life-giving power which belongs to Christ not only as God but also as man, and to exclude the humanity of Christ from that light is to turn away in blindness from the true mystery of the one Christ. To know Christ *only* as a 'divine essence' is little better than knowing Him only as a frail and mortal man. The Christian and monastic contemplation of Christ is that of a man who is God, who is totally transfigured in the light of God and who calls us, His brothers, out of darkness to a participation in that 'admirable light' (1 Pet. 2.9).

The true call to monastic contemplation is, then, a call to renounce all that opposes this 'ineffable light' of God in Christ, to submit totally and without reservation to the *lumen Christi*, to accept one's own helplessness and one's own deficiency, indeed one's own impurity and darkness in the presence of His light, and yet to seek with all one's heart to become transformed by contemplation and love into the very purity of the light itself. The ineffable and indefinable light of Christ is a light of extreme simplicity and purity, but it is also a tender and merciful light which does not reject any darkness that is aware of itself and laments its alienation from His truth. The chief desire of the monk is, then, to surrender to the light of Christ, to remove all that acts as an obstacle between ourselves and that light. This presupposes a perfect honesty and a complete readiness to accept the light on its own terms, obedience to the light in total humility. It means, of course, first of all, the obedience of faith, the submission of our intelligence to God and the acceptance of His way and His plan for us in the mystery of Christ. With this submission comes love, which gives us eyes with which to apprehend the invisible reality of the *lumen incircumscriptum:* this demands a supernatural gift of vision, since the 'light' is invisible to a created intelligence as such.

Preaching on the parable of the woman who lost a groat, lit a lantern and turned her whole house upside down until she found it,[47] St Gregory says that the woman seeking the groat is like God seeking His image in man. God lit a lantern to seek man when He enkindled the light of His wisdom in human nature. 'For a lamp', says St Gregory, 'is a light burning in an earthenware vessel, and the light in the earthenware vessel is the divinity in flesh: *lumen in testa divinitas in carne.*'[48]

Now if we look a little closely at this expression, we will find that, as it stands, it does not give a fully satisfactory description of the union of the two natures in Christ. To describe the Incarnation as 'divinity in flesh' is to make it not so much a *union* of the two natures as their *juxtaposition.* And objects that are merely set one within another can easily be separated again. The vessel that has been filled can also be emptied. But such is not the case with Christ. We must understand St Gregory in his own terms, and we must take these comparisons in their context. St Gregory adds: 'An earthenware vessel is hardened in the fire, and the power [of Christ] was dried up like a potsherd (Ps. 21.16) because the flesh that He assumed, He made strong by the tribulation of the passion, for the glory of the resurrection'. Here we have once again the paschal theme, the 'passage' or 'passover' of Christ the man into the glory of the Father.

In these simple approximations and popular comparisons, St Gregory is hinting at a deeper mystery: the fact that the distinct and inseparable natures united in the Person of Christ were manifested in an even more intimate and perfect unity after the Resurrection so that the man Christ is now totally penetrated not only with hidden divinity but with the manifest and glorious light of His Godhead. Whereas before the resurrection the divine life of Christ was completely hidden, so that he could be thought of as a mere man, *this is no longer possible*. Christ the man is truly God of God and light of light, and can never be otherwise. Nor can His divinity and His humanity ever be separated except by the logical operations of our abstract thought. Our faith and our contemplation have absolutely no need for such a separation, since they are directed to the *Person of the God-Man in whom the two natures are perfectly united*. And this union makes the glorious Redeemer the source of all our spiritual illumination and our sanctification.

St Gregory, therefore, goes on to say that when the light of glory is lit in the 'lamp' of the risen Christ, it is able to strike directly into our conscience, and in the presence of this invisible light our conscience is shaken from top to bottom: *mox ut ejus divinitas per carnem claruit, omnis se conscientia nostra concussit*. The consequence is that the lost drachma, or man's likeness to God, is found when the *lumen incircumscriptum* enters the conscience, turning everything upside down and purifying the heart with tribulation.

In the twenty-second and twenty-third books of the *Moralia in Job*, St Gregory gives one of his classical expositions on compunction, which is essential to true monastic prayer. Compunction is one of the first effects of the light of Christ in the soul, and it has a twofold character. First, sorrowful compunction, which springs from an experience of the contrast between our sinfulness and His love for us; secondly, a compunction, which bursts out in tears of gladness at the recognition of God's mercy. 'The light of truth, gliding into our hearts, sometimes moves us to sorrow by showing us the severe justice of God, at other times, opening up the springs of inward joy, it makes us serenely happy.'[49] The *lumen incircumscriptum* thus enters our hearts as a purifying fire consuming our sins, and 'then, when the eyes of our heart are cleansed, the joy of our heavenly homeland opens up to us. . . . First the burning ray of sorrow clears away from our interior vision (*mentis acie*) the darkness of our sins which stands in the way of sight. And then in a flash our mind is lit up with the dazzling blaze of indefinable light'.[50] He goes on to describe the way in which our spirit, in this light, seems to be created anew, rapt out of itself into a totally new life which is the life of the world to come. At the same time (and this too is characteristic of the Gregorian teaching on contemplation) it apprehends its own complete incapacity to grasp the *lumen incircumscriptum*. Hence it is at the same time flooded with joy from the 'immense source' of grace (Christ) and baffled by its own complete inability to grasp His light as it is in Himself. In the end, the spirit of man is blinded by the 'dazzling presence of His immensity all about us'.[51]

This, then, is the light of Christ as it is poured out in monastic contemplation, the light of His personal presence, not the presence of the divine essence in its immensity, but the presence of the Man-God in His transcendent glory.

In these typical passages of St Gregory we can see a profound development of the implications hidden in a simple phrase of the Prologue to St Benedict's *Rule*: 'with our eyes open to the deifying light: *apertis oculis ad deificum lumen*'.

Ambrose Autpert

In conclusion, and in confirmation of what has been said, we may consider a text ascribed to a Benedictine master of the eighth century who is less well known than he deserves to be, Ambrose Autpert,[52] Abbot of St Vincent on the Volturno, one of the spiritual heirs of St Gregory the Great. In a homily on the transfiguration he reminds us of the text of Cassian which we considered at the beginning of this study.

First he speaks of the body of the glorified Christ as being 'new in glory but not new in nature': *alterius gloriae sed non alterius naturae*.[53] 'He who was evident in His flesh suddenly blazed forth in majesty, full of glory.'[54]

Yet as long as this glory is not manifested in the risen Lord, Autpert suggests that the human nature and actions of Christ tend to *hide* his real Person and His divine nature rather than reveal it. For instance, in the mystery of the

Purification, Christ *hid* the sacrament (mystery) of His incarnation: *claudit impiis sacramentum divinae incarnationis.*[55] Mary, in keeping the law, hides the *majestas* of her Son, which is revealed by the spirit of prophecy to Simeon and Anna alone. In the same sermon, Ambrose Autpert calls the *caro redemptionis* before the Passion a seal set upon the secret of the divinity: *Quoddam divinitatis ejus sigillum absconsionis.*[56] And yet Mary herself is fully aware both of the divinity and humanity in Her Son.

> O how small, and O how great is He whom you have brought into the world! Small in His humanity, great in His divinity. Small in the kingdom of the Jews, great in the kingdom of the Gentiles. . . . You, beyond all others, recognized the immensity, of Him whom you saw truly born of yourself; surely you adored with trembling the God whom you had brought into the world as an infant; but you suckled, cherished and nourished Him whom, according to His humanity, you recognized as your Son.[57]

Now obviously, though there is great tenderness toward the humanity of the saviour in these lines, what Ambrose Autpert contemplates in adoring wonder is not the humanity as such, but *the union of humanity and divinity in the one Person of the incarnate word.* It is not the humanity of Christ that constitutes the mystery of the incarnation, but the fact that this human nature has been assumed by a divine Person and subsists in an inseparable unity with His divine nature.

Returning to the transfiguration, we find in this mystery a certain inchoative manifestation of Christ's divinity in and through His humanity, but the manifestation is not yet perfect because the body of Christ has not yet won the complete victory over death. It has not yet 'passed over' into the new state which is destined for His humanity. 'He was as yet mortal and the very mortality of His body did not permit Him to show forth the light of His divinity as it really was.'[58] At this point, Autpert advances a theory which is curiously reminiscent of the Christian Orient. He says that the light of the transfiguration was not the light of Christ's full glory as head of His Church, but the light which would be bestowed on the members of His mystical body in heaven.[59] The light of Tabor which came forth and transformed even His garments, making them 'white as snow' was only a partial emanation of His inner and divine light: *ab illa interiore luce processit quam nullus humani generis corporeus oculus intueri potest.* He goes on to say that this inner light of Christ is the source of all visible light: from it comes the light of the sun and the stars, but it is also the light which illumines the minds of angels and men. Hence, while we consider in faith the miracle of the transfiguration, we should seek *to see in contemplation the light of Christ shining by His divinity within us: miremur potius hunc divinitate micantem interius.* At the last judgement, he continues, all, both sinners and just, will see the exterior glory of Christ as He was in the transfiguration, but only the just will see His inner glory, which will be hidden from the others. At the same time all the great contemplatives, both before Christ and after Him, were illumined by His inner and divine light. Moses, for instance, saw the light of the divine *majestas* in Christ, and it was this that gave him strength to fast for forty days and nights 'without feeling hunger or thirst or darkness'.[60]

Ambrose Autpert says that monks ought to seek with all their hearts, in perfect humility and unalterable desire, this inner light of the divine majesty shining in Christ, and sent by Him into our hearts. In order to do this, we must imitate Him (as Cassian said) by ascending the mountain to pray in solitude.

> He went up on the mountain in order that He might pray; that is to say, He went in order that by this action of His He might show all who are to seek the sight of His *majestas* that they must pray without ceasing, and that they must not stay in the lowlands, but must always pray on the mountain. Those only can do this without obstacle who do not give in to earthly desires through the allurement of vices. But, with their eyes fixed on the heights, by love they gaze upon heavenly things.[61]

Then Bl. Ambrose, abbot as he was of a cenobium, added a note that is in strict accord with primitive monastic tradition: the lesson of Christ praying on the mountain is that the monk also, with his abbot's permission, should seek that degree of exterior solitude which is appropriate to his own spiritual maturity. 'In this action [going up on the mountain to pray] the Lord shows that, if permission is given, exterior solitude itself should be sought for the sake of prayer, so that the monk may call upon God with all the more intimacy, when he is not surrounded by a tumult of other men.'[62]

Our conclusion is evident. The Patristic tradition distinguishes the humanity and divinity of Christ, not in order to separate but in order to unite them, because the Christ of monastic contemplation is neither the divinity alone nor the humanity alone, but the unity of the two natures in one Person. Ambrose Autpert sums up the tradition in these words:

> IN THE ONE PERSON OF OUR REDEEMER, GOD AND MAN, we confess there is the perfect nature of God and the perfect nature of man. By reason of one nature He is Lord, by virtue of the other, a servant . . . to be Lord is one thing, to be servant another (*aliud Dominus, aliud servus*), AND YET THE LORD IS NOT OTHER THAN THE SERVANT (*non tamen alius Dominus, alius servus*) FOR THERE IS BUT ONE AND THE SAME SON OF GOD AND MAN.[63]

It is precisely because this is so that the mysteries of Christ's human life on earth can become the object of our admiration and our love. But they are not, strictly speaking, the ultimate resting place of contemplation, which is a light received in the inner depths of our being from the risen saviour, God and Man, reigning in the glory of the Father.

CONVERSION OF LIFE

The vow of *conversatio morum* (conversion of life) is the essential monastic vow, and monastic renewal is only really comprehensible in the light of it. Such renewal must consist first of all in a rethinking, an adaptation of the monastic *conversatio*, the whole monastic life of prayer and penance (*si revera Deum quaerit*) which is the heart of the monastic vocation.

The task of monastic renewal today is something more than that of a restoration of an existing discipline, of returning to the strict observance of seventeenth century interpretations of twelfth century customs based on a supposed sixth century monastic practice. The renewal of monastic prayer is not simply a revival of certain prayers, and the restoration of monastic penance is not simply the restoration of certain penances. Our age of transition and crisis demands a restoration of the monastic idea of *conversatio morum* in its purity and its depth, in a way that is timeless, transcends the peculiarities of age and culture, and is therefore able to be as actual and authentic to us in our time as it was to men in the time of St Benedict. The term indeed is archaic but the reality is as new and as old as the actuality of the Gospel. Our study of *conversatio morum* is therefore a study of the monastic vocation, of the monk's essential 'task' (though in fact he has no task but to pursue that peace and liberty of spirit which enable him to rest in God). An understanding of *conversatio morum* is necessary if we are to evaluate the aspirations of some modern monks toward 'incarnational witness' in the world on one hand and toward greater solitude on the other. This study is not however directly concerned with the problem of monks going out to work in factories. It is concerned simply with the heart of the monastic vocation to prayer and penance, to liberty of spirit, to freedom from vain preoccupation as well as from active pastoral works. Such a study may help to make prayer and penance fully significant again for modern man, and may also help to liberate the monastic life from the dead hand of conventionalism, so that the monk's turning to Christ, his openness to the living word of the Gospel and to the sanctifying word of the Church, may be completely authentic and alive in our time.

'The vow of conversion of life', as it is habitually called, is by no means easy to understand. The term itself is both ambiguous and quaint. We are fully aware of the confusions that proliferate in the chapter devoted to this vow in the *Spiritual Directory*, which treats it as an engagement 'to advance without intermission', 'tending to perfection by the purgative, illuminative and unitive ways', purposing 'to go forward without ever believing that they have arrived at the bourne'.[1] Thus the vow is seen as an explicit commitment to make constant progress in virtue so that 'as soon as one says it is enough one is undone'. This might seem to imply that to 'say it is enough' is to 'sin against the vow'. But the author catches himself in time and sets a limit which, instead of making his idea precise, is so broad that it no longer defines anything specifically monastic: the vow is sinfully violated (he says) when one is 'habitually transgressing in a serious degree the duties of the Christian life' along with the duties of 'the religious state'.

It is obvious that this brave attempt to treat the vow of *conversatio morum* in terms of the scholastic manual and to discuss its obligation as one discusses the precise obligations of the 'three vows' taken by modern Orders, leads only to confusion.

Nevertheless it must be said that the *Directory* has good things to say about the spirit of the vow of conversion of life and describes the purpose of the vow fairly accurately as: 'transforming one's habits of thought and one's general behaviour from those of a worldling to those of monk, imitating Christ' (p. 186), hence vowing 'to tend to perfection all one's life according to our Rule'. But it must nevertheless be admitted that *conversatio morum* does not permit a precise scholastic treatment, with clear definition of the 'matter of the vow' and a strict limit where one sins or does not 'sin against the vow'. In St Benedict's mind it is simply a formal commitment to live until death as a fervent monk.

First of all, let us recall that the earliest text of the Rule definitely uses the term *conversatio morum*, whereas later manuscripts change this to *conversio morum*. The term *conversatio morum* is unusual, and was already considered unusual even by monks close to the time of St Benedict. Indeed from a very early date, the tendency to prefer *conversio* in the phrase *conversio morum* is everywhere evident. And as a matter of fact, the two terms *conversio* and *conversatio* are taken as more or less synonymous. Note too that the expression *conversatio morum* is not found in the *Rule of the Master*.

As early as Benedict of Aniane we find *conversatio morum* disappearing from profession formulas, indeed all reference to the vow may be absent in some formulas where only obedience and stability are explicitly promised. Other profession formulas of the Carolingian period give phrases like *stabilitas conversationis in congregatione*.[2]

Something of a problem may seem to arise from the fact that the earliest commentators on the Rule all speak of *conversio morum* and not of *conversatio morum*. This indeed matters little if you assume that *conversio* and *conversatio* mean substantially the same thing. But we shall find authors who hold that the two are so significantly different that any discussion of the vow in terms of *conversio* seems to them to be misleading. Thus they may refuse to accept anything said about *conversio morum* as applying to *conversatio morum*.

Let us rapidly look over the choice of definitions and descriptions of *conversio morum* offered by the commentators, from the earliest times to the present.[3]

Conversio morum is simply defined by Paul the Deacon as *eradicatio vitiorum et plantatio virtutum*. This is the most primitive meaning, and we can hardly doubt that it fits in roughly with the probable intention of the Legislator himself, assuming that *conversio morum* more or less fits his idea of *conversatio morum*. It is, however, too general. Bernard of

Monte Cassino gives a more precise description: *ut non saeculariter vivat sed mores per conversionem a saecularibus habeat distinctos*. This is perhaps the most practical definition. It fits the monastic life, whereas that of Paul the Deacon does not distinguish the monk from the ordinary Christian in any way. Boherius takes up the same idea: *conversio morum idem est quod abrenuntiatio mundanorum*. It is the classic *apotage*, the definitive farewell to the world, to one's home, family, to married life, to property, to the cares of worldly business, to all worldly pleasure, in order to follow Christ and indeed to follow Him into the desert. This implies eventually life ordered to transformation in Christ, as we find with Turrecremata. For him the vow of *conversio morum* leads the monk to be changed truly into another man so that he (the monk) might say in all truth 'I live now not I but Christ liveth in me'.

These definitions follow the classic monastic pattern. Post-Tridentine commentators tend to stress the keeping of the Rule as the matter of the vow. Calmet says *conversio morum* means renouncing one's former vices and ordering one's life by the Rule of St Benedict. For Haeften it is a vow 'to follow the monastic observance and the customs of the place'. This is substantially the same as the expression we find in the nineteenth-century Trappist usages.[4] But if the vow of conversion of manners is a vow to live according to the Rule, to observe with exactitude all the observance and even the customs of the house, then violations of Rule and even of observances would appear to be sins against the vow. This problem implies a casuistical view of the vow which was probably alien to the mind of St Benedict, and there would be little value in discussing it here, as the discussion would lead to a loss of perspective.

Modern commentators and scholars have returned to the traditional expressions of primitive monasticism, with formulas that are more or less felicitous. 'L'adieu à la vie mondaine avec direction de notre activité vers les choses surnaturelles' (Delatte); 'Auswerkung des Mönchsseins im Leben der Tugend. . . . Streben nach Heiligkeit. . . . Nachfolge Jesu

Christi' (Herwegen); 'Asketische Lebensweise' (Rothen-
häusler); 'Monastic life or *politeia*' (Butler); 'Monasticity of
behaviour' (Chapman); 'Self-discipline' (McCann).[5]

We might summarize all this by saying that the vow of
conversio morum is a vow of renunciation and penance, a
vow to abandon the world and its ways in order to seek God
in the solitude, ascesis, obedience, prayer, poverty and labours
of the monastic way. It is the vow to respond totally and
integrally to the word of Christ, 'Come, follow Me' by renouncing all that might impede one in following Him
untrammelled, all that might obscure one's clarity of intent
and confuse one's resolve. It is the vow to obey the voice
of God, to place oneself under a Rule and an Abbot in order
to follow the will of God in all things (which does not exclude
a hermit life since this may be, however exceptionally, a fruit
of monastic ascesis in community, as we shall see).

There can be no doubt that one of the most important
aspects of *conversatio morum* is the persevering determination
to bear with patience and courage all the trials one may meet
in the monastic life, carrying one's cross and following Christ.
True monastic *conversatio* is not possible without a radical
and generous disposition to accept all the sufferings and tribulation willed for one in God's divine plan, since these are
a consequence of one's response to His call, and therefore
play an important part in one's vocation. It is in a sense
precisely to these trials that one has been called by grace,
so that fidelity to grace demands this acceptance. Evasion and
rebellion would be a failure of monastic *conversatio*, and
might lead to loss of one's vocation.

To really understand the traditional basis of *conversio* or
conversatio morum we would need to go back to some of the
classic New Testament texts, such as Matthew 4.18–22 (the
vocation of the Apostles). The monastic life is traditionally
regarded as a *vita apostolica* in so far as the monk in the
perfection of his metanoia, his conversion and renunciation,
imitates the Apostles most perfectly. When the Cistercian
Exordium Magnum calls the Cistercian life a *formula perfectae paenitentiae* it is thinking of Christ's call to 'sell all

and follow Me'.[6] This is at once the 'form of perfect penance' and the 'word of consummate justice'. The author of the *Exordium* uses the traditional distinction between offering one's possessions to God and offering one's very self. The way of monastic *conversatio* is to renounce all and offer oneself totally to God, *licet legamus non nullos in divitiis et omni gloria mundi continentes et humiles vixisse*.[7] The true way of penance is to renounce all and become a disciple, travelling the narrow way, the *sublimis conversatio*[8] of apostolic renunciation and community life as exemplified in Acts 2.44–7, and 4.32–5.[9] St Anthony, says the *Exordium* (Dist. I, ch. 3), had the law of love written in his heart by the Spirit of the living God and left this law of *perfectissima conversatio* by the example of his life to 'most perfect disciples, Macarius, Paphnutius, Pambo, Isidore and many others' (p. 50). Above all, St Benedict '*superexcellenti puritate conversationis*' (ch. 4, p. 52) showed he had in himself the spirit of all the Monastic Fathers of the East, and by his discretion opened the monastic way to all who desired to seek God.

Perfecta paenitentia is then equivalent to *conversio morum*, and is *perfectissima religio, sublimis conversatio*.

Perhaps the best Gospel text for a full understanding of *conversatio morum* in its radical and essential demands (which are simply those of the Christian life itself, taken literally and perfectly) is Mark 8.34–8, and the corresponding passages in the other synoptics. The Christian, therefore in a very special sense the monk, is called to 'deny himself and take up his cross and follow Me'. *Conversatio morum* is a life which renounces care according to the teaching of the Sermon on the Mount in order to fix all the love and attention of the heart on Christ alone. 'Whoever would save his life will lose it, and whoever will lose his life for My sake will save it' (Mark 8.35). Comparing the gain of the whole world and the loss of one's own soul, *conversatio morum* elects rather to lose all and save one's life in and for Christ (Mark 8.36). The life of the monk bears witness before the world to the truth of the Gospel and gives expression to the eschatological hope which takes the promises of Christ in full and literal seriousness. 'Whoever is ashamed of Me and of My word in this adulterous and sinful generation, of him also will the Son of Man be ashamed.' The vow of *conversatio morum* is then a total commitment with all one's being to Christ and to His word, so that one renounces all that might tend in the slightest way to make one 'ashamed' of the Gospel. Understood in this light, the vow obviously includes within its scope the obligations of poverty and chastity. The monk of St Benedict and of Citeaux does not make explicit vows of poverty and chastity since they are implicit in *conversatio morum.*

The recently published *Collectio Monastica* of Ethiopian monastic texts,[10] though from late manuscripts, gives many passages that sum up the monastic tradition on this point.

'O brother monks who have left the business of this passing world, take care lest you return to your former business. . . . Thou art renewed as an eagle, seek the things that are above; thou hast come forth from Sodom, do not look back. Pass over the mountain lest thou be as Lot's wife. . . . Thou hast been made a disciple, do not become a traitor with Judas. . . . Thou hast become a free man, do not become a slave of desires' (op. cit., p. 3).

The ancient monastic fathers are proposed to the new novice as models because 'keeping their word, they went on through conflict and patience to inherit the kingdom of heaven' (p. 3). The spirit of indifference, complacency, neglect is foreign to that of true metanoia and penance. 'O *monache, ne sis negligens sed paenitentiam age in hoc saeculo*' (p. 5).

Smaragdus in his commentary on the Rule (ch. 58) shows that the vow (which he calls *conversio morum*) was understood in this sense. The *promissio* of stability, *conversio morum* and obedience is in fact regarded simply as one inclusive promise, not as 'three vows'. By this promise the monk is subjected to monastic rules and observance in order to 'please God by zeal in good works'. In the petition formula written out by the novice before vows, Smaragdus indicates that the Novice Master has formally warned him: 'Sciendo scias quoniam si praeter promissionem regularis observantiae *retro convertens respexeris*, aptus regno caelorum non eris.' *Conversio morum* is turning toward God in monastic ascesis and good works and implies the refusal to 'turn back' to the works of the world or to negligence. But if he 'turns back' he will be thrown out of the monastery. The real spirit of monastic conversion is summed up by the novice in Smaragdus in these words: '*Certissime (scio) quia si particeps passionis Christi fuero, et resurrectionis ero*'.[11]

Traditional texts which sum up the *vita monachi* also by that very fact describe *conversio* or *conversatio morum*. 'Vita monachi haec est, opus, obedientia meditatio, non obloqui, non murmurare . . . neque examinare et audire quod alienum est, neque manibus suis rapere sed magis dare, neque in corde suo superbire, . . . neque satiari in ventre suo, sed omnia agere cum discrimine cogitationis et hic est monachus'.[12]

Many texts in the *Collectio Monastica* insist on the necessity to accept and fear with tribulation. This one attributed to Ephrem, says:

> He who desires to please the Lord and to become a son of the Lord must above all get rid of anger and firmly hold on to patience and silence. In all things that come upon him, in tribulation of all kinds, in need, and bodily care . . . sickness and conflict . . . struggle with evil spirits . . . insults from other men . . . in all these things he who desires to please the Lord must consequently rejoice and love and exult and be fervent with the zeal of the Lord and approach Him with perfect conduct—*cum perfectis moribus ad eum accedat.*[13]

This is *conversio morum!*

The *Rule of the Master* especially in the early pages, the *thema* and the prologue sums up the *conversio* of the monk (the word *conversatio* is not found in the RM, but the word *conversio* is frequent).

Clamat nobis cottidie Dominus dicens convertimini ad me

et ego convertar ad vos. Conversio ergo nostra ad Do-
minum, fratres, non est nisi a malis reversio, dicente Scrip-
tura, *deverte a malo et fac bonum.* A quibus autem malis
cum avertimur Deum intuemur, et ille nos statim suo
illuminans vultu, donans nobis adjutorium suum, mox gratiam suam petentibus tribuit, quaerentibus ostendit, pul-
santibus patefacit. Haec tria Domini dona concessa ipsi
conveniunt qui Dei voluerint non suam facere volunta-
tem.[14]

Here we find one of the essentials of *conversio morum:* the
complete abandonment of one's own will. The true monk, according to the Regula Magistri, is he who 'walks by the
judgement of his teacher, *doctoris arbitrio ambulans,* and has
learned how not to know the way of his own will: *iter volun-
tatis propriae nescire.*

No need to insist that in spite of the crucial importance of
fasting, prayer, solitude, labour, works of charity and so on,
all in the life of the monk hangs on the renunciation of self-
will, and this is consequently not simply a special obligation
of the vow of obedience, as modern thought would insist, but
is also an essential note of *conversio morum.* Texts could be
multiplied and a whole book could be written on the subject.
Let us remember only the Prologue of St Benedict, which
echoes the Master here, as well as his 'instruments of good
works' and the seventh chapter (humility) and we will get
some idea of what *conversio* means for a monk of St Benedict.

Needless to say the works of Abbot de Rancé offer a somewhat neglected source of rich traditional material on this subject. It is true that one must discount a certain vehemence
and exaggeration in some of the statements made by the
reformer of La Trappe. Nevertheless his conferences, particularly his talks at profession and the vesting of novices, give
us the traditional monastic view of 'conversion'.[15] 'St Bernard
teaches us that our profession is that of the Apostles; and
that if we cannot raise ourselves entirely to the holiness of
these quite divine men, we must imitate them as far as we
can in their mortification, their poverty, their humility, their

renunciation, their privations. And we must strive to follow
Jesus Christ as they did in a total stripping and perfect
nakedness'.[16] In his application of this traditional principle,
Abbot de Rancé is, however, extremely rigorous. He indicates
that the possession of a merely 'common level' of Christian
virtue is, for the monk, so insufficient that the monk who
does not strive with all his might to be a saint is likely to be
damned. Monastic tradition certainly abhors negligence, but
it is generally more compassionate and understanding toward
human weakness.

A modern scholar, Dom O. Lottin, has questioned all the
traditional interpretations of St Benedict that accept the expression *conversio morum* instead of *conversatio morum*.[17]
These two, Dom Lottin insists, are so profoundly different
that an interpretation of *conversio* does not really give St
Benedict's true mind regarding *conversatio morum*. The relation of *conversatio* to *conversio* is, says Dom Lottin, that of
means to ends. *Conversatio* is the means by which the monk
arrives at *conversio*. Now the means by which the monk at-
tains to true *conversio* is the cenobitic life. Dom Lottin insists on this. It is the cenobitic life *only*, says he, in the mind
of St Benedict. So definite is Dom Lottin in this conviction
that he finally reaches the point of declaring that the vow of
conversatio morum is simply and strictly a vow to persevere
in the community with the *explicit intention of never becoming a hermit*. How does Dom Lottin reach this conclusion?
He does indeed admit that St Benedict declares the excel-
lence of the eremitic life, but he insists that the vow of *conversatio morum* is none the less explicitly a *renunciation* of
eremitic solitude. There can be no doubt of Dom Lottin's
categorical insistence on this point. The vow means nothing
less than 'l'exclusion de la vie érémitique et dès lors le choix
de la vie cénobitique'. This is based first of all on a dictionary
definition in which *one* of the meanings given for *conversatio*
is *commoratio, convictus, societas conversantium*.

Dom Lottin's conclusion also rests quite heavily on an
artificially schematic comment of Bernard of Monte Cassino,
in which Bernard says that the three Benedictine vows are intended to emphasize a contrast between the cenobite and the

three other categories of monks enumerated in Chapter One of the Rule. According to this pattern, *conversio morum* protects the cenobite from sarabaitism; stability keeps him from becoming a gyrovague, while obedience, without being precisely *against* hermits, distinguishes the cenobite from the hermit who is on his own and not under a superior. Dom Lottin, arguing that an interpretation based on the reading *conversio morum* must be wrong, revises it as follows. Stability is against gyrovagues, yes: but obedience is against sarabaites. Therefore by a process of exclusion the vow of *conversatio morum* must be *against* hermits and indeed a vow never to become one. This is an oversimplification.

To consider the vow of *conversatio morum* nothing more and nothing less than an explicit vow never to become a hermit is to fly in the face of primitive monastic tradition which St Benedict himself, with all his preference for cenobites, accepts without question. And, as a matter of fact, in taking note of criticisms of his position, Dom Lottin shifts his emphasis to a more common and less debatable ground. 'St Benedict took into account the special condition of monasteries in his time, where candidates for the eremitic life had to spend several years in common life in houses of cenobites.' In order to prevent a spirit of restlessness, says Dom Lottin, 'St Benedict obliges by vow all the members of his community (*cenobites and future hermits*) to follow his rule which manifestly organizes the cenobitic life alone'.[18] This view admits that St Benedict does not close off absolutely and without appeal a way of perfection which, while being exceptional and fraught with danger, is nevertheless a normal (though rare) outcome of the cenobitic ascesis. To bind oneself by vow never to go beyond a certain level of the monastic life, never to listen to any voice calling *ad interiora deserti*, would be an arbitrary limitation of the monastic vocation to one of its aspects. One may admit the superiority of the cenobitic life, and assert that the cenobitic life is the safe way to the perfection of the Gospel and even is somewhat better than the way of total solitude (as Cassian's Abbot John declared in his Conference), but it is quite another matter to assert that the true mind of St Benedict is that a monk who has made vows according to his Rule is thenceforth in a position where his very vows themselves prevent him from ever seeking a solitary life. This would in one stroke annihilate and reprobate the existence of Benedictine hermits which nevertheless a constant tradition attests, whether among the Camaldolese or in hermitages attached to Cluny and other great monasteries, or even in the intransigently cenobitic Cistercian family.

A still more serious consequence of this theory would be a threat to the authentic spirit of cenobitic monasticism itself. Dom Leclercq quotes a traditional statement on the relation of cenobitism to the hermit life: *vita eremitica quae est radix vitae monasticae vel cenobiticae*.[19] All monasticism is in some sense solitary and even the common life has its spiritual roots in eremitical solitude. The desert ideal is the monastic ideal as such, and the value of cenobitism is that it makes a certain solitude, austerity and renunciation of the world possible to the average man who would have no desire and no need to become a real hermit. Nevertheless there will always be some in the *cenobium* drawn by God to a greater solitude and to a life of more continuous silence and prayer. To interpret the most characteristic of the monastic vows as an obligation *not* to seek the radical and ultimate perfection to which the monastic life tends by its very nature is to reject and exclude a perfection of surrender that may, in exceptional cases, be demanded by God.

Conversio morum or *conversatio morum* in the light of the first chapter of St Benedict's Rule, seems to be rather the way of life of the genuine monk, be he cenobite or hermit, as opposed to the way of life of the false monks (sarabaites and gyrovagues) who are said to 'lie to God by their tonsure' and who in the *Regula Magistri* are dismissed as 'laici'.

Both *conversio* and *conversatio* can have the same meaning of 'living as a monk'. *Conversatio* can certainly indicate any way of life followed in common with others, *communis vivendi ratio*, but this does not apply exclusively to the life of a cenobitic monastery. It applies equally well to the *conversatio* of hermits following similar customs and having the same orientation in their life of solitary combat with the devil.

Du Cange in his *Glossarium* gives many examples, including one from St Gregory's *Life of St Benedict*, in which *conversatio* simply means 'monachismus, vita monachica'. When St Benedict became a hermit, St Gregory tells us, he received the habit of monk *sanctae conversationis habitus*. It is clear from this example that in the earliest Benedictine circles the word *conversatio* was by no means restricted to cenobites.

Conversari can mean, in late Latin, to embrace the monastic life or any other well-defined way of life. This latter is also its classical meaning. *Conversari* can also mean simply to live and work in a certain milieu. *Aquila conversatur in montibus*, said Pliny. In this sense the monk is simply one whose *conversatio* is not in the world but in the desert, in 'paradise' or according to St Paul's phrase 'in heaven' (Phil. 3.20). To say that only cenobites are living the monastic *conversatio* is the same as saying that only cenobites have *consuetudines*. But the hermit can have his 'customs' as well as anyone else, and his usages may be those of other hermits. The term *solitaria conversatio* for the hermit life is just as common as *conversatio* in any other combination. Theofrid, Abbot of Echternach, speaks of the hermit St Wilgis retiring to a chapel on a point overlooking the sea *'ubique solitariae conversationis in sudavit exercitio . . . caelestem in terris vitam excoluit'*.[20] Negatively described, the monk is one who has chosen not to live among men of the world and according to their standards. *'Non vult cum hominibus conversari, in heremo cum angelis philosophatur.'*[21] St Honoratus and his brother sought an angelic life in solitude, far from the *conversatio* of ordinary men (humanam conversationem et gratiam fastidientes eremi amore flagrarunt—Vita Honorati, PL, 50.1254). A very early document, the *Constitutiones Zacchaii et Apollonii*, speaks of various levels of ascetic life. The most fervent is that of the ones who seek the desert (soli eremum ac squalentia deserti loca habitant) while the least fervent are those who remain to live virtuous lives in the world (rebus communis conversationis intersunt et secreta non expetant).[22] Each level has its proper duties and modes of action, or as we would say today, duties of state. St Anselm urges the layman, the cleric and the monk to live as perfectly as possible in their respective states.[23] *Conversatio morum* is simply the genus vivendi of the monk living apart from the world, whether in community or in solitude, faithful to his vocation.

In the first chapter of the Rule, when St Benedict speaks of true and false monks, we see that the false monk is the one who instead of resisting his passions and fighting the devil, is one who yields to his own will and therefore succumbs to the devil, even though he may think he is living a holy life. But this life of negligence, sloth and self-will constitutes what St Benedict calls *miserrima conversatio*, a way of life about which it is better to keep silent than to speak. The *miserrima conversatio* deplored by St Benedict applies both to sarabaites and gyrovagues but obviously not to hermits.

In speaking of the hermit, St Benedict implicitly describes the monastic *conversatio*, the *apotage* and ascesis of the monk, on two levels. First, on the cenobitic level, the 'long probation in the monastery' in which probation is not necessarily to be taken in our modern sense of a preparatory trial, but according to the last sentence of the prologue, persevering under the doctrine of Christ in the monastery and sharing in His sufferings. This is the *vita activa*, the *bios praktikos* in which the monk grows in virtue and of this growth St Benedict uses the phrase *processu conversationis*.

The cenobitic *conversatio* consists in fighting against the devil in company with many brethren, supported and consoled by them 'multorum solatio docti pugnare'. But the same *conversatio* can be carried into the desert where the hermit continues the battle single-handedly.

Smaragdus, commenting on the hermit passage in Chapter One of the Rule, explicitly equates the 'spiritual combat' with monastic *conversatio*: 'Sicut in luctaminibus hujus saeculi sine agone, sine certamine non coronatur, *ita et in spiritali conversatione* et proposito sancto, nemo sine luctamine potest immarcescibilem coronam accipere. . . .'[24] The word *conversatio* is equivalent to another interesting term, *propositum*, which we cannot examine here. The monastic 'militia' is therefore one, both in community and in solitude. The hermits are among the *'perfectissimi luctatores et continentis-*

simi monachi', and the true hermit *'cum Domini tantum adjutorio victor exstitit in eremo'* (id.).

All true monks are engaged in the same battle, the same *conversatio*, and what St Benedict ascribes to the hermit is not the *bios theoretikos* or the *vita contemplativa* but rather a prolongation of the same ascetic *conversatio* under more difficult, more perilous and more heroic conditions. It is still the same warfare to which the monk as *miles Christi* is committed by his vow of *conversatio*. The terms used by St Benedict are familiar from the Desert Tradition, a struggle against the vices of the flesh and against temptations in thought, *contra vitia carnis vel cogitationum*.

It is not clear that St Benedict considers *conversatio* precisely as a means and *conversio* as the end attained by this means. On the contrary, *conversio* is the act of entering upon the monastic life in order to give oneself for the rest of his days, in an ever renewed 'conversion', to God. The hermit is precisely one who has not just entered and in his first fervour, *non conversionis fervore novitio*. The novice in Chapter 58 is spoken of as *noviter veniens ad conversionem*, and some, coming from slavery, are *ex servitute convertentes*.

Conversatio is rather a more precise view of *conversio* with emphasis on the monastic ascesis or the monastic way of life. *Conversio* may be a result of monastic *conversatio*, but it is also and first of all the cause of *conversatio*. The two go together, they influence each other, they are, so to speak, two sides of the same coin. One is converted from the *conversatio* of the world to that of the monastery, and by the *conversatio* of monastic life one is gradually 'converted' or 'transformed' in the likeness of Christ. Dom Winandy, opposing Dom Lottin and following Christine Mohrmann, shows that in monastic parlance *conversare* is the frequentative of *convertere* and hence *conversatio* is simply a *conversio* that reaches into all the details of one's daily life.[25] Monks are to receive bedclothes *pro modo conversationis*, that is to say appropriate to their way of life as monks. Brethren whose *conversatio* is holy and edifying are to be chosen as deans (ch. 21). Finally, at the end of the Rule, in Chapter 73, St Benedict humbly declares that he has only set down standards for those who wish to make a beginning of the monastic life, *initium conversationis*. But he urges the reader interested in the height of perfection to consult the works of 'the Holy Fathers'. Some of these may, like Basil, look askance at the hermit life, but the *Conferences* of Cassian have a great deal to say in favour of eremitic solitude, indeed assuming that it is a normal fruit of the active life in the cenobium. The last sentence of St Benedict's Rule has nothing in it to imply a prohibition of the hermit life, although it does not necessarily imply either that the only way to be a perfect monk is to be a hermit. Dom Winandy advises us not to be too quick to regard Chapter 73 as 'une invitation a dépasser la règle'.[26]

Let us therefore conclude that for St Benedict the vow of *conversatio morum* is the vow to live as a true monk, in renunciation of the world, in perfect obedience to the voice of Christ. But since there can be many kinds of illusion in the way of the untrained ascetic, St Benedict wants to make quite clear in what renunciation of the world and monastic *conversatio* essentially consist.

To renounce the world means not only to leave the world physically and to live apart from it, to follow ways that differ from those of the world and to devote oneself to a life of ascesis and prayer which has as its end the glory of God in all things; it is above all the renunciation of *one's own will.* 'Beatus est qui continuit cupiditatem carnis suae sponti nec aperuit ianuam suam propria voluntate.'[27] Only he who renounces his own will can survive in the battle against vices and evil thoughts.

That is why for all practical purposes the life of the cenobite takes priority over all others in the mind of St Benedict. It is in this life that the monk can devote himself most effectively and continuously to the *labor obedientiae* and will therefore more quickly and surely divest himself of his own will in order to follow Christ and become like Christ in His passion, so as to share His glory. The characteristic of the false monks, sarabaites and gyrovagues, is precisely that their *conversatio* is rooted in their own will, and thus it is without value and without substance, indeed it is vitiated and full of sin. One may certainly infer from the description of these monks that a wandering eremitism was reproved by St Benedict, and that a loose knit organization of hermit lauras without fixed Rule is considered by him to be nefarious. 'He has nothing against the solitary life,' says Dom Winandy (*Collectanea*, 1960, p. 385), 'and it is not to the solitary life that he opposes his cenobitism, but to the counterfeits of true monasticism.' While legislating only for cenobites, whom he prefers, St Benedict admits of a true eremitism which is however rooted in genuine monastic renunciation, the renunciation of the monk's own will. From this one can reasonably conclude that the vow of *conversatio morum* (along with obedience and stability) is indeed aimed against the inauthentic hermit who throws off the Rule and separates himself from the Abbot and the brethren by an act of his own will, but it is certainly not 'the exclusion of all eremitism'.

MONASTIC ATTITUDES:
A MATTER OF CHOICE

Let us suppose that there are two ways in which the monastic community can look at the postulant whom it expects to recruit from 'the world'. These two ways will reflect differences, and perhaps rather profound differences, in one's concept of the Church, the monastic life and 'the world'. The first way considers the monastic order (and the Church too, by implication) as the embodiment and the guardian of a fixed traditional ideal.

Without examining too closely what the authentic monastic tradition really is, this outlook simply assumes that what is 'there' is 'given', that what is more or less 'established' is also, in fact, traditional. Thus we find that an 'accepted spirituality' is considered without investigation or serious question to embody a living tradition and to say the last word on what is and is not 'monastic'. Though not really official, this 'spirituality' has common currency and has, in fact, been received without much criticism and even without serious interest, as if it could not really be questioned. As a result, the real monastic tradition has at times become drained of life and sap. In the presence of a passively accepted, vague, indefinite and static 'spirituality', tradition tends to be transformed into routine. Yet this accepted attitude towards monastic observance, embodied in formal regularity, and in a somewhat schematic teaching, stands radically opposed to all other ideologies, especially to those of 'the world'.

Hence the postulant is regarded as one who comes to the Order with the intention of being stripped of an old ideology and clothed with a new one—the 'monastic spirituality'. And, of course, more than ideas are at stake: a whole new way of life will reflect the new ideas, or indeed the new ideas will perhaps come as a *result* of the new behaviour. If the novice learns to walk humbly, sit humbly, cough humbly, etc., he will also think humble thoughts. At least, we hope so. But, in any case, he now has the wrong ideas and he must be given the right ideas as soon as possible.

There is, of course, a genuine charitable concern for the spiritual needs of the postulant. But it is taken for granted that the community perfectly well understands his needs and his possible problems (they are all characteristic problems of 'the world' and can all be schematically reduced to a few simple headings: pride, self-satisfaction, self-seeking, self-will). It is also taken for granted that the solution to his problems and the fulfilment of his needs is ultimately a simple matter. It is, in fact, assumed that the postulant, by the mere fact of desiring to enter the monastic order, thereby signifies his recognition that he is 'wrong', that he wishes to escape from the errors and the ambiguities of his worldly state, that he is resolved to have done with these errors in their totality, and that indeed he recognizes that all that is of the world is simply error and sin. Thus there is no necessity to examine his needs with subtle and discrete analysis. He has one need: the need for the doctrine and discipline he is to receive in the monastery. And in order to do this he needs to escape from the world. Having once escaped from it, there remains one need above all: the need to be kept from returning to it, at any cost.

Therefore, the novice has only to embrace the rule and the observances, just as they are, to renounce and forswear his own ideas and opinions, and accept with perfect docility any teaching that is given him in the monastery. This teaching need not be especially stimulating or 'intellectual'. Indeed, the value of intellectuality is questioned, though learning is theoretically respectable, provided that it means the learning of acceptable and well-understood and time-tried attitudes: the 'accepted spirituality'. (Note that the teaching given tends to be not so much the personal doctrine of a 'spiritual father', based on his experience, but rather what is taken for granted by a whole generation. Not that this 'spirituality' has a definite authoritative status—it is not so much 'official' as simply 'taken for granted').

Why is this doctrine rather than another to be taught? First, because it is already accepted. In actual fact, this accepted spirituality recommends itself because it is the most complete justification of the community in its actual condition. If it permits changes, they will all be very slight, because, in fact, only the slightest changes are felt to be needed. Anything else would strike at the 'essence of the monastic life'. It is true that 'times have changed'. But do times change in a monastery? Are not the times that change rather the 'times' of 'the world'? The truth is one and eternal. It does not change. Of course, there must be accidental modifications. But they are worthwhile precisely in so far as they can be made with the minimum of disturbance. In fact, their chief recommendation is perhaps that they are more apparent than real.

A 'good monk' is, then, one who has thoroughly learned this accepted spirituality and put it into practice, thus becoming at once an exemplar of the current teaching and its confirmation. The presence of the 'good monk' is a kind of concrete guarantee that the teaching itself is practical, and that it can and does succeed (if it can succeed in some cases, it must, therefore, be capable of succeeding in all cases). The successful carrying out of this programme is rewarded by a life of happiness and peace. The monk feels that he is approved, accepted, and that his efforts are rightly directed, in fact blessed by God. This being the case, the average postulant can be judged by his willingness to understand, accept and follow the accepted spirituality and the ordinary rules. The ability to do this is a sign that he is capable of being formed 'according to the spirit of the Order'. To put it quite simply, such a one shows unmistakable signs of having a divine vocation. He agrees with us from the very start and we have reason to be assured that he will cause us no trouble, nor will he raise any doubts in our own minds as to the absolute rightness of what we have always accepted ourselves.

There is no question that this approach is in many ways quite simple and practical. It may, in its application, be somewhat oversimplified, even to the point where it becomes slightly inhuman in its apparent indifference to the peculiar and personal needs of some modern vocations. But it assumes that these special needs can legitimately be sacrificed to the common good, which is reduced to the peaceful, efficient application of one common and accepted norm to all without exception. And, in times of general stability, it may happen that in fact exceptional vocations consent to this without too much anguish, though of course not without effort and self-immolation. They can accept the sacrifice demanded of them without too much questioning and are able to adjust their motives. And because this happens in some cases, or many cases, it is taken to be reasonable evidence that it ought to happen in *all* cases. It is even elevated to the rank of a universally valid principle for all situations and at all times.

Today, for serious reasons the Church herself, in a time of crisis and of reform, calls into question certain human and practical principles, 'traditions of men' that have been accepted for a long time. Upon examination, many of these are seen to have possessed a validity that was temporary rather than permanent and universal. As a result, the whole idea of a passively accepted and static spirituality is questioned, the more so because in becoming quasi-official it has, in fact, lost some of the necessary elements of suppleness, of life, and of *charis* (in the sense of spiritual beauty, attractiveness, appeal) which inspire genuine love of the monastic vocation. Many younger monks are looking critically both at the ideal and at the performance of seniors who embody the 'accepted spirituality'. It seems that those who have devoted themselves with all sincerity and trust to carrying out the teachings of the accepted spirituality have suffered certain human impoverishments and limitations in consequence, though they have perhaps developed and have attained a certain poise and even wisdom, supported by the observances which they faithfully practise. Yet the relevance of the monastic ideal itself comes to be questioned, and it is asked whether the most basic doctrines of the spiritual life, as taught and practised in the monastery, have any real significance. When this questioning begins, the whole structure of faith suddenly seems to be threatened, in so far as the mere questioning of the validity of an accepted spirituality seems to involve a doubt of a principle of authority, doubt of the Church, doubt of God revealing himself in and through the Church, and ultimately doubt of God himself. Thus the monk who is convinced that he must identify everything that is 'accepted' as traditional and therefore as the teaching and the will of God himself, suddenly finds that in doubting the meaningfulness of this or that monastic observance, he appears to be doubting God. This lamentable misapprehension can hardly be articulated. Nor is any encouragement offered for it to be so. It sometimes remains unspoken and often unconscious. Perhaps more often the monastic conscience is formed in such a way that the mere 'temptation' to question the absolute and eternal validity of this or that practice may cause terror in the heart of the monk who sees himself, as it were, putting his foot on the slippery path to total apostasy. In any case, conscious or unconscious, where this misapprehension exists, it can become the cause of grave difficulties.

Unfortunately, the monk is still trained to accept as axiomatic the idea that he belongs in the monastery, that his needs can be satisfied only in and by the monastery, and that any needs he may have which cannot be fulfiled in the monastery are highly questionable, indeed 'natural' and therefore suspect of degeneracy or at least of uselessness. When it becomes necessary for such a monk to leave the monastery, in which he is no longer able to extricate himself from intellectual confusion and spiritual anguish, he returns to the world without really getting rid of his doubts and hesitancies. He goes back to secular life with a heart full of ambiguity, self-questioning, perhaps self-hatred, and, in any case, profound distress. One hopes at the best that he will readapt himself to secular life with some understanding of his plight and without too many unresolved and irrational guilt feelings, or without simply losing his faith altogether.

The consequence of this first way of looking at the postulant and at the Order's obligations to him is that at the present time there will be very few postulants who will be able to assimilate this rigid and absolute idea of monasticism and resign themselves to live by it. One can simply tighten up the requirements, writing off the new generation as more or less monastically hopeless, and then at the same time attempt quietly and unobtrusively to adapt the accepted spirituality, relaxing its rigidities and making room for a more tolerant consideration of the needs of the modern postulant, while assuming it to be obvious that this is what we meant to do all along.

The principle, however, remains this: that the postulant comes to the Order with the wrong ideas, and consequently even his expression of what he feels to be urgent personal and spiritual needs will usually be wrongheaded and inspired by unregenerate self-love (or perhaps by a neurosis), which cannot be reconciled with the monastic life. The right idea of the monastic life is the idea which is commonly held and taught in the community, and the first requirement of faith and humility in a prospective monk is to accept this in all docility as an unquestionable premise.

Let us now consider another possible attitude. There is another concept of the monastic life which implies a somewhat different view of the Church, and which is perhaps more complex and less absolute. It is doubtless more difficult to understand in theory and certainly more difficult to put into practice. It involves definite risks of misinterpretation and of misapplication, and from the institutional point of view it may seem, and indeed may actually be, less practicable and more hazardous than the other. Basing itself on more general principles from the Bible and from the Rule of St Benedict and primitive monastic documents (rather than on detailed and more recent legislation, observance and 'spirituality') this view understands the monastic community as an assembly of men called together by the grace of God in order that they may live the life of discipleship together under a Rule and an Abbot, helping one another to attain to eternal life by means which will (in their minor details) depend largely on the situation in which they are actually living.

According to this view, the monastic community is in possession not so much of a body of detailed and more or less infallible and rigid principles, governing all the minutiae of one's daily life and worship, and systematizing all one's communal relationships: but rather the Holy Spirit, working through the humility and charity of the brethren in their loving acceptance of their Rule and their Spiritual Father, enables them all to keep the commandments and counsels of Christ within the framework of rather flexible observances and practices which are not regarded as so perfect that they cannot be changed without extraordinary legislation.

Depending less on the support of legislation in black and white, the community puts its trust in the love and grace of Christ. Believing that the Holy Spirit has been granted to the community to be a source of light and life, and acting in a spirit of openness and sincerity, the brothers under their Father seek to work out together actual solutions to their own problems. They may certainly come up with answers that are far from ideal in theory, but it may happen by God's grace that these are the particular answers which bring to all of them a possibility of authentic peace, fruitfulness and growth in Christ. Naturally, these solutions will not lack the support of whatever official approval may be necessary.

Into this conception of the monastic life enters a correlative conception of the world. There is no question, of course, that the monk lives as one who is basically alien to the ways of the world (*a saeculi activus se facere alienum*). Nevertheless, the peculiar difficulties and vicissitudes of life in the world are relevant to the monastic life which is considered precisely as a *remedy* and as a *fulfilment*: a remedy for the ills contracted in the world, and a fulfilment of legitimate needs which the world of this particular time arouses without being able to satisfy them.

The first, static, concept of the monastic life also promises a fulfilment which the world cannot give, a fulfilment which is attained by the simple and uncompromising way of renunciation (of the world) and obedience (to the accepted observances and practices of the monastery, as applied in detail by the Superior). But in this first case there is no concern for needs, legitimate or otherwise, that may have been brought to consciousness by the mentality of 'the world'. Whatever came to mind in the world remains more or less irrelevant to the monastic calling which is so far 'out of this world' that it has nothing more to do with it. So the 'needs of modern man' precisely as *modern and contemporary* are regarded as irrelevant.

Contemporary man is regarded, by the first view, as 'contemporary' precisely in his worldliness. In having a 'need' to renounce his worldliness, he has *ipso facto* a need to renounce his contemporaneousness. He ceases to be *contemporary* with his fellow men in entering the monastery, just because in that same act he ceases to be worldly, and becomes an unworldly being, concerned only with the needs of his soul and with eternity. Of course, it can be argued that eternity is contemporaneous with all time, and in this sense the monk becomes contemporary, in an abstract and universal way, with absolutely all ages and all times. A malicious intelligence might also conclude that in doing so the monk became contemporary with no one and, in fact, altogether abandoned the realm of the human.

The second view, on the contrary, recognizes, not without a certain anguish, that there is no other time than the present, and that to be contemporary is the price of existence itself. Man has a responsibility to his own time, not as if he could seem to stand outside it and donate various spiritual and material benefits to it from a position of compassionate distance: but man has a responsibility to *find himself where he is*, namely in his own proper time and place, in the history to which he belongs and to which he must inevitably contribute either by his responses or evasions, either truth and act or slogan and gesture. Even the gestures of evasion and withdrawal may unfortunately be decisive contributions to a void in which history can take on a demonic orientation. And so the second form of monasticism exists in confrontation with a world and with a time to which it feels it must *respond*. Not that it must become *implicated* in pure secularity by a loss of its own special perspective. For the first thing that the monk can contribute to the world of his time is precisely a perspective that is not of the world. The monk owes the world of his time an unworldliness proper to this time, and the contemporary monk is real in so far as he manages, by the grace of God and the charism of his vocation, to achieve a contemporaneous unworldliness. He is in the world and *not of it*. He is both in his time and *of it*.

Hence we see the error of imagining that being out of the world also involves being out of one's own time, i.e. in the past, since the past is imagined as having acquired an eternal validity by the fact that it is past. It would, perhaps, be more truly monastic to say that the monk who is effectively liberated from the servitudes and confusions of 'the world' in its negative and sterile sense, ought to be enabled by that very fact to be more truly present to his world and to his time by love, by compassion, by understanding, by tolerance, by a deep and Christ-like hope.

The second view of monasticism can therefore be called in a certain sense 'worldly'; not that it concerns itself with the ends and means of secular life as such, but it takes into account with sympathy and understanding the legitimate aims which 'the contemporary world' feels itself called to obtain for man, such as peace, civil rights, remunerative work, personal fulfilment, communion with other men in a warm and creative social environment etc. It regards these aspirations as real and relevant to everyone and therefore to monks, and it sees with compassion that man today is frustrated in his most sincere efforts to attain these things. It does not despise or condemn him because his efforts are undertaken seemingly 'without God' or in an 'irreligious' spirit since it sees that he is basically sincere and in good faith and that these aspirations, good in themselves, doubtless come from God. The monk should be in the world of his time as a sign of hope for the most authentic values to which his time aspires.

Thus the monastic community will take seriously the earnest and valid efforts of secular thought to reach out towards these values, but will understand that thought in the light of the Bible and of the Fathers (finding there a very propitious climate for ideas which seem to a great extent doomed to sterility in the aridity and violence of modern urban and technological life).

This is not the place to develop this idea in all its implications. One consequence of it concerns us here: in looking at the postulant, the monastic community will no longer assume that he comes to the monastery with ideas and aspirations that are *all wrong,* but that some of the deepest needs of his heart, even though they may not be explicitly religious needs, are genuinely *human* and specifically *contemporary* needs *which the monastic life is also called upon to fulfil.* And so to ignore these human needs, to reject them as irrelevant, and to turn the whole attention of the postulant to other seemingly more lofty, more eternal, more unworldly, more spiritual and more religious aims, may in fact turn out to be arbitrary, unjust, and even unrealistic. For that reason, this procedure will ultimately tend to vitiate the postulant's vocation precisely in its *religious and spiritual* authenticity. For one cannot establish the religious authenticity of a vocation by trying to distil away all the human contemporary components that there may be in it. On the contrary, the truth of a vocation, its religious truth, depends on the fundamental respect for the human components which have been placed there by heredity, by the postulant's history, by his own freedom acting in union with grace, and therefore by God himself.

There is no question that in implementing the postconciliar legislation of the religious life, the monastic order will naturally wish to adopt the second of the two attitudes we have outlined above.

The Council's decree *Perfectae Caritatis* on the renewal of the religious life praises the contemplative orders and urges them to maintain 'at their holiest' their 'withdrawal from the world and the practices of their contemplative life'. But it also states that the language of praise and approval for the contemplative orders as 'the glory of the Church and an overflowing fountain of heavenly graces' does not exempt them from the obligation of complete renewal. The decree says significantly: 'Nevertheless (i.e. in spite of the above praise), their manner of living should be revised according to the aforementioned principles and standards of appropriate renewal' (n. 7). Among the principles referred to are the following: 'Communities should promote among their members a suitable awareness of contemporary human conditions and of the needs of the Church' so as to enable their members to make 'wise judgements in the light of faith concerning the circumstances of the modern world (and) to come to the aid of men more effectively (n. 2, d.). 'The manner of living, praying and working should be suitably adapted to the physical and psychological conditions of today. . . . The way in which communities are governed should be re-examined in the light of these same standards. . . . Constitutions, directories, custom books . . . are to be suitably revised. . . . This task will require the suppression of outmoded regulations' (n. 3). But 'the fact must also be honestly faced that even the most desirable changes made on behalf of contemporary needs will fail of their purpose unless a renewal of spirit gives life to them. Indeed such an interior renewal must always be accorded the leading role even in the promotion of exterior works' (n. 2, e.).

In the section that deals specifically with monks, the decree says: 'While safeguarding the proper identity of each institution, let the monasteries be renewed in their ancient and beneficial traditions and so adapt them to the modern needs of souls that monasteries will be seed beds of growth (seminaria aedificationis) for the Christian people' (n. 9). The injunction to 'safeguard the proper identity' of each 'institution' refers to the previous sentence in which the decree says that some monks serve God 'by devoting themselves entirely to divine worship in a life that is hidden' and others 'by lawfully taking up some apostolate or works of Christian charity'. Note that in speaking of papal enclosure for nuns, the decree says that, while the enclosure is to be maintained, 'outdated customs are to be done away with' and 'in such matters, consideration should be given to the wishes of the monasteries themselves' (n. 16).

Without doubt a notable change of attitude has taken place. Communities certainly show an increased willingness to consider realistically the needs of the new generation, and no one any longer categorically assumes that the new wave is made up entirely of morons, rebels, neurotics and dope-fiends. It is almost conceded that in their quixotic way the young manifest a certain amount of good sense. Unfortunately, there is still very much of a spirit of patronage in this benign endeavour to recognize the engaging and positive qualities of youth. Do we really believe that monasticism can actually survive in an actual *dialogue* with the modern postulant? Or with the novice? Or with the young monk?

Here we must admit that there are problems, some of them rather complex. It would be a little silly to take for granted that one who has no experience whatever of the monastic life is, upon entering, in a secure position to reform everything in the first week. When all monastic tradition unanimously assumes that the worthy postulant manifests a sincere desire to listen and to learn rather than immediately to teach, this is surely not to be taken as an eccentric and antique formula fit for the museum. It is, after all, not unfamiliar to modern man, for example, in the world of athletics. Coaches are not normally patient with temperamental freshmen who know more about football than anyone else.

On the other hand, let us admit that we can no longer safely insist that the postulant passively accepts our cursory diagnosis of his ills just because we have a familiar remedy at hand to fit that particular diagnosis. ('You are proud, therefore you need to submit to humiliation, and to begin with you must accept the fact that I know you better than you know yourself; and if you don't agree on that point, it shows from the very start how proud you really are.' A most convenient vicious circle which dispenses with all effort to understand the subject's real needs.)

The postulant who has come to the monastery looking for something may not necessarily be looking for what we think. Yes, of course, *si revera Deum quaerit*. 'Does he truly seek God?' But what entitles me, as novice master, to imagine that *my* particular way of seeking God is the only way possible and that *my* spirituality, *my* prayer, *my* idiosyncrasies, *my* monastic likes and dislikes, *my* interpretations are normative for all monks of all time? Such an assumption teaches, louder than any words, that I have no humility myself and am therefore disqualified from trying to teach it to another. I do not have the elementary humility to respect his own personal integrity, his uniqueness, his differences, his own singular and personal need.

All this is quite simply to say that the Holy Spirit speaks in very many ways, and one of the ways in which he speaks is precisely through the *need*, the *poverty*, the *limitation* of our fellow man. (Or perhaps we ought to listen well enough to realize that what we imagine to be poverty and limitation is in fact a richness and an unexpected capacity that we ourselves have not yet learned to appreciate because of our *own* narrowness of mind.) Let us suppose that the *needs of modern man are such that they impose a radical change* in areas of the monastic life which are so dear to us as to seem absolutely essential. In other words, let us suppose that our own understanding and love of a profound ideal, say, of silence, prayer and contemplation, may be radically menaced by a genuine need in modern man. We are, let us imagine, faced with a choice in which we must either take a whole new view of silence, prayer, enclosure, and so on, or else resign ourselves to having no more postulants. (Parenthetically, let us also admit that quite possibly if we are too ready to sacrifice silence, solitude, etc., we may all the more quickly find ourselves deserted by vocations.) If by relinquishing my own favourite interpretation of what the perfect life of silence and contemplation ought to be (whether I practise it myself is, of course, another matter: but it is the idea of monastic life which happens to *please me*), if by relinquishing this and submitting to certain adaptations I can make the monastic life possible for others who would not otherwise be able to live it, then it would seem that charity itself ought to tell me that this 'need' of others is an appeal to my own generosity, in a way very different from that which I anticipated when I made my vows. Let us recall that precisely such generosity as this characterized St Benedict.

This is just an example, and examples can be misleading. It is not intended to suggest that we ought to introduce recreative conversation in our monasteries, or to abolish our silence or to encourage our many frustrated preachers and apostles. A case in point might however be the practice of mental prayer in common and in choir. This is an exercise which, for one reason or another, most modern novices and young monks seem to find unduly frustrating, and which, even though they may accept it, seems to be entirely un-profitable for them—in fact, in many cases actually stultify-ing. On the other hand, it has the advantage of keeping ev-erybody there under the eyes of the abbot and the seniors, and it guarantees that at least formally and externally an 'ex-ercise of the contemplative life' is going on. But if, in fact, this exercise does become a sterile formality, then we must courageously try to find an alternative—and the search for a re-ally valid way of prayer may entail considerable work: a real return to monastic tradition on prayer, *lectio divina*, etc., and also a real discipline of inner awareness and enlightened faith. The imaginative and affective methods popular in the last cen-tury will no longer do, and the 'prayer of simple regard' leads the undeveloped mind easily to the prayer of sleep.

A merely external practice of silence and enclosure will never do anything to guarantee a spirit of interior prayer, and since all this hangs together, we have to re-examine all of it with a serious willingness to admit that our present concep-tions are often simply inadequate and need to be made much deeper and much more alive—and perhaps given an entirely new perspective. In this way we will show ourselves truly alert to the needs of a new generation, aware that in this alertness we are being open to grace, obedient to the love of the Holy Spirit, and in the end more authentically monks, than if we simply insisted on making two fatal assumptions: 1. that the idea of monasticism which we happen to hold, and which happens at the moment to have a quasi-official look, is the only right view, and is therefore of the essence of the monas-tic life and therefore unchangeable; 2. because we are right in this respect, we are right in every other respect too; we can safely assume that the man who comes in from the world is infected with every error, and that if he does not manage to assimilate our own favourite view of monasticism this is merely a proof that he is bad material, dead wood, a fruitless tree, fit only to be rooted up and cast into the fire. Attach-ment to these two rather arrogant assumptions will guarantee the early end of the monastic life in any community that clings to them with perseverance.

PART THREE

The Solitary Life

PROJECT FOR A HERMITAGE

Need for a Hermitage[1]

The solitary life in the strict sense is the crown of the monastic vocation. Though not all monks are called to the solitary life permanently, and though the relative solitude of a silent community may normally be sufficient, there are nevertheless some monks who need a greater degree of solitude than is offered by the cenobitic life.

It must be admitted that the environs and atmosphere of the large monastery tend sometimes to become increasingly noisy and active and unfavourable for the development of a deep, silent, contemplative life. It is more and more necessary for those called to a more intense and simple life of prayer to be able to seek silence and solitude at a distance from the monastery.

Those who need a greater degree of solitude may easily be permitted to spend some of their time apart from the community, whether on a *lectio day* or at least on long feast day afternoons. This is now admitted and practised, and with good effects.

It is conceivable that some monks might be permitted to spend several days alone on private retreat. A small house near the monastery might serve this purpose.

But eventually we must face the fact that at least a few or perhaps only one monk in a generation may develop a genuine vocation to permanent solitude, either relative or complete.

Relative solitude: in or close to the monastery but apart from the community for some of the exercises. Complete solitude: permanently in a hermitage.

For those who develop an apparent vocation to the eremitic life, not only in their own judgement but above all in the judgement of those who know them well, especially their

Spiritual Father and their Abbot, it becomes necessary at least to make a trial of their vocation. Where? Should they go through all the complications required to transfer to the Camaldolese or to some Benedictine monastery that has a hermitage? Or should they not rather work out this problem in their own monastic milieu, in dependence on a monastery of their own Order?

All these and other such practical considerations show that there is a real need to construct a hermitage at some distance from the monastery, with facilities for both relative and complete solitude, to provide for temporary and permanent vocations to solitude, without severing the bonds of the monk with the community of his vocation and of his profession.

This should be regarded as a project of general interest and advantage to the community, even though it would directly concern a few with special needs. All would in fact benefit because all would have the opportunity to make at least short retreats at the hermitage whenever they had a need for it.

Layout of the Hermitage

There is an excellent site for a hermitage in a wooded valley, completely enclosed and secluded, a few miles south of the monastery in a thinly populated area of wooded hills.

The hermitage would consist of a central building, which can be called the *Skete* (a traditional term in Athonite monasticism), and scattered hermit cottages which can be called the *cells*.

The *Skete* would be at the terminus of the road leading to the area. Here would be the *Gatehouse*, a building with residence for two or three persons charged with the material care of the area. Here would be the kitchen, storeroom, refectory, chapel and several rooms for monks spending a short time at the Skete. Here also would be the telephone to the monastery (only). Here would be showers, and a small infirmary or a dispensary with a sick-room attached.

The purpose of the Skete

(*a*) A centre for supplies, food, contact with the monastery, etc., for the hermits living apart in cells. Their needs would be furnished from this centre. In sickness they would be cared for at the Skete.

(*b*) A place of preparation for those trying out their solitary vocation, in the hope of being admitted to a cell after their vocation was clear.

(*c*) A place of relative solitude for those not definitely called to the life of the cells but needing a more secluded life than that of the monastery. Such would be the three or four permanently charged with the care of the Skete, cooking, material needs of the hermitage, etc.

(*d*) A place of temporary retreat for monks coming from the monastery for a few days or a month.

(*e*) The Skete would follow the horarium of the monastery but not all the exercises would be in common. The following would be in common: Lauds—Mass, Sext—Dinner, Vespers—Supper. Other offices would be recited privately.

(*f*) Hermits in cells could come to the Skete and participate in common exercises there if there was need for them to do so. Hermits with special dietary needs requiring more elaborate cooking would take dinner and/or supper at the Skete, in which case they would participate in the office immediately preceding the meal.

(*g*) Offices at the Skete would be in the vernacular. Hermits in cells could have the choice of any liturgical language permitted by the Church. Hermits might obtain an indult to follow some other rite.

The *Cells* would be the real raison d'être of the hermitage. At first four cells could be constructed, in view of a period of ten years experimentation with the hermitage. If it then became clear that the project was successful, more cells could be added according to need.

Each cell would consist of two rooms, a sleeping alcove, and a small oratory. The smaller room would be a kitchen and work room. The other would be a 'living room' with alcove and oratory opening into it. The oratory would have an altar at which the hermit would say Mass if he were a priest. Each hermitage would also have a porch. Care would be taken to construct the hermitage so that it would have a good view, catch the breeze in summer, be well-lighted, dry, etc.

The hermitages would be provided with electric light but not with telephone or running water. Electric stoves would be permitted for heating water and some cooking. A small refrigerator would be allowed. The hermit would go to the Skete for showers. Water would have to be carried from a spring or from the Skete. A pond could be made in the valley where a hermit could bathe if he preferred this to going to the Skete for a shower. The cottage would be heated by wood fire. There would be no gas at the cells, only at the Skete.

Each hermit could have a garden and grow some vegetables if he wished. Or he could have fruit trees. The cells would be about a quarter of a mile apart. They could not normally be reached except via the Skete. Cars and machines would not be able to come any further into the hermitage area than the gate at the Skete. The entire area could be enclosed with a high fence and the enclosure could be kept strictly.

Life in the Cells

Admission

To be eligible for a permanent hermit life in a cell, one would have to be a monk five years solemnly professed. One would have to have solid and long-standing evidence of a call to the solitary life, vouched for by one's Spiritual Father.

A period of trial consisting of at least one year in the Skete would be required.

Before admission to the period of 'novitiate' the candidate

would require the permission of the Abbot of the monastery with the advice of his private council and the assent of the Superior of the hermitage.

After one year of trial the Chapter of hermits in conjunction with the Abbot of the monastery would vote on the candidate, and if he were not accepted in a cell they could signify whether his probation could usefully be prolonged or whether he should return to the monastery.

All permanent residents in the Skete or cells would vote on the candidates.

After a year in the cell, with the assent of the Superior of the hermitage and the other hermits, the hermit could make a promise of fidelity to his solitary life in this place.

Mode of Life

The resident of the cells would be strictly bound to remain in the hermitage area (i.e. the whole valley or the property on which the hermitage would be located. He could go out of the enclosure with permission to walk in the woods.). He would seldom or never return to the monastery. He would go to the Skete for any needs, to get supplies, for showers, for medicine, and he would be allowed to use the phone at the Skete to call the Father Abbot at the monastery if necessary.

The hermits would remain apart from one another and would not visit one another's cells without special permission, except in the case of the Spiritual Father. If, however, a hermit wished to have daily access to the sacrament of penance or to (brief) direction, this would be granted him if it were really useful and not an evasion.

There would be no offices or exercises in common, at least ordinarily. However, it would be permitted to a hermit if necessary to attend some of the common offices at the Skete where Lauds, Mass and Vespers would be in common. If there were a real need for relaxation the hermit could also go to meals at the Skete, or if under tension he could live for a time at the Skete until he recovered his balance. There should be a certain flexibility in the hermit's life while he is getting adapted, and he would not have to feel himself rigidly confined to the cell until the cell became delightful to him. On the other hand he would have to realize that if he spent too much of his time at the Skete he could be asked to forfeit his cell, and give it up to someone who would be more serious about the solitary life.

Meals

One meal a day, at least the substance of one meal, could be cooked at the Skete and delivered. That is to say, the Skete would provide one complete hot cooked portion, plus fruit, bread, etc. The hermit would have to provide for himself at frustulum (breakfast) and collation (supper). It would be possible to cook simply in the hermitage tea, coffee, soup, oatmeal, simple vegetables. All supplies would be furnished by the Skete.

Eggs and fish would be allowed to those who needed them.

Meat would not be allowed in the cells. If a hermit for reasons of health needed meat, he would go to the Skete and eat it there in the kitchen (not in the refectory).

Horarium

In general, the hermit, provided he remained in his solitude, would work out pretty much his own horarium with his Spiritual Father. Normally all would rise a little earlier than the monastic community, that is to say, at two o'clock or earlier. It would be understood that all would be saying Vigils and making their meditation and so on in the night hours, and all would say Lauds about dawn and Vespers about sunset. Each hermitage would have a bell, which the hermit would ring for his Mass as well as for Lauds and Vespers.

The Angelus would be rung at the Skete at the regular times.

Since the Skete would stick closely to the horarium of the monastery the cells would regulate their dinner time according to that of the Skete. But frustulum would be taken when desired, and collation, also. The amount of food at these extra meals would be regulated with the consent and advice of the Spiritual Father.

Work

Besides the necessary work caring for their cell and their personal needs, the hermits might perhaps undertake to do some piece work for one of the departments at the monastery, or secretarial work (of a non-worldly character) or else they might do gardening and contribute to the food supply of the group.

It might be desirable for the hermits to be charged with the care of some cows and goats, contributing to the needs of the monastery as well as their own.

Hermits could help one another in heavy work such as felling and sawing trees for firewood.

It is conceivable that the work of the hermits and of those at the Skete might contribute something to their support. If one were a writer, he could continue to write books for publication, but at a reduced tempo (!) and of a more strictly spiritual nature. A hermit would obviously not be writing about topical matters.

Penance

The life of the cells would be austere, but the chief penitential emphasis would be on solitude and silence, on remaining alone in prayer, simplicity and poverty, casting one's care upon the Lord and abandoning all ambition, in order to surrender to the purifying action of the Holy Spirit in solitude and draw near to the Lord in love and trust. Each one would adopt those penances which his Spiritual Father recommended.

Charity

However, the hermits would have some relation with one another, particularly to help one another spiritually and materially. Though they would not have recreation, they would recognize themselves as living together as brothers. It might be worked out to what extent they would celebrate feasts together, with a Mass in common. Probably it would be best to assume that they would have a Mass and Agape together on Sundays and big feasts: the Mass would be a dialogue Low Mass celebrated by one of their number, and the Agape would be a common meal with a spiritual conference and a discussion of necessary practical business. The hermits would collaborate together in running the hermitage and dealing with its practical problems, but one of them would be elected Superior or Spiritual Father each year by the others. He could be re-elected indefinitely.

The 'Superior' or Spiritual Father of the hermitage would normally take care of the spiritual needs of all those in the cells or at the Skete, and normally one would be elected who would be best qualified for this. However, each individual would be free in seeking direction and absolution from any priest available in the hermitage area having faculties.

Prayer

The great work of the hermit would be *prayer*. He would consider himself set apart by God for this above all. His prayer would take the forms inspired by the Holy Spirit, dictated by his own needs and those of the Church, and approved by his Spiritual Father. His prayer would be supported by solid *Lectio* and perhaps also by some study according to his temperament and needs.

Relations with outsiders

The hermit could go to the Skete whenever necessary and could speak to those in charge there. But it should be remembered that if he spent too much time there it would reflect on the seriousness of his vocation. He could not speak to those who came to the Skete on retreat, nor could they visit him without special permission from the Abbot and the Superior of the Hermitage.

Once a year the hermit could receive a visit from his family at the Skete but not in his cell. Other visits would be only most exceptional. Visits would normally be for one day only.

The hermit would hope and desire that on entering the hermitage he was bidding farewell to the outside and even to the monastery, and would be ready to die there.

However, in regard to those coming from the monastery for retreat or those monks living temporarily at the Skete, a hermit priest would be able to hear their confessions or give them spiritual help when needed. But this should not become a full-time occupation, nor should penitents be coming regularly from the monastery or elsewhere to confess to one of the hermits.

Correspondence would be restricted, and hermits would certainly not give spiritual direction by mail. No letters would be received in Advent or Lent.

If a hermit decided to eliminate all correspondence completely, with the approval of his Spiritual Father, he might do so. In this case, any important mail for that hermit would be read by the Spiritual Father who would decide what ought to be done.

Normally it would be simpler if each one in a spirit of discretion took care of whatever mail was really necessary. In this, each would have different requirements.

However, all unsolicited secular correspondence from strangers and not concerned with unusual and important business would be intercepted at the monastery and not delivered at the hermitage. Mass stipends would be acknowledged by the Mass Secretary at the monastery.

Spiritual Needs of the Hermits

The Spiritual Father would attend to the needs of the hermits. They could confess to any priest in the hermitage. If necessary a confessor could be summoned from the monastery in an exceptional case.

The nature and number of spiritual conferences could be worked out. They would be infrequent (not exceeding one a week) and would remain usually optional.

However, it would be desirable to invite *periti*, priests and theologians especially qualified, to visit the hermitage, to give instruction and direction when necessary (people like Dom Jean Leclercq, and others who know this field in history and in theology).

Visits of 'top brass' whether ecclesiastical, civil or political would definitely not be encouraged. Visits of mere curiosity would be strictly prohibited. No outsiders would be allowed beyond the gate of the Skete without an explicit permission of the Abbot at the monastery and the Superior of the Hermitage.

Organization

The permanent community would consist of the hermits in the cells and two or three established permanently at the Skete.

The 'Superior' of the whole hermitage would be the Spiritual Father, one of the hermits elected annually by the other hermits and approved by the Abbot of the monastery.

The 'Procurator' would be either a priest or a brother who would be *ex officio* in charge of the Skete and of the material needs of the whole hermitage and who would be in contact with the outside world, going down to the monastery or even to town when necessary. He would be elected annually with the Spiritual Father.

The Chapter of the Hermits would consist of all those living permanently either in the cells or the Skete.

Promises

After a year or two in the hermitage, the hermit could make a promise of fidelity to the hermit life which, however, would not have the force and obligation of a vow.

Reclusion

In special cases, after several years of fidelity to the promise, the possibility of complete reclusion might be considered at first for one year, then perhaps permanently.

WILDERNESS AND PARADISE

In recent years some curious theories have been proposed which, in order to emphasize the importance of an active turning to the world and a 'secular Christianity', have felt it necessary at the same time to discredit monastic solitude. The 'contemplative' life of the monk is then discovered to be 'Greek rather than Christian'. The struggle with temptation in the wilderness is seen as a curious relic of gnosticism or some other heresy. Solitude is declared essentially alien to the Christian message and life which are communal. In a word, the whole monastic idea becomes theologically suspect.

How seriously should we take these theories? Should they induce us to adopt a purely defensive and apologetic attitude toward our monastic vocation? Or must we, while remaining monks, find ways of living unmonastically so as to disarm this criticism? Are we required to prove that we too are all 'secular' at heart and that our monasticity of behaviour—or *conversatio morum*—is really a turning *to* the world and not away from it?

We do not here pretend to solve this intricate question of the monk's relation to the modern world. Before that question can be solved the monk must have a definite idea of what he himself is supposed to be. If he begins by compromising *himself* he cannot avoid ambiguity and compromise in considering his relationship to the world.

Monastic theology is not merely a search for a few specious texts in Scripture and the Fathers which will excuse or justify the monastic vocation. It is rather a study and meditation of revealed truth which enables the monk to understand how he, in a most special way, can respond to the call to follow Christ in the wilderness.

Two studies by Protestants[1] show that the theme of a call into the wilderness, a vocation to recover the paradise life after suffering temptation with Christ in desert solitude, is but a variant of the fundamental themes of all Biblical theology: the *pascha Christi*, the call of the People of God out of Egypt, through the Red Sea into the Desert and to the Promised Land; the theme of the Cross and Resurrection; dying to sin and rising in Christ; the theme of the old and new man; the theme of the fallen world and the new creation. Not only is a Christian withdrawal to a 'desert solitude' excusable, licit and even praiseworthy, but the whole theology of the second Gospel is built upon the theme of Christ in the desert.

The study of Dr Ulrich Mauser is confined to the biblical use of the desert theme, especially in St Mark. Dr George Williams in his survey of biblical, patristic, medieval and radical Protestant thought, gives us a remarkably interesting picture of the 'Paradise-Wilderness' motif running through the whole history of Christian spirituality and playing a most important part not only in monasticism but also in Protestantism and particularly in the universities and seminaries founded by Protestants in the 'wilderness' of the New World. Both these books are of considerable importance to monks, and we will attempt here to give a brief survey of their contents, assessing their implications for a monastic theology relevant to our own needs.

The *Eremos*, the desert wilderness 'where evil and curse prevail', where nothing grows, where the very existence of man is constantly threatened, is also the place specially chosen by God to manifest Himself in His 'mighty acts' of mercy and salvation. Obedience to a divine call brings into this dreadful wilderness those whom God has chosen to form as His own people. The convocation of Israel in the wilderness of Sinai is the story of God leading men on what appears to be a 'march into the open gates of death' (Mauser). God places Israel in a seemingly impossible situation where, however, He reveals His name to His chosen, and thus places them directly in communication with Him as a source of unfailing help. On the basis of this free relationship rests the covenant of God with His people.

Failure to trust Yahweh in the wilderness is not simply an act of weakness: it is disobedience and idolatry which, substituting the golden calf for the ineffable name, seek to shorten the time of suffering by resort to human expedients glossed over with religious excuses. Only a free act of grace can restore the violated covenant by reawakening in the people a true sense of the meaning of their desert vocation. They must recover their understanding that the desert calling implies a *complete and continual dependence on God alone*. For Israel, the desert life was a life of utter dependence on a continued act of grace which implied also a recognition of man's own propensity to treachery and to sin. We know how the prophets urged Israel under her Kings and at the time of the Babylonian exile, to remember the desert time of espousals and to anticipate a new Exodus which would restore the authentic relationship of bridal love between Israel and her God in a 'renewed wilderness time'. We know that this theme was taken over in the Pauline writings.

Dr Ulrich Mauser shows that this is the message of John the Baptist at the opening of the second Gospel. The fact that the Baptist preaches 'in the wilderness' is of *theological* significance in Mark, for whom 'the wilderness is a theme full of theological implications and not primarily a locality'. John is in fact announcing what the prophets announced before him: One who is to come from God will appear in the wilderness and initiate the final work of salvation. Israel must go out to meet this one in the wilderness in an act of sincere repentance which acknowledges her whole history as one of disobedience and infidelity. The Baptism of John is a sign of recognition that God's people are under judgement. Even Christ is baptized, thus showing His willingness to 'endure God's judgement' and indeed to die for the sins of the people. Immediately after this, Jesus goes out to be tempted in the desert, for 'only Jesus fully realized what it meant to go out into the wilderness: it meant the determination to live under the judgement of God'. His going out into the desert is then the necessary outcome of His baptism.

For all others, baptism is simply a gesture of temporary repentance. They return to the cities. But Jesus goes on into the wilderness as the sign that His baptism is fully serious, and that He is 'the only true penitent whose return to the desert is (not merely a token gesture) but unfeigned'. One might argue that Christ's stay in the desert is itself only a temporary retreat, a pause for thought and recollection in preparation for his active mission. Not at all. 'The forty days', says Dr Mauser, are not 'a period passed forever once Christ starts his public ministry,' but as in the case of Moses and Elias, the desert retreat 'sounds the keynote of his whole mission.'

Mauser then traces the development of the wilderness theme throughout the whole Gospel of Mark. 'Mountain' and 'Sea' are variants of the 'wilderness' in Mark. Invariably all stories of Jesus, in Mark, which have an 'epiphany character' take place in the 'wilderness', that is to say 'on the mountain' or by or on the sea. The underlying concept of Mark is in fact the confrontation between Jesus and Satan in the wilderness, the overcoming of the powers of evil in the world by the struggle in the desert, the agony in the garden and death on Calvary. Hence the whole Gospel of Mark is, for Dr Mauser, a development of the struggle of Jesus and Satan in the desert. To live in this state of struggle with the adversary of God, and to sustain this conflict in direct and complete dependence on God Himself, is the 'wilderness life'. Even if one lives this confrontation far from the actual desert, one is in fact living 'in the wilderness' and 'with Christ in the desert'. We see here the basic idea of all monastic theology firmly rooted in the second Gospel.

What of 'contemplation'? The Gospels do not use the expression 'contemplative life', but the idea is expressed in other language. Christ is transfigured on the mountain, i.e., in the wilderness. The cloud, which would later have such fruitful destiny in Christian mystical literature, is since Exodus a permanent feature of the desert tradition: the 'visible form of the governing, guiding yet hidden form of Yahweh's presence'. The desert life is not only darkness and battle, it is also light and rest in the Lord who is our only help. 'The epiphany of the glory of God is an indispensable element in the desert tradition.' In fact, says Dr Mauser, the transfiguration is the sign of the Father's approval of the obedience of Jesus in His desert vocation, His fidelity to a life of persistence in the desert'.

This persistence will of course lead finally to death, because the mountain of Calvary is the culmination of the desert vocation. 'Jesus's determination to persist in the desert . . . finds its conclusion in His decision to suffer and to die.' Why? Because the very secret of life itself is that by renunciation one overcomes death and suffering (Mark 8.35) and enters upon life everlasting. The disciples of Christ who are called in a very real sense to follow Him 'in the wilderness' do not really understand the meaning of their calling. They are to a certain extent blind to the teaching of their master and to the significance of His life. The real cause of this blindness is their incapacity to surrender totally to their own desert vocation. 'The unwillingness to endure tribulation and persecution, the care for security in the world, in one word the unwillingness to suffer'—prevent the disciples from seeing and accepting all the implications of Christ's teaching in their own lives. Even the apostolic mission of the followers of Jesus is marked with the sign of the wilderness. They are, in fact, called 'on the Mountain' and this, for Dr Mauser, is the 'indication of (the) basic condition of their mission'. When they are sent out to preach in Mark 6.8 ff, the instructions given them are similar to those given to Israel at the beginning of the desert journey. In one word: the disciples of Christ are to be kept alive by nourishment from God, and they must not waste time and energy caring for themselves. The miraculous feeding of the multitudes in the wilderness in Mark 6 represents at once the convocation of the new Israel in the desert and the messianic and eschatological rest of God's people with their King in the desert which has become His Kingdom and where He feeds them with His might in the new manna, the eucharist.

From this brief résumé we can see at once that Dr Mauser has given us a monastic reading of Mark's Gospel which is more thorough and more solid than almost anything we have in monastic literature since the Fathers. As monks we owe him thanks for a treatise in biblical theology which sums up the whole meaning of our own vocation to follow Christ in the wilderness, in temptation, to the cross, strengthened by His epiphany in the 'cloud' of contemplation, nourished by his eucharist and by the hope of the 'eschatological rest' with Him in the paradise of the transformed and flowering desert which is His Kingdom.

The intricate relationship between the themes of desert and paradise is developed in a fascinating manner by Dr George Williams. The Church of the martyrs believed that the desert had become the *arena*, the sandy place where they fought the beasts and overcame the adversary of God in their *agonia*. Then the monks went out into the actual desert as Christ had done and their monastic struggle with temptation became a 'martyrdom' in witness to the faith, in obedience to Christ, in direct dependence on God for the grace without which one could not resist. This struggle was rewarded and the Church of martyrs and monks became also a 'provisional paradise' in anticipation of the eternal Kingdom.

These themes are quire familiar to anyone who has read the monastic Fathers. But what is particularly interesting about Dr Williams' book is the way in which he traces the development of the wilderness-paradise theme through the medieval universities (with their traditional autonomy from outside control) to Protestant sectarians who sought refuge in the 'desert' and 'paradise' of the New World, and who there built seminaries and colleges as 'gardens in the wilderness'. Dr Williams sums up his thesis in these words: 'Many major and minor movements in Christian history have been in substantial degree the history of the interpenetrations of the biblical and post-biblical meanings of the wilderness and paradise in the experience of God's ongoing Israel'.

Besides exploring the wilderness-paradise theme in the Bible, especially in the prophetic writings, Dr Williams gives special attention to Qumran and to Christian monasticism. Qumran was an 'apocalyptic community that imitated the ancient sojourn in the wilderness of Sinai', seeking to prepare the way for a priestly and a royal Messiah (two Messiahs in fact) by a paradisic covenant and communal life. The aim of Qumran is summed up in a phrase that has most fruitful implications for monastic theology: 'the purity of paradise truth recovered within the fellowship of a disciplined wilderness encampment sustained by the Spirit'. Williams traces the themes of desert and paradise through Christian monasticism, shows the gradual *interiorization* of this theme in the mystical literature of the Middle Ages, especially of the Victorines. He demonstrates that it persisted in the spirituality of the Mendicants and in the Universities, and quotes many texts from radical Protestantism which have the authentic ring of ancient monasticism, except that they apply to sectarian communities rather than to conventual families living under monastic vows.

These texts incidentally offer much food for thought to anyone interested in ecumenical dialogue with Protestant visitors to our American monasteries. They show how completely a theme which is fundamental to monastic theology was taken over in the theology of radical Protestantism in the seventeenth century and hence entered into the formation of the Christian ideal of North American culture that grew up out of the Puritan colonies of New England. These words of John Eliot, a seventeenth-century New England Puritan, might equally well have come from one of the Trappist founders of the Abbey of Gethsemani: 'When the enjoyment of Christ in his pure Ordinances is better to the soul than all worldly comforts, then these things (the hardships of the wilderness) are but light afflictions'. Roger Williams is said to have practically 'made an incantation of the word wilderness'. Kentucky, we know, is still haunted by the thought of that 'wilderness road' through the Appalachian Mountains, over which the settlers came from Maryland and Virginia, including those Catholics who gathered around Bardstown where the first Cathedral west of the Alleghenies was dedicated in 1816. Bishop Flaget of Bardstown invited the first monks to North America.

In conclusion, one very important aspect of Dr Williams' book must not be passed over in silence. He is acutely aware, as too few Americans still are, of the criminal wastefulness with which commercial interests in the last two centuries have ravaged and despoiled the 'paradise-wilderness' of the North American mountains, forests and plains. The struggle to protect the natural beauties and resources of this country has not ended, and it is by no means to be regarded as an eccentricity of sentimental souls, bird watchers and flower gardeners. The disastrous storms of the thirties in the south-western dust bowl finally brought home more or less to everyone that conservation of soil and natural resources was an absolute necessity. Yet this does not prevent wastefulness, stupidity, greed and sheer destructive carelessness from going on today. So Dr Williams says, in words that monks above all should be ready to understand and appreciate: 'Ours is the age of the bulldozer as much as it is the age of the atomic bomb. For good or ill, we need no longer conform to the contours of the earth. The only wilderness that will be left is what we determine shall remain untouched and that other wilderness in the heart of man that only God can touch.' Anyone who reads the book will find this theme developed with its theological and religious implications. Meanwhile we might reasonably draw at least one obvious lesson from it. If the monk is a man whose whole life is built around a deeply religious appreciation of his call to wilderness and paradise, and thereby to a special kind of kinship with God's creatures in the new creation, and if technological society is constantly encroaching upon and destroying the remaining 'wildernesses' which it nevertheless needs in order to remain human, then we might suggest that the monk, of all people, should be concerned with staying in the 'wilderness' and helping to keep it a true 'wilderness and paradise'. The monk should be anxious to preserve the wilderness in order to share it with those who need to come out from the cities and remember what it is like to be under trees and to climb mountains. Surely there are enough people in the cities already without monks adding to their number when they would seem to be destined by God, in our time, to be not only dwellers in the wilderness but also its protectors.[2] This judgement may, admittedly, reflect a personal preference. The two books discussed here certainly show that even a monastic life in an industrial setting can also find a theological basis in the Bible and monastic tradition provided it is in fact a true 'wilderness life' in the spirit of the theology of the apostolate in the Gospel of St Mark.

THE SOLITARY LIFE

Like everything else in the Christian life, the vocation to solitude can be understood only within the perspective of God's mercy to man in the incarnation of Christ. If there is any such thing as a Christian hermit, then he must be a man who has a special function in the mystical body of Christ—a hidden and spiritual function, and perhaps all the more vital because more hidden. But this social function of the hermit, precisely because it has to be invisible, cannot be allowed in any way to detract from his genuinely solitary character. On the contrary, his function in the Christian community is the paradoxical one of living outwardly separated from the community. And this, whether he is conscious of it or not, is a witness to the completely transcendental character of the Christian mystery of our unity in Christ.

The hermit remains to put us on our guard against our natural obsession with the visible, social and communal forms of Christian life which tend at times to be inordinately active, and become deeply involved in the life of secular non-Christian society. The average Christian is in the world but not of it. But in case he might be likely to forget this—or worse still in case he might never come to know it at all—there must be men who have completely renounced the world: men who are neither in the world nor of it. In our day, when 'the world' is everywhere, even and perhaps especially in the desert, the hermit retains his unique and mysterious function. But he will fulfil it perhaps in many paradoxical ways. Wherever he does so, even where he is unseen (for he ought not to be conscious that he is a visible witness) he testifies to the essentially mystical bond of unity which binds Christians together in the Holy Spirit. Whether he is seen or not, he bears witness to the unity of Christ by possessing in himself the fullness of Christian charity. In fact, the early Christians who went out into the desert to see the solitaries of Nitria and Scete admired in them not so much their extreme asceticism as their charity and discretion. The miracle of the desert Fathers was precisely that a man could live entirely separate from the visible Christian community with its normal liturgical functions, and still be full of the charity of Christ. He was able to be so only because he was completely empty of himself.

The vocation to solitude is therefore at the same time a vocation to silence, poverty and emptiness. But the emptiness is for the sake of fullness: the purpose of the solitary life is, if you like, contemplation. But not contemplation in the pagan sense of an intellectual, esoteric enlightenment, achieved by ascetic technique. The contemplation of the Christian solitary is the awareness of the divine mercy transforming and elevating his own emptiness and turning it into the presence of perfect love, perfect fullness.

Hence a Christian can turn his back on society—even on the society of his fellow Christians—without necessarily hating society. It can be, in him, a sign of love for his fellow man to leave the company of others and live alone. This withdrawal should not be a rejection of other men; but it may well be a quiet and perhaps almost despairing refusal to accept the myths and fictions with which social life is always full—and never more than today. But to despair in the lies with which man surrounds himself is not to despair of man. Perhaps, on the contrary, it is a sign of hope. For is not our involvement in fiction, especially political and demagogic fiction, an implicit confession of spiritual despair?

The Christian hope in God and in the 'world to come' is something drastically spiritual and pure, which jealously clings to its invisibility. To be sure, it must take on visible and symbolic forms, in order to communicate its message. But when these symbolic forms in turn become submerged in other secular symbols, and when the Christian message becomes involved in mundane hopes, then faith itself tends to be corrupted by these human fictions with which it has been confused. At such a time, some men will seek clarity in isolation and silence, not because they think they know better than the rest, but because they want to see life in a different perspective. They want to withdraw from the babel of confusion in order to listen more patiently to the voice of their conscience and to the Holy Spirit. And by their prayers and their fidelity they will invisibly renew the life of the whole Church. This renewal will communicate itself to others who remain 'in the world' and will help them also to have a clearer vision, a sharper and more uncompromising appreciation of Christian truth. These will give themselves to apostolic work on a new level of seriousness and of faith, and will be able to discard fictitious gestures of zeal in favour of humble and patient labour.

So when, as in our time, the whole world seems to have become one immense and idiotic fiction, and when the virus of mendacity creeps into every vein and organ of the social body, it would be abnormal and immoral if there were no reaction. It is even healthy that the reaction should sometimes take the form of outspoken protest, as long as we remember that where Christian obedience is concerned, even manifest errors on the part of hierarchical authority are no justification for rebellion and disobedience, and the observations made by subjects should never be lacking in the respect due to Superiors, or in submission to authority as such. Solitude, in other words, is no refuge for the rebellious. And if there is an element of protest in the solitary vocation, that protest must be a matter of rigorous spirituality. It must be deep and interior, and intimately personal, so that the hermit is one who is critical, first of all, of himself. Otherwise he will delude himself with a fiction worse than that of all the others, becoming a more insane and self-opinionated liar than the worst of them, cheating no one more than himself. Solitude is not for rebels like this, and it promptly rejects them. The desert is for those who have felt a salutary despair of accepted values, in order to hope in mercy and to be themselves merciful men to whom that mercy is promised. Such solitaries know the evils that are in other men because they experience these evils first in themselves.

Such men, out of pity for the universe, out of loyalty to mankind, and without a spirit of bitterness or of resentment, withdraw into the healing silence of the wilderness, or of poverty, or of obscurity, not in order to preach to others but to heal in themselves the wounds of the entire world.

The message of God's mercy to man must be preached. The word of truth must be proclaimed. No one can deny this. But there are not a few who are beginning to feel the futility of adding more words to the constant flood of language that pours meaninglessly over everybody, everywhere, from morning to night. For language to have meaning, there must be intervals of silence somewhere, to divide word from word and utterance from utterance. He who retires into silence does not necessarily hate language. Perhaps it is love and respect for language which impose silence upon him. For the mercy of God is not heard in words unless it is heard, both before and after the words are spoken, in silence.

There have always been, and always will be, hermits who are alone in the midst of men without realizing why. They are condemned to their strange isolation by temperament or circumstance, and they get used to it. It is not of these that I am speaking, but of those who, having led active and articulate lives in the world of men, leave their old life behind and go out into the desert.

Such a vocation is not, generally speaking, for the young. It cannot spring merely from a ferment of idealism or from callow rebellion, from mere disgust with conventional attitudes and ways of living. But there comes a time when one is simply tired of keeping up the pretences that are necessarily involved in social living. He sees that he has no further use for them.

Of course, everyone with any sense sees, from time to time, in a lucid moment, the folly and triviality of our conventional attitudes. It is possible for anyone to dream of liberty. But to undertake the wretched austerity of living in complete honesty, without convention and therefore without support, is quite another matter. That is why there exist communities of artists, of esoteric thinkers and cultists, of religious hermits in communities under vows. The break with the big group is compensated by enrolment in the little group. This is not yet the desert. But it is perhaps a long way in the right direction, if the little group is moderately honest.

And in demanding 'honesty' of the hermit, let us not be too hypocritically exacting. He too may have his eccentricities. He may rely heavily on certain imperfect solutions to problems which his human weakness does not allow him to cope with fully. Let us not condemn him for failing to solve problems we have not even dared to face.

It is at any rate significant that the religious hermit is once more getting to be almost officially recognized in the Church. He has always been there. He is now even closer to having a canonical status of his own. The eremitic orders have always been the objects of reverence or of envy among those who really understood the cloistered life. But now, too, we find Orders like the Benedictines rather readily granting some of their members permission to live alone, for the sake of contemplation. And the Carmelite Friars are reopening their 'desert' communities, where they are able to retire for a year of solitude amid their active works.

But the solitary life is an arid, rugged purification of the heart. St Jerome and St Eucherius have written rhapsodies about the flowering desert, but Jerome was the busiest hermit that ever lived and Eucherius was a bishop who admired the hermit brethren of Lerins only from afar. The *eremi cultores*, the farmers of the desert sand, have had less to say about the experience. They have been washed out by dryness, and their burnt lips are weary of speech.

If a solitary should one day find his way, by the grace and mercy of God, into a desert place in which he is not known, and if it is permitted to him by the divine pity to live there, and to remain unknown, he may perhaps do more good to the human race by being a solitary than he ever could have done by remaining the prisoner of the society where he was living. For anyone who breaks the chains of falsity, and strives, even unsuccessfully, to be true to God and to his inner self, is doing more for the world than can be done even by a saint in politics—assuming that such a miracle as a saint in politics were to happen in this age.

Physical solitude sometimes takes on the aspect of a bitter defeat. It is an earthly paradise only in the imaginations of those who find their solitude in the crowded city, or who are able to be hermits for a few days or a few hours at a time, no more. But the call to perfect solitude is a call to suffering, to darkness, and to annihilation. Yet when a man is called to it, he prefers this to any earthly paradise.

The solitary who no longer communicates with other men except for the bare necessities of life is a man with a special and difficult vocation. He soon loses all sense of his significance for the rest of the world. And yet that significance is great. The hermit has a very real place in a world like ours that has degraded the human person and lost all respect for solitude.

But in such a world the vocation of the hermit is more terrible than ever. In the eyes of our world, the hermit is nothing but a failure. He has to be a failure—we have absolutely no use for him, no place for him. He is outside all our projects, plans, assemblies, movements. We can countenance him as long as he remains only a fiction, or a dream. As soon as he becomes real, we are revolted by his insignificance, his poverty, his shabbiness, his dirt. Even those who consider themselves contemplatives, often cherish a secret contempt for the hermit. For in the contemplative life of the hermit there is none of that noble security, that intellectual depth, that artistic finesse which the professional contemplative seeks in his sedate communities.

Yet the hermit must always remain the true model of the monk. The man in the warm, freshly ironed cowl, should remember that what he is trying to be is something like the solitary with chapped hands, working foolishly outside his shack in the woods—or perhaps pottering aimlessly in some job without honour. It is the aimlessness of the hermit that is the great scandal. He is shiftless, insecure, in a sense idle. He looks too much like (let's face it) a mere bum. And evidently there is something about him that makes him want to be that. He seems to have a strange inner need to be a bum. In this, we assume, he is a pathological case, no? And yet the windows of the monastery are supposed to open, not upon the world, but upon the desert in which this shiftless creature lives without too much respectable discipline. Unfortunately, the cenobite is more likely to have, as his ideal, a purely abstract hermit, and this abstraction permits him, with a quiet conscience, to turn his mind more readily toward the world than toward the desert. Thus he is saved from the painful necessity of admitting that the highest form of contemplative life is a life that has absolutely no practical use or purpose whatever. It is not even supposed to be practical.

One of the things that most strikes the visitor to a 'good' monastery, is the practicality of what takes place there. There is plenty of zeal and hard work. The machines hum. Much is 'accomplished'. Very well. But in reality, practicality should enter the monastic life purely as a concession to human weakness. Nowhere does it form part of the genuine monastic ideal.

It has never been either practical or useful to leave all things and follow Christ. And yet it is spiritually prudent. Practical utility and supernatural prudence are sometimes flatly opposed to one another, as wisdom of the flesh and prudence of the spirit. Not that the spirit can never allow itself to accomplish things in a practical, temporal way. But it does not rest in purely temporal ends. Its accomplishments belong to a higher and more spiritual order—which is of course necessarily hidden. Practical utility has its roots in the present life. Supernatural prudence lives for the world to come. It weighs all things in the balance of eternity. Spiritual things have no weight for 'practical' man. The solitary life is something that cannot even tip his scales. It is 'nothing', a non-entity. Yet St Paul says: 'The foolish things of the world hath God chosen that He may confound the wise, and the weak things of the world hath God chosen that He may confound the strong. And the base things of the world, and the things that are contemptible that He might bring to nought things that are'. (1 Cor. 1.27–8)

And why is this? 'That no flesh should glory in His sight.' It is the invisible glory that is real. The empty horizons of the solitary life enable us to grow accustomed to a light that is not seen where the mirage of secular pursuit fascinates and deludes our gaze.

Of course monks must legitimately make their living, and sell what they produce. Presumably they ought to be able to

do this without turning into men of business. Their attempts
to square this circle are quite sufficient to keep them amused
and out of worse mischief. Therefore, and with every good
reason, practical utility enters into the cenobitic life as the
servant of supernatural prudence. And still, when practical
utility begins to outweigh monastic poverty and becomes an
end in itself, it destroys supernatural prudence, roots the
monk in secular life, makes him a prisoner of his endeavours,
and robs him of his liberty to fly freely into eternity.

The hermit remains there to prove, by his lack of practical
utility and the apparent sterility of his vocation, that monks
themselves ought to have little significance in the world, or
indeed none at all. They are dead to the world, they should
no longer cut a figure in it. And the world is dead to them.
They are pilgrims in it, isolated witnesses of another kingdom. This of course is the price they pay for universal compassion, for a sympathy that reaches all. The monk is compassionate in proportion as he is less practical and less successful, because the job of being a success in a competitive
society leaves one no time for compassion.

The hermit has all the more of a part to play in our world,
because he has no proper place in it. The monk is not yet
enough of an exile. That is why we need hermits. The monk
can be understood and appreciated. As soon as one can com-
pare the monastery to a 'power house of prayer' the world is
ready to grant it, if grudgingly, a certain respect. A power
house produces something. And, so it appears, the prayers of
the monks produce a kind of spiritual energy. Or at least the
monks take care of their own needs, and make a little money.
They are there as a comforting presence. The presence of the
hermit, when it is known at all, is no comfort; it is disturbing. He does not even look good. He produces nothing.

One of the most telling criticisms of the hermit may well
be that even in his life of prayer he is less 'productive'. You
would think that in his solitude he would quickly reach the
level of visions, of mystical marriage, something dramatic at
any rate. Yet he may well be poorer than the cenobite, even
in his life of prayer. His is a weak and precarious existence,
he has more cares, he is more insecure, he has to struggle to

preserve himself from all kinds of petty annoyances, and often he fails to do so. His poverty is spiritual. It invades his whole soul as well as his body, and in the end his whole patrimony is one of insecurity. He enjoys the sorrow, the spiritual and intellectual indigence of the really poor. That is precisely the hermit vocation, a vocation to inferiority on every level, even the spiritual. Obviously it has in it a grain of folly. Otherwise it is not what it is meant to be, a life of direct dependence on God, in darkness, insecurity and pure faith. The life of the hermit is a life of material and physical poverty without visible support.

Of course, one must not exaggerate or be too absolute in this matter. Absolutism itself can become a kind of 'fortune' and 'honour'. We must also face the fact that the average human being is incapable of a life in which austerity is without compromise. There comes a limit, beyond which human weakness cannot go, and where mitigation itself enters in as a subtle form of poverty. Maybe the hermit turns out, unaccountably, to have his ulcer just like the next man. And he has to drink large quantities of milk and perhaps take medicines. This finally disposes of any hope of him becoming a legendary figure. He, too, worries. Perhaps he worries even more than others, for it is only in the minds of those who know nothing about it that the solitary life appears to be a life free from all care. We must remember that Robinson Crusoe was one of the great myths of the middle-class, commercial civilization of the eighteenth and nineteenth centuries: the myth not of eremitic solitude but of pragmatic individualism. Crusoe is a symbolical figure in an era when every man's house was his castle in the trees, but only because every man was a very prudent and resourceful citizen who knew how to make the best out of the least and could drive a hard bargain with any competitor, even with life itself. Carefree Crusoe was happy because he had an answer to everything. The real hermit is not so sure he has an answer to anything.

True, the hermit should not be a completely helpless person. He should have something of Crusoe's skill with his hands, for he has to be self-sufficient at least to a degree. But there is a limit to self-sufficiency. And in the spiritual order too, the eremitic life is not completely independent. The hermit is not subject to the complexities of religious institutionalism, and to its vanities, but he sometimes needs a director, and if he does not have one, his life is apt to be an altogether absurd confusion. (Yet even of this confusion, if it is nobody's fault, God will make sense and order in His own way.)

If being a hermit meant being a hero, we might after all respect such a vocation. If it means simply being a tramp, even then some of us can accept it insofar as it suggests the idea, perhaps, of preaching to the birds.

But what if, in the end, our hermit turns out to be not even a contemplative in the ordinary sense of the word? He may not have 'a high degree of prayer'. Worse still, he may not even aspire to one. He may not care to be enlightened. He may have some sardonic, silent, hopeless idea that if there is for him some way to enlightenment, it consists of fleeing as far as possible from every suggestion of professional illumination.

It is true that his life must be a life of prayer and meditation, if he is an authentic hermit. For the hermit in our context is purely and simply a man of God. This should be clear. But what prayer! What meditation! Nothing more like bread and water than this interior prayer of his! Utter poverty. Often an incapacity to pray, to see, to hope. Not the sweet passivity which the books extol, but a bitter, arid struggle to press forward through a blinding sandstorm. The hermit, all day and all night, beats his head against a wall of doubt. That is his contemplation. Do not mistake my meaning. It is not a question of intellectual doubt, an analytical investigation of theological, philosophical or some other truths. It is something else, a kind of unknowing of his own self, a kind of doubt that questions the very roots of his existence, a doubt which undermines his very reasons for existing and for doing what he does. It is this doubt which reduces him finally to silence, and in the silence which ceases to ask questions, he receives the only certitude he knows: the presence of God in the midst of uncertainty and nothingness, as the only reality, but as a reality which cannot be 'placed' or identified. Hence the hermit says nothing. He does his work, and is patient (or perhaps impatient, I don't know) but generally he has peace. It is not the world's kind of peace. He is happy, but he never has a good time. He knows where he is going, but he is not 'sure of his way', he just knows by going there. He does not see the way beforehand, and when he arrives he arrives. His arrivals are usually departures from anything that resembles a 'way'. That is his way. But he cannot understand it. Neither can we.

Beyond and in all this, he possesses his solitude, the riches of his emptiness, his interior poverty: but of course, it is not a possession. It is an established fact. It is there. It is assured. In fact, it is inescapable. It is everything—his whole life. It contains God, surrounds him with God, plunges him in God. So great is his poverty that he does not even see God; so great are his riches that he is lost in God and lost to himself. He is never far enough away from God to see Him in perspective, or as an object. He is swallowed up in Him, and therefore, so to speak, never sees Him at all.

All that we can say of this indigence of the true hermit must not make us forget the fact that he is happy in his solitude, but especially because he has ceased to regard himself as a solitary in contradistinction to others who are not solitary. He simply is. And if he has been impoverished and set aside by the will of God, this is not a distinction, but purely a fact. His solitude is sometimes frightening, sometimes a burden, yet it is more precious to him than anything else because it is for him the will of God. Not a 'thing' willed by God, not an object decreed by a remote power, but the pressure, upon his own life, of that pure actuality which is the will of God, the reality of all that is real. His solitude is, for him, simply reality. He could not break away from this will even if he wanted to. To be prisoner of this love is to be free, and almost to be in paradise. Hence the life of physical solitude is a life of love without consolation, a life that is fruitful because it is pressed down and running over with the will of God: and all that has this will in it is full of significance, even when it appears to make no sense at all.

The terror of the solitary life is the immediacy with which the will of God presses upon our soul. It is much easier, and gentler, and more secure to have the 'will of God' filtered to us quietly through society, through decrees of men, through the orders of others. To take this will straight in all its incomprehensible, baffling mystery, is not possible to one who is not secretly protected and guided by the Holy Spirit and no one should try it unless he has some assurance that he really has been called to it by God. One has to be born into solitude carefully, patiently and after long delay, out of the womb of society.

The hermit remains in the world as a prophet to whom no one listens, as a voice crying in the desert, as a sign of contradiction. The world does not want him because he has nothing in himself that belongs to the world, and he no longer understands the world. Therefore it does not understand him. But this is his mission, to be rejected by the world which, in that act, rejects the dreaded solitude of God Himself. For that is what the world resents about God: His utter otherness, His absolute incapacity to be absorbed into the context of worldly and practical slogans, His mysterious transcendency which places Him infinitely beyond the reach of catchwords, advertisements and political slogans. It is easier for the world to re-create a god in its own image, a god who justifies its own slogans, when there are no solitaries about to remind men of the solitude of God: the God who cannot become a member of any purely human fellowship. And yet this solitary God has called men to another fellowship, with Himself, through the passion and resurrection of Christ— through the solitude of Gethsemani and of Calvary, and the mystery of Easter, and the solitude of the ascension: all of which precede the great communion of Pentecost.

Fear is close to love. Even those who fear the solitary nevertheless allow themselves to be fascinated by him, because his very uselessness does not cease to proclaim that he has, after all, some incomprehensible function in our world.

And this function is to be in the world as solitary, as poor and as unacceptable as God Himself in the souls of so many men. The solitary is there to tell them, in a way they can barely understand, that if they were able to discover and appreciate their own inner solitude they would immediately discover God and find out, from His speech to them, that they are really persons.

The habitual argument of those who protest against exterior solitude is that it is dangerous, besides being totally unnecessary. Unnecessary because all that really matters is interior solitude, or so they say. And this 'can be obtained without physical isolation'. There is in this statement a truth more terrible than can be imagined by those who so glibly make it, as a justification for their lives without solitude, silence or prayer.

There are some who equate the purely solitary life with selfishness, and praise solitude in community as 'more charitable'. But in effect, the solitude in community they praise tends to become a comfortable and secure life that is made possible by the sacrifices and efforts of others. It makes contemplation easier by virtue of the charity of others and as long as the contemplative is supported by them, he 'enjoys his solitude'. As soon as he becomes insecure, he leaves his solitude for something else, and seeks support elsewhere. If that is the case his solitude is a sham.

But there is a terrible irony about solitude in community: that if you are called to solitude by God, even if you live in a community, your solitude will be inescapable. Even if you are surrounded by the comfort and the assistance of others, the bonds that unite you with them on a trivial level break one by one so that you are no longer supported by them, that is, no longer sustained by the instinctive, automatic mechanisms of collective life. Their words, their enthusiasms become meaningless. Yet you do not despise them, or reject them. You try to find if there is not still some way to comprehend them and live by them. And you find that words have no value in such a situation. The only thing that can help you is the deep, wordless communion of genuine love.

At such a time it is a great relief to be put in contact with others by some simple task, some function of the ministry. Then you meet them not with your words or theirs, but with the words and sacramental gestures of God. The word of

God takes on an ineffable purity and strength when it is seen as the only way in which a solitary can effectively reach the solitudes of others—the solitudes of which these others are unaware. Then he realizes that he loves them more than ever, perhaps that he now loves them really for the first time. Made humble by his solitude, grateful for the work that brings him into contact with others, he still remains alone. There is no greater loneliness than that of an instrument of God who realizes that his words and his ministry, even though they be the words of God, can do nothing to change his loneliness and yet that, beyond all distinction between mine and thine, they make him one with everyone he encounters.

This loneliness is the loneliness of God Himself in man; the solitude of the hidden and unknown God who has 'emptied Himself' and identified Himself with man, in whom He is forgotten, ignored and infinitely poor. To share in such solitude, such poverty, is a joy beyond human comment and appreciation.

About such joy nothing adequate can be said. Silence alone can worthily express it. It has a logic of its own which is beyond discursive thought. Words reduce that logic to absurdity.

Appendixes

MONASTIC RENEWAL:
A MEMORANDUM

The monastic vocation is an ascetic charism, not a call to a special work in and for the Church. The monk is called 'out of this world' to seek God truly in silence, prayer, solitude, renunciation, compunction and simplicity. Even in its cenobitic form (which must not be taken to be the only form) the monastic life maintains something of the desert atmosphere of a life alone with God. The work of the monk is to seek God first and Him alone.

In monastic reform, care should be taken first of all to maintain or restore the special character of the monastic vocation. The monastic life must not be evaluated in terms of active religious life, and the monastic orders should not be equated with other religious institutes, clerical or otherwise. The monastic community does not exist for the sake of any apostolic or educational work, even as a secondary end. The works of the monk are not justified by their external results but only by their relevance to his monastic life alone with God. They are meaningful insofar as they are appropriate to a life out of this world, which is also a life of compassion for those who remain in the world, and of prayer for the salvation of the world.

In reflecting on the current task of *aggiornamento* in the Church at large those concerned with monastic reform must take care not to be misled by their rightful admiration of other charisms, foreign to monasticism. Now experiments which are signs of genuine life and apostolic renewal, in vital contact with the world and in sympathy for the secular spirit of the time, are not to be taken as germane to monastic reform merely because they are necessary and good.

However, the concept of a 'pure contemplative life', especially in a juridical sense, does not necessarily fit the monastic

vocation, in which room can and should be left for certain
cases of exceptional openness to the world and contacts with
certain individuals or groups in an informal and rather personal apostolate, in hospitality, small conferences, or spiritual
direction. These contacts remain exceptional. No monastic
community should be obliged to regard them as normal and
systematic.

The first concern of monastic reform should be the
clarification of monastic principles by a return to sources, in
order that monastic life may recover its authenticity and simplicity, liberated from all that is foreign to it. But this will
not be possible if, in fact, those monastic institutions which
are active rather than contemplative, are taken as the norm.
The monastic life as lived in the large active communities
today devoted to education or to business is not fully normal,
for in such communities the spirit of solitude and the life of
prayer are the exception rather than the rule.

Monastic reform will therefore not be authentic or effective if it consists mainly in adjustments of liturgy and regular
observance, with exhortations to a greater spirit of prayer and
a more exact observance of silence and enclosure. If the life
within the enclosure is a life of preoccupation and great activity, a mere tightening of discipline will not make it more monastic. Nor will a greater emphasis on 'family life' attain this
end, for this emphasis may, itself, serve the purpose of an increasingly active and busy spirit, and draw the monk further
and further from a life of silence and prayer.

When, therefore, the familiar monastic structures tend in
fact to frustrate some of the deep aims of the monastic vocation, it would be a serious error to regard them as the norm.
This does not mean that such community structures are not
very admirable and useful to the Church in their own way.
There is no need to criticize them or to insinuate that they
are not fervent and regular communities. Yet we must admit
that genuine monastic reform must be looked for elsewhere.
It is therefore important that when members of these communities seek a more simple and authentic form of monastic
life, whether in communities that already exist or in solitude,
or perhaps even in new monastic communities to be founded,

they should not be impeded merely because their aspirations do not seem to accord with what is regarded as 'normal' in the big and familiar monastic structures of our day. The fact that a proposed new form of monastic life does not fit in with the pattern that is generally accepted in large, prosperous and well-established monasteries, does not mean that it is either dangerous or undesirable. The norm must be sought in authentic monastic tradition, adapted to the special needs of our time. A certain amount of 'risk' may naturally be expected when there is a question of the wager of an experiment.

Monastic superiors should be ready to see and encourage in their subjects any exceptional and genuine desire for a deeper life of prayer and for a return to simpler monastic ways. The Abbot is a Spiritual Father and not merely an administrator. He is not simply a head of an organization responsible for getting his men to serve the purposes of the community. He is responsible to God for the development and true sanctification of his monks. When therefore they believe they should seek a simpler, more solitary and more fervent life of prayer, they should not be prevented from investigating reasonable possibilities of doing so. They should not be discouraged from their attempt, still less ridiculed, but should be helped in various ways to test their abilities and prove the reality of their higher vocation. One may perhaps be able to lead a simpler and more prayerful life within the framework of a large community of the familiar type. Another may perhaps be permitted to live apart from the community temporarily or permanently, under obedience to his Abbot. Still others may need to transfer to new communities or even receive permission to live alone as hermits. All these possibilities should be recognized as legitimate and practical. Thus no one would be prevented from putting to the test any aspiration which might be considered serious. The fact that others might be 'influenced' does not constitute 'scandal'. It may well be an edification.

The situation of the monk living apart from the world as a man of God gives him a special advantage and authority in spiritual things, provided that he is really living up to his vocation. Hence a monastic apostolate, which has a special character of its own, will not be justified if it merely reproduces in every detail the activity of preaching orders or of the secular clergy. A monk who is caught in the organized pressures of a systematic and uninterrupted active life cannot truly live as a monk and his apostolate therefore loses its true character, useful though it may be. A true monastic apostolate therefore should always be 'occasional' in character, and should not be subject to unusual pressures or constant, uninterrupted demands. It should always be an overflow of a deep life of silence and prayer. The monk has no obligation to share directly with others, in word or work, the 'fruits of contemplation'. Hence if he leaves his solitude without reason in order to engage in activity, he cannot rely on the special graces that support others who are officially engaged in active or apostolate work. On the other hand if the monk, directly or indirectly (for instance by the pen) is able to reach souls, his apostolate will be effective insofar as it springs obviously and manifestly from his monastic life. Whether the individual monk reaches 'the world' or not, the monastery itself can always offer to men a place of peaceful meditation where they can seek spiritual guidance and hours of restful prayer, benefiting by the hospitality which is a traditional obligation of the monastic life.

Monastic education should be adapted to the monastic life, and should not merely follow the lines laid down for active orders and seminaries. The novitiate training should be longer than in other orders and after the novitiate the monastic formation should be continued, with studies of Scripture, Liturgy, Asceticism, the Fathers and other subjects proper to the monastic life. When monks study for the priesthood (which is traditionally regarded as *exceptional* for a monk) their course should correspond to the needs of the monastic life and they should not be obliged to take the full seminary course prescribed for priests in the active life.

The monastic life is a life of love for God and for man. The social aspect of the monastic life is therefore very important, but its importance must not be overemphasized to the detriment of the spirit of prayer and solitude. The apostolate of the monk need not necessarily be confined to prayer and reparation, but if in active work the monk merely imitates what can be done better by other orders or by the secular clergy, his apostolate loses its meaning and its justification.

On the other hand, a truly monastic apostolate is urgently needed in the sphere of monasticism itself. For instance retreats and conferences in monasteries should be given by members of monastic orders deeply imbued with the traditional monastic spirit in preference to members of active orders who are not aware of the special problems and needs of the monastic life.

A LETTER ON THE CONTEMPLATIVE LIFE

Abbey of Gethsemani, 21 August 1967

Reverend and dear Father,[1]

This morning I received your letter of 14 August and I realize I must answer it immediately in order to get the reply to you before the end of the month. This does not leave me time to plan and think, and hence I must write rapidly and spontaneously. I must also write directly and simply, saying precisely what I think, and not pretending to announce a magnificent message which is really not mine. I will say what I can. It is not much. I will leave the rest of you to frame a document of good theology and clearly inspiring hope which will be of help to modern man in his great trouble.

On the other hand I must begin by saying that I was acutely embarrassed by the Holy Father's request. It puts us all in a difficult position. We are not experts in anything. There are few real contemplatives in our monasteries. We know nothing whatever of spiritual aviation and it would be the first duty of honesty to admit that fact frankly, and to add that we do not speak the language of modern man. There is considerable danger that in our haste to comply with the Holy Father's generous request, based on an even more generous estimate of us, we may come out with one more solemn pronouncemnt which will end not by giving modern man hope but by driving him further into despair, simply by convincing him that we belong to an entirely different world, in which we have managed, by dint of strong will and dogged refusals, to remain in a past era. I plead with you: we must at all costs avoid this error and act of uncharity. We must, before all else, whatever else we do, speak to modern man as his brothers, as people who are in very much the same difficulties as he is, as people who suffer much of what he suffers, though we are immensely privileged to be exempt from so many, so very many, of his responsibilities and sufferings. And we must not arrogate to ourselves the right to talk down to modern man, to dictate to him from a position of supposed eminence, when perhaps he suspects that our cloister walls have not done anything except confirm us in unreality. The problem of the contemplative orders at present, in the presence of modern man, is a problem of great ambiguity. People look at us, recognize we are sincere, recognize that we have indeed found a certain peace, and see that there may after all be some worth to it: but can we convince them that this means anything to them? I mean, can we convince them professionally and collectively, as 'the contemplatives' in our walled institution, that what our institutional life represents has any meaning for them? If I were absolutely confident in answering yes to this, then it would be simple to draft the message we are asked to draw up. But to me, at least, it is not that simple. And for that reason I am perhaps disqualified from participating in this at all. In fact, this preface is in part a plea to be left out, to be exempted from a task to which I do not in the least recognize myself equal. However, as I said before, I will attempt to say in my own words what I personally, as an individual, have to say and usually do say to my brother who is in the world and who more and more often comes to me with his wounds which turn out to be also my own. The Holy Father, he can be a good Samaritan, but myself and my brother in the world we are just two men who have fallen among thieves and we do our best to get each other out of the ditch.

Hence what I write here I write only as a sinner to another sinner, and in no sense do I speak officially for 'the monastic Order' with all its advantages and its prestige and its tradition.

Let us suppose the message of a so-called contemplative to a so-called man of the world to be something like this:

My dear Brother, first of all, I apologize for addressing you when you have not addressed me and have not really asked me anything. And I apologize for being behind a high wall which you do not understand. This high wall is to you a problem, and perhaps it is also a problem to me, O my brother. Perhaps you ask me why I stay behind it out of obedience? Perhaps you are no longer satisfied with the reply that if I stay behind this wall I have quiet, recollection, tranquillity of heart. Perhaps you ask me what right I have to all this peace and tranquillity when some sociologists have estimated that within the lifetime of our younger generations a private room will become an unheard-of luxury. I do not have a satisfactory answer: it is true, as an Islamic proverb says 'the hen does not lay eggs in the market place'. It is true that when I came to this monastery where I am, I came in revolt against the meaningless confusion of a life in which there was so much activity, so much movement, so much useless talk, so much superficial and needless stimulation, that I could not remember who I was. But the fact remains that my flight from the world is not a reproach to you who remain in the world, and I have no right to repudiate the world in a purely negative fashion, because if I do that my flight will have taken me not to truth and to God but to a private, though doubtless pious, illusion.

Can I tell you that I have found answers to the questions that torment the man of our time? I do not know if I have found answers. When I first became a monk, yes, I was more sure of 'answers'. But as I grow old in the monastic life and advance further into solitude, I become aware that I have only begun to seek the questions. And what are the questions? Can man make sense out of his existence? Can man honestly give his life meaning merely by adopting a certain set of explanations which pretend to tell him why the world began and where it will end, why there is evil and what is necessary for a good life? My brother, perhaps in my solitude I have become as it were an explorer for you, a searcher in realms which you are not able to visit—except perhaps in the company of your psychiatrist. I have been summoned to explore a desert area of man's heart in which explanations no longer suffice, and in which one learns that only experience counts. An arid, rocky, dark land of the soul, sometimes illuminated by strange fires which men fear and peopled by spectres which men studiously avoid except in their nightmares. And in this area I have learned that one cannot truly know hope unless he has found out how like despair hope is. The language of Christianity has said this for centuries in other less naked terms. But the language of Christianity has been so used and so misused that sometimes you distrust it: you do not know whether or not behind the word 'cross' there stands the experience of mercy and salvation, or only the threat of punishment. If my word means anything to you, I can say to you that I have experienced the cross to mean mercy and not cruelty, truth and not deception; that the news of the truth and love of Jesus is indeed the true good news, but in our time it speaks out in strange places. And perhaps it speaks out in you more than it does in me; perhaps Christ is nearer to you than he is to me. This I say without shame or guilt because I have learned to rejoice that Jesus is in the world in people who know Him not, that He is at work in them when they think themselves far from Him, and it is my joy to tell you to hope though you think that for you of all men hope is impossible. Hope not because you think you can be good, but because God loves us irrespective of our merits and whatever is good in us comes from His love, not from our own doing. Hope because Jesus is with those who are poor and outcast and perhaps despised even by those who should seek them and care for them more lovingly because they act in God's name. . . . No one on earth has reason to despair of Jesus, because Jesus loves man, loves him in his sin, and we too must love man in his sin.

God is not a 'problem' and we who live the contemplative life have learned by experience that one cannot know God as long as one seeks to solve 'the problem of God'. To seek to solve the problem of God is to seek to see one's own eyes. One cannot see one's own eyes because they are that with which one sees and God is the light by which we see—by which we see not a clearly defined 'object' called God, but everything else in the invisible One. God is then the Seer and the Seeing and the Seen. God seeks Himself in us, and the aridity and sorrow of our heart is the sorrow of God who is not known to us, who cannot yet find Himself in us because we do not dare to believe or trust the incredible truth that He could live in us, and live there out of choice, out of preference. But indeed we exist solely for this, to be the place He has chosen for His presence, His manifestation in the world, His epiphany. But we make all this dark and inglorious because we fail to believe it, we refuse to believe it. It is not that we hate God, rather that we hate ourselves, despair of ourselves. If we once began to recognize, humbly but truly, the real value of our own self, we would see that this value was the sign of God in our being, the signature of God upon our being. Fortunately, the love of our fellow man is given us as the way of realizing this. For the love of our brother, our sister, our beloved, our wife, our child, is there to see with the clarity of God Himself that we are good. It is the love of my lover, my brother or my child that sees God in me, makes God credible to myself in me. And it is my love for my lover, my child, my brother, that enables me to show God to him or her in himself or herself. Love is the epiphany of God in our poverty. The contemplative life is then the search for peace not in an abstract exclusion of all outside reality, not in a barren negative closing of the senses upon the world, but in the openness of love. It begins with the acceptance of my own self in my poverty and my nearness to despair, in order to recognize that where God is there can be no despair, and God is in me even if I despair: that nothing can change God's love for me, since my very existence is the sign that God loves me and the presence of His love creates and sustains me. Nor is there any need to understand how this can be or to explain it or to solve the problems it seems to raise. For there is in our hearts and in the very ground of our being a natural certainty that says that insofar as we exist we are penetrated through and through with the sense and reality of God even though we may be utterly unable to believe or experience this in philosophic or even religious terms.

O my brother, the contemplative is not the man who has fiery visions of the cherubim carrying God on their imagined chariot, but simply he who has risked his mind in the desert beyond language and beyond ideas where God is encountered in the nakedness of pure trust, that is to say in the surrender of our own poverty and incompleteness in order no longer to clench our minds in a cramp upon themselves, as if thinking made us exist. The message of hope the contemplative offers you, then, brother, is not that you need to find your way through the jungle of language and problems that today surround God; but that whether you understand or not, God loves you, is present to you, lives in you, dwells in you, calls you, saves you, and offers you an understanding and light which are like nothing you ever found in books or heard in sermons. The contemplative has nothing to tell you except to reassure you and say that if you dare to penetrate your own silence and dare to advance without fear into the solitude of your own heart, and risk the sharing of that solitude with the lonely other who seeks God through you and with you, then you will truly recover the light and the capacity to understand what is beyond words and beyond explanations because it is too close to be explained: it is the intimate union in the depths of your own heart, of God's spirit and your own secret inmost self, so that you and He are in all truth One Spirit. I love you, in Christ.

Such are the few ideas I have had, written in haste—so much more will be said so much better by others.

Yours in Christ Jesus,
br. M. Louis
(Thomas Merton)

CONTEMPLATIVES AND
THE CRISIS OF FAITH

While the Synod of Bishops is meeting in Rome,[1] we, a group of contemplative monks, feel ourselves closely united with our bishops in their pastoral cares. We are thinking especially of the difficulties which many Christians are experiencing at the present time concerning their faith—difficulties which even go so far as to lead them to call into question the possibility of attaining to knowledge of the transcendent God who has revealed himself to men.

In this situation, it seems to us that our way of life puts us in a position where we can address a few simple words to all. Since we do not want to make our silence and solitude an excuse for failing to render what may be a service to our brothers, especially to those who are struggling to keep or to find faith in Jesus Christ, we are addressing ourselves in a spirit of sonship to you who are the witnesses to that faith, and the guides and masters of souls, so that you can judge in what measure our message might be useful to the people of God in the world of today.

Our personal qualifications for offering such a testimony are poor indeed. But it is more in the name of the way of life that we lead, rather than in our own names, that we dare to speak.

On the one hand, the cloistered contemplative life is simply the Christian life, but the Christian life lived in conditions which favour the 'experience' of God. It could be described as a sort of specialization in relationship with God which puts us in a position to offer a testimony to this aspect of things.

On the other hand, while the contemplative withdraws from the world, this does not mean that he deserts either it or his fellow-men. He remains wholly rooted in the earth on which he is born, whose riches he has inherited, whose cares and aspirations he has tried to make his own. He withdraws from it in order to place himself more intensely at the divine source from which the forces that drive the world onwards originate, and to understand in this light the great designs of mankind. For it is in the desert that the soul most often receives its deepest inspirations. It was in the desert that God fashioned his people. It was to the desert he brought his people back after their sin, in order to 'allure her, and speak to her tenderly' (Hos. 2.14). It was in the desert, too, that the Lord Jesus, after he had overcome the devil, displayed all his power and foreshadowed the victory of his Passover.

And in every generation, surely, the people of God has to pass through a similar experience in order to renew itself and to be 'born again'. The contemplative, whose vocation leads him to withdraw into this spiritual desert, feels that he is living at the very heart of the Church. His experience does not seem to him to be esoteric, but, on the contrary, typical of all Christian experience. He can recognize his own situation in the trials and temptations which many of his fellow-Christians are undergoing. He can understand their sufferings and discern the meaning of them. He knows all the bitterness and anguish of the dark night of the soul: *My God, my God, why have you forsaken me?* (Ps. 21.1; cf. Matt. 27.46). But he knows, too, from the story of Christ, that God is the conqueror of sin and death.

The world of today is sorely tempted to fall into atheism—into the denial of this God who cannot be grasped on its own level, and is not accessible to its instruments and calculations. Some Christians, even, moved by the desire to share the condition of their fellow-men in the fullest possible way, are yielding to this outlook when they proclaim the need for a certain measure of unbelief as a necessary basis for any fully human sincerity. According to some of them, it is just not possible to reach a God who is, by definition, transcendent—'wholly other'. To be a Christian, it is enough, they say, to devote oneself generously to the service of mankind.

We are not insensitive to everything that is attractive in such a standpoint, although it leads to absurd results. The contemplative Christian, too, is aware of that fundamental datum, so firmly anchored in mystical tradition, that God who has revealed himself to us in his word, has revealed himself as 'unknown', inasmuch as he is inaccessible to our concepts in this life (Exod. 33.20). He lies infinitely beyond our grasp, for he is beyond all being. Familiar with a God who is 'absent', and, as it were, 'non-existent' as far as the natural world is concerned, the contemplative is, perhaps, better placed than most to understand the attitude of those who are no longer satisfied by a mystery whose presentation is reduced to the level of *things*. But he knows very well, nevertheless, that God does allow the attentive and purified soul to reach him beyond the realm of words and ideas.

In the same way, the contemplative can more readily understand how the temptation to atheism which is confronting many Christians at the present time can affect their faith in a way which may, in the long run, be salutary. For this is a trial which bears a certain analogy with the 'nights' of the mystics. The desert strips our hearts bare. It strips us of our pretensions and alibis; it strips us, too, of our imperfect images of God. It reduces us to what is essential and forces us to see the truth about ourselves, leaving us no way of escape. Now this can be a very beneficial thing for our faith, for it is here, at the very heart of our misery, that the marvels of God's mercy reveal themselves. Grace, that extraordinary power from God, works at the very heart of our dullness and inertia, for 'his power is made perfect in weakness' (2 Cor. 12.9).

It is precisely here that the sympathy and understanding of the contemplative make him want to offer a word of comfort and hope. For his experience is not a negative thing, even though it leads him along the paths of the desert with which the temptation to atheism may well have something in common. The absence of the transcendent God is also, paradoxically, his immanent presence, though it may well be that recollection, silence and a certain measure of withdrawal from the agitation of life are necessary for perceiving this. But all Christians are called to taste God, and we want to proclaim this fact in order to put them on their guard against a certain lassitude and pessimism which might tend to create for them conditions which, from this point of view, are less favourable than our own.

Our Lord was tempted in the desert; but he overcame the tempter. Our faith constantly needs to be purified and disentangled from the false images and ideas which we tend to mix with it. But the night of faith emerges into the unshakable assurance placed in our hearts by God whose will it has been to test us.

The cloistered life in itself bears witness to the reality of this victory. It still attracts hundreds of men and women in our own day. But what meaning would it have if grace did not provide the remedy for our blindness, and if it were not true that the Father, 'after having spoken many times and in many ways to our fathers through the prophets, has spoken to us in these latter days through the Son'? (Heb. 1.1–2). For 'if it is only for this life that we have set our hope in Christ, then we are of all men the most to be pitied' (1 Cor. 15.19).

The truth is that this experience is indescribable. But, fundamentally, it is that which Paul, John and the other Apostles proclaimed as being the experience of every Christian; and it is by using the same expressions as they used that we can best speak about it. We are dealing here with a gift of the Spirit which is, as it were, a guarantee of our inheritance (Eph. 1.14). We are dealing here with a gift of that Spirit through whom love has been poured into our hearts (Rom. 5.5), the Spirit who knows what is of God, because he searches everything, even the depths of God (1 Cor. 2.10), the Spirit whose anointing teaches us all things, so that we have no need for anyone else to teach us (1 John 2.27), the Spirit who unceasingly bears witness to our spirit that we are truly sons of God (Rom. 8.16).

It is in this same Spirit that we have come to understand how true it is that Christ died for our sins and rose again for our justification (Rom. 4.25), and that in him we have access through faith to the Father and are restored to our dignity as sons of God (cf. Rom. 5.2; Heb. 10.19).

The mystical knowledge of the Christian is not only an obscure knowledge of the invisible God. It is also an experience of God—a personal, loving encounter with the one who has revealed himself to us and saved us, in order to make us sharers in the dialogue of the Father and the Son in the Holy Spirit. For it is surely in the Trinity of Persons that God appears to us most clearly as the 'wholly other', and, at the same time, as closer to us than any being.

This, then, is the good fortune which we have felt it our duty to declare to our Shepherds upon whom the trials of the faith bear most heavily at the present time. We ask them for their blessing, and we remain constantly united with them in prayer. In communion with the whole Church, we unite ourselves to the sufferings of the world, carrying on before God a silent dialogue even with those of our brothers who keep themselves apart from us.

Our message can only end on a note of thanksgiving. For that is the feeling which will always predominate in the hearts of those who have experienced the loving-kindness of God. The Christian, that pardoned sinner whom God's mercy has qualified beyond all expectation to share in the inheritance of the saints in light (Col. 1.12), can only stand before God endlessly proclaiming a hymn of thanksgiving: 'He is good, for his love is eternal' (Ps. 135).

It is our wish to offer our own testimony to this sense of wonder and thankfulness, while inviting our brothers everywhere to share them with us in hope, and in this way to develop the precious seeds of contemplation implanted in their hearts.

Notes
Select Bibliography

NOTES

PART TWO—MONASTIC THEMES

THE HUMANITY OF CHRIST IN MONASTIC PRAYER

1 St Teresa of Avila, *Life*, ch. 22.
2 It is better for you that I should go away; the Paraclete will not come to you unless I go,' etc. (John 16.7 ff).
3 J. De Guibert, *Documenta Ecclesiastica Christianae Perfectionis Studium Spectantia* (Rome, 1931), nn. 445, 446.
4 *Ibid.*, n. 461.
5 *Ibid.*, n. 495.
6 *Con.* I, 15; cf. *Con.* I, 18, *Con.* XIV, 9.
7 *Haec itaque supplicationum genera sublimior adhuc status ac praecelsior subsequitur, qui contemplatione Dei solius et caritatis adore formatur, per quam mens in illius dilectionem resoluta atque rejecta, familiarissime Deo, velut Patri proprio, peculiari pietate colloquitur* (*Con.* IX, 18). Note that this is in no sense a Platonic contemplation of the divine essence. Here Cassian is commenting on the *Pater Noster* as the way to the highest contemplative prayer which is attained together with the *perfecta charitas filiorum*, the pure love which is inseparable from the 'spirit of sonship'. Hence there is implied that contemplation is union with the Father in and through Christ. In the next chapter when we pray for the coming of the Father's Kingdom we must realize also that this is 'the Kingdom by which Christ reigns in His saints'.
8 *In modum cujusdam incomprehensibilis ac rapacissimae flammae cuncta pervolitans, [mens coepit] ineffabiles ad Deum preces purissimi vigoris effundere, quas ipse Spiritus interpellans gemitibus inenarrabilibus, ignorantibus nobis, emittit ad Deum* (*Con.* IX, 15).
9 *Non est perfecta oratio in qua se monachus, vel hoc ipsum quod orat, intelligit* (*Con.* IX, 31).
10 *Con.* X, 6 (the entire chapter should be read).
11 *Ibid.*
12 *Ibid.*

13 *Ibid.*
14 *De Incarnatione Christi* (P.L., 50, 9–272).
15 *Con.* X, 6.
16 *Ibid.*
17 *Eam naturam in Dei Patris consessuram throno quae jacuerat in sepulchro* (Serm. 73, P.L., 54, 396).
18 P.L., 54, 397.
19 P.L., 54, 398.
20 *Serm.* 77 (P.L., 54, 414). This last phrase, originating with St Irenaeus, is constantly reiterated by the Fathers.
21 *Hom.* 29 (P.L., 76, 1218).
22 *Serm.* 74 (P.L., 54, 937). On 'Paradise' in patristic mysticism, see Dom A. Stolz, *The Doctrine of Spiritual Perfection* (St Louis, 1946) pp. 17–36.
23 *Ibid.*
24 *Serm.* 77 (P.L., 54, 414).
25 *Serm.* 74 (P.L., 54, 399).
26 *Hom.* 27 *in Evang.* (P.L., 76, 1207). Note this is the source for the famous principle used so frequently by William of St Thierry.
27 See St Leo, *Serm.* 76 (P.L., 54, 397).
28 St Gregory, *Hom.* 8 *in Evang.* (P.L., 76, 1105).
29 *Serm.* 74 (P.L., 54, 397).
30 *Ibid.*
31 St Gregory, *Hom.* 34 *in Evang.* (P.L., 76, 1249).
32 *La spiritualité du moyen âge* (Paris, 1961), p. 27.
33 Cf. *Moralia in Job*, XXXI, 51 (P.L., 76, 630).
34 P.L., 145, 557.
35 *Moralia*, XXXI, 53 (P.L., 76, 631).
36 *Serm.* 74 (P.L., 54, 397).
37 St Bede, *Hom.* II, 13 (*Corpus Christianorum*, 122, p. 268).
38 *Hom.* II, 10 (p. 247).
39 *Ibid.*
40 *Ibid.* (p. 248).
41 *Ibid.*
42 *Hom.* II, 111 (p. 254).
43 *Ibid.*
44 *Ibid.*
45 *Serm.* 74 (P.L., 54, 399).
46 *Ibid.* (P.L., 54, 398).
47 *Hom.* 34 *in Evang.* (P.L., 76, 1249).
48 *Ibid.*

49 *Moralia*, XXIII, 6 (P.L., 76, 292).

50 *Tunc resplendente raptim coruscatione incircumscripti luminis illustratur* (ibid.).

51 *Immensitatis ejus coruscante circumstantia reverberatur.* Cf. *Hom. in Ez.* I, 5, 12 (P.L., 76, 926).

52 Ambrose Autpert is probably the most original theologian in the Latin world in the eighth century. See Dom Berlière's 'Ambroise Autpert' in the *Dictionnaire d'histoire et de géographie ecclésiastiques*. Dom J. Winandy has written a study of Autpert with some of his texts in Latin and French: *Ambroise Autpert, moine et théologien* (Paris, 1953). In an article on him in *La Vie Spirituelle*, 1950 (p. 149), Dom Winandy says of him: 'Chez Autpert, la théologie est vraiment sagesse, elle ne fait qu'un avec elle.'

53 P.L., 89, 1308.

54 *Ut qui erat in carne conspicuus subito appareret in majestate coruscus.*

55 P.L., 89, 1293. Cf. Origen, *Hom. in Luc.* I, 4 (*Sources Chrétiennes*, 87, p. 106).

56 P.L., 89, 1300.

57 P.L., 89, 1294.

58 *Adhuc mortalis erat et ipsa carnis mortalitas claritatem divinitatis ejus, ut erat ostendere non sinebat* (P.L., 89, 1309). In a very interesting article by G. Habra, 'La signification de la Transfiguration dans la théologie byzantine,' *Collectanea, O. C. R.*, 25 (1963), we find several Patristic quotations to this same effect (pp. 136–7).

59 *Figura membrorum suorum qualia . . . in futuro fulgebunt in sua claritate monstrabat* (ibid.). Cf. St Bede, *Hom. in Luc.* III, 9 (*Corpus Christianorum*, 120, p. 205).

60 P.L., 89, 1319.

61 P.L., 89, 1308.

62 *Ibid.*

63 P.L., 89, 1299.

CONVERSION OF LIFE

1 *Spiritual Directory*, pp. 186–9.

2 See A. Schroll, *Benedictine Monasticism*, p. 71.

3 See Schmidt's article *Conversatio Morum* in DS, Vol. II.

4 *Règlement de la Trappe*, 1878, p. 15.

5 *Vision of Peace*, ch. XXI, 'The Monastic Way of Life'.

6 Mat. 19.21, Luke 18.22.
7 Dist. I., cap. 1, Griesser, Ed, p. 48.
8 Idem., p. 50.
9 Dist. II, cap. 2.
10 *Collectio Monastica*, Ed. V. Arras, CSCO, Vol. 239, Louvain, 1963.
11 P.L., 102, col. 901–2.
12 *Collectio Monastica*, XVI, 16, p. 99.
13 Idem., XXXI, p. 129.
14 *Regula Magistri*, ch. 1.
15 Cf. XLIXe *Conférence sur le détachement du Monde*.
16 Migne, *Orateurs Chrétiens*, II^eSerie, Vol. 90, col. 309.
17 See RTAM, 1961.
18 Bulletin de Théologie Ancienne et Médiévale, 1961, 2926.
19 'Erémitisme en Occident' in *Le Millénaire du Mont Athos*, p. 178.
20 Quoted by Dom Leclercq, *Studia Anselmiana*, 40, p. 104.
21 St Jerome, Epist. 108.23.
22 P.L., 20. 1153.
23 Conentur in suo ordine viriliter semper proficere. Epistle 189, Schmidt, IV, p. 75.
24 P.L., 102.726.
25 See *Collectanea*, 1960, p. 381.
26 Idem., p. 385.
27 *Collectio Monastica*, Vol. 32, p. 132.

PART THREE—THE SOLITARY LIFE

PROJECT FOR A HERITAGE

1 It has often been stated that Thomas Merton lacked organizational and administrative abilities. He, himself, admitted as much on a number of occasions. But this blueprint for a Skete is very well mapped out, and reveals a man with uncommon foresight and practical vision. It could be useful for persons today involved in small contemplative communities.—*Editor*.

WILDERNESS AND PARADISE

1 *Christ in the Wilderness*, by Ulrich Mauser, Naperville, Ill., 1963.

Wilderness and Paradise in Christian Thought, by George H. Williams, New York, 1962.

2 It would be interesting to develop this idea. Obviously the life of forest ranger or fire guard in the vast forests of North America offers a natural opportunity for the hermit life today, and some of the hermit vocation have adopted it.

APPENDIXES

A LETTER ON THE CONTEMPLATIVE LIFE

1 This hastily written letter addressed to the Abbot of the Cistercian monastery of Frattocchie near Rome was in response to a request of Pope Paul VI for a 'message of contemplatives to the world'.—*Editor*.

CONTEMPLATIVES AND THE CRISIS OF FAITH

1 The following is a translation of a message sent to the Synod of Bishops, which met at Rome in October 1967. It is the joint work of Dom J. B. Porion, Procurator General of the Carthusians, Dom André Louf, Abbot of Mont-des-Cats, and Father Thomas Merton. The original French version appeared in the *Osservatore Romano* on 12 October 1967.—*Editor*.

SELECT BIBLIOGRAPHY

These books by Thomas Merton deal either directly or indirectly with the monastic life, beginning with the second part of *The Seven Storey Mountain*. Some of the books, such as *The Asian Journal* and works on Zen make many passing references to Christian and non-Christian monasticism, while others like *Thoughts in Solitude* are applicable to both the monk and the lay-person.

	PUBLISHER: U.S.	PUBLISHER: U.K.
The Seven Storey Mountain (1948)	Doubleday Image 1948	Sheldon Press 1975
The Waters of Siloe (1949)	Doubleday Image 1951	Sheldon Press 1976
Bread in the Wilderness (1953)	Liturgical Press 1971	Burns & Oates 1955
The Sign of Jonas (1953)	Doubleday Image 1956	Sheldon Press 1976
No Man is an Island (1956)	Doubleday Image 1967	Burns & Oates 1955
The Silent Life	Farrar Straus 1957	Sheldon Press 1975
Thoughts in Solitude	Farrar Straus 1958	Burns & Oates 1958
Spiritual Direction & Meditation	Liturgical Press 1960	Anthony Clarke 1975
The Wisdom of the Desert	New Directions 1960	Sheldon Press 1973
Disputed Questions (*The Power & Meaning of Love* in U.K.)	Farrar Straus 1960	Sheldon Press 1976
New Seeds of Contemplation	New Directions 1961	Burns & Oates 1962
Mystics & Zen Masters	Farrar Straus 1967	(parts of these two volumes were published in U.K. under the title: *Thomas Merton on Zen*) Sheldon Press 1976
Zen & the Birds of Appetite	New Directions 1968	
The Climate of Monastic Prayer	Cistercian Pub. 1969	Ecclesia Press 1969
Reissued as *Contemplative Prayer*	Doubleday Image 1971	Darton, Longman & Todd 1973

| *Contemplation in a World of Action* | Doubleday Image 1971 | Allen & Unwin 1972 |
| *The Asian Journal of Thomas Merton* (Edited by Naomi Burton, Brother Patrick Hart and James Laughlin) | New Directions 1973 | Sheldon Press 1974 |

OTHER IMAGE BOOKS

ABANDONMENT TO DIVINE PROVIDENCE – Jean Pierre de Caussade. Trans. by John Beevers

AGING: THE FULFILLMENT OF LIFE – Henri J. M. Nouwen and Walter J. Gaffney

AND WOULD YOU BELIEVE IT – Bernard Basset, S.J.

ANOTHER KIND OF LOVE/Homosexuality and Spirituality (Revised Edition) – Richard Woods

APOLOGIA PRO VITA SUA – John Henry Cardinal Newman

AN AQUINAS READER – Ed., with an Intro., by Mary T. Clark

THE ART OF BEING HUMAN – William McNamara, O.C.D.

ASCENT OF MOUNT CARMEL – St. John of the Cross – Trans. and ed. by E. Allison Peers

AN AUGUSTINE READER – Ed., with an Intro., by John J. O'Meara

AUTOBIOGRAPHY OF ST. THÉRÈSE OF LISIEUX: THE STORY OF A SOUL – A new translation by John Beevers

BELIEVING – Eugene Kennedy

BIRTH OF THE MESSIAH – Raymond E. Brown

CATHOLIC AMERICA – John Cogley

CATHOLIC PENTECOSTALISM – Rene Laurentin

THE CHALLENGE OF JESUS – John Shea

CHRIST IS ALIVE! – Michel Quoist

CHRIST THE LORD – Gerard S. Sloyan

THE CHURCH – Hans Küng

CITY OF GOD – St. Augustine – Ed. by Vernon J. Bourke. Intro. by Étienne Gilson

THE CLOUD OF UNKNOWING (and THE BOOK OF PRIVY COUNSELING) – Newly ed., with an Intro., by William Johnston, S.J.

CLOWNING IN ROME – Henri J. M. Nouwen

A CONCISE HISTORY OF THE CATHOLIC CHURCH (Revised Edition) – Thomas Bokenkotter

THE CONFESSIONS OF ST. AUGUSTINE – Trans., with an Intro., by John K. Ryan

CONJECTURES OF A GUILTY BYSTANDER – Thomas Merton

THE CONSPIRACY OF GOD: THE HOLY SPIRIT IN US – John C. Haughey

CONTEMPLATION IN A WORLD OF ACTION – Thomas Merton

CONTEMPLATIVE PRAYER – Thomas Merton

CREATIVE MINISTRY – Henri J. M. Nouwen

DAILY WE TOUCH HIM – M. Basil Pennington, O.C.S.O.

DAMIEN THE LEPER – John Farrow

DARK NIGHT OF THE SOUL – St. John of the Cross. Ed. and trans. by E. Allison Peers

THE DAYS AND THE NIGHTS – Candida Lund

OTHER IMAGE BOOKS

THE DEVIL YOU SAY! – Andrew M. Greeley

THE DIARY OF A COUNTRY PRIEST – Georges Bernanos

DIVORCE AND REMARRIAGE FOR CATHOLICS? – Stephen J. Kelleher

A DOCTOR AT CALVARY – Pierre Barbet, M.D.

EVERLASTING MAN – G. K. Chesterton

FIVE FOR SORROW, TEN FOR JOY – J. Neville Ward

THE FOUR GOSPELS: AN INTRODUCTION (2 vols.) – Bruce Vawter, C.M.

THE FREEDOM OF SEXUAL LOVE – Joseph and Lois Bird

THE FRIENDSHIP GAME – Andrew M. Greeley

THE GREATEST STORY EVER TOLD – Fulton Oursler

GUIDE TO CONTENTMENT – Fulton J. Sheen

GUILTY, O LORD – Bernard Basset, S.J.

HANS KÜNG: HIS WORK AND HIS WAY – Hermann Häring and Karl-Josef Kuschel

HAS SIN CHANGED? – Seán Fagan

HE LEADETH ME – Walter J. Ciszek, S.J., with Daniel Flaherty, S.J.

A HISTORY OF PHILOSOPHY: VOLUME 1 – GREECE AND ROME (2 Parts) – Frederick Copleston, S.J.

A HISTORY OF PHILOSOPHY: VOLUME 2 – MEDIAEVAL PHILOSOPHY (2 Parts) – Frederick Copleston, S.J. Part I – Augustine to Bonaventure. Part II – Albert the Great to Duns Scotus

A HISTORY OF PHILOSOPHY: VOLUME 3 – LATE MEDIAEVAL AND RENAISSANCE PHILOSOPHY (2 Parts) – Frederick Copleston, S.J. Part I – Ockham to the Speculative Mystics. Part II – The Revival of Platonism to Suárez

A HISTORY OF PHILOSOPHY: VOLUME 4 – MODERN PHILOSOPHY: Descartes to Leibniz – Frederick Copleston, S.J.

A HISTORY OF PHILOSOPHY: VOLUME 5 – MODERN PHILOSOPHY: The British Philosophers, Hobbes to Hume (2 Parts) – Frederick Copleston, S.J. Part I – Hobbes to Paley. Part II – Berkeley to Hume

A HISTORY OF PHILOSOPHY: VOLUME 6 – MODERN PHILOSOPHY (2 Parts) – Frederick Copleston, S.J. – The French Enlightenment to Kant

A HISTORY OF PHILOSOPHY: VOLUME 7 – MODERN PHILOSOPHY (2 Parts) – Frederick Copleston, S.J. Part I – Fichte to Hegel. Part II – Schopenhauer to Nietzsche

A HISTORY OF PHILOSOPHY: VOLUME 8 – MODERN PHILOSOPHY: Bentham to Russell (2 Parts) – Frederick Copleston, S.J. Part I – British Empiricism and the Idealist Movement in Great Britain. Part II – Idealism in America, the Pragmatist Movement, the Revolt against Idealism

OTHER IMAGE BOOKS

A HISTORY OF PHILOSOPHY: VOLUME 9 – Maine de Biran to Sartre (2 Parts) – Frederick Copleston, S.J. Part I – The Revolution to Henri Bergson. Part II – Bergson to Sartre

HOW TO BE REALLY WITH IT – Guide to the Good Life – Bernard Basset, S.J.

THE HUMAN ADVENTURE – William McNamara, O.C.D.

THE IMITATION OF CHRIST – Thomas à Kempis. Ed., with Intro., by Harold C. Gardiner, S.J.

IN SEARCH OF THE BEYOND – Carlo Carretto

INTERIOR CASTLE – St. Teresa of Avila – Trans. and ed. by E. Allison Peers

IN THE SPIRIT, IN THE FLESH – Eugene C. Kennedy

INTRODUCTION TO THE DEVOUT LIFE – St. Francis de Sales. Trans. and ed. by John K. Ryan

INVITATION TO ACTS – Robert J. Karris

INVITATION TO JOHN – George MacRae

INVITATION TO LUKE – Robert J. Karris

INVITATION TO MARK – Paul J. Achtemeier

INVITATION TO MATTHEW – Donald Senior

INVITATION TO PAUL II – Eugene A. LaVerdiere

INVITATION TO PAUL III – Luke Timothy Johnson

THE JESUS MYTH – Andrew M. Greeley

THE JOY OF BEING HUMAN – Eugene Kennedy

KEY TO THE BIBLE – Wilfrid J. Harrington, O.P.
　　Vol. 1 – The Record of Revelation
　　Vol. 2 – The Old Testament: Record of the Promise
　　Vol. 3 – The New Testament: Record of the Fulfillment

LIFE AND HOLINESS – Thomas Merton

LIFE FOR A WANDERER – Andrew M. Greeley

LIFE IS WORTH LIVING – Fulton J. Sheen

THE LIFE OF ALL LIVING – Fulton J. Sheen

LIFE OF CHRIST – Fulton J. Sheen

LIFE OF TERESA OF JESUS: THE AUTOBIOGRAPHY OF ST. TERESA OF AVILA – Trans. and ed. by E. Allison Peers

LIFT UP YOUR HEART – Fulton J. Sheen

LILIES OF THE FIELD – William E. Barrett

LITTLE FLOWERS OF ST. FRANCIS – Trans. by Raphael Brown

LIVING FLAME OF LOVE – St. John of the Cross. Trans., with Intro., by E. Allison Peers

LIVING IN HOPE – Ladislaus Boros, S.J.

OTHER IMAGE BOOKS

LOVE IS ALL – Joseph and Lois Bird

LOVE IS A COUPLE – Fr. Chuck Gallagher

THE MAN IN THE SYCAMORE TREE: The Good Times and Hard Life of Thomas Merton – Edward Rice

MARRIAGE IS FOR GROWNUPS – Joseph and Lois Bird

MEETING GOD IN MAN – Ladislaus Boros, S.J.

MR. BLUE – Myles Connolly

MODELS OF THE CHURCH – Avery Dulles

THE MONASTIC JOURNEY – Thomas Merton

MORALITY FOR OUR TIME – Marc Oraison

MY LIFE WITH CHRIST – Anthony J. Paone, S.J.

MY WORDS ARE SPIRIT AND LIFE: Meeting Christ through Daily Meditation – Stephanie M. Herz

THE NEW SEXUALITY: MYTHS, FABLES AND HANG-UPS – Eugene C. Kennedy

NEW TESTAMENT ESSAYS – Raymond E. Brown, S.S.

THE NEW TESTAMENT OF THE JERUSALEM BIBLE: Reader's Edition – Alexander Jones, General Editor

THE NEW TESTAMENT OF THE NEW AMERICAN BIBLE (complete and unabridged)

THE OLD TESTAMENT OF THE JERUSALEM BIBLE: Reader's Edition – Alexander Jones, General Editor
  Volume 2: 1 Samuel – 2 Maccabees; Volume 3: Job – Ecclesiasticus; Volume 4: The Prophets – Malachi

THE OLD TESTAMENT WITHOUT ILLUSION – John L. McKenzie

ORTHODOXY – G. K. Chesterton

OUR LADY OF FATIMA – William Thomas Walsh

THE PAIN OF BEING HUMAN – Eugene Kennedy

PARENTS ARE LOVERS – Fr. Chuck Gallagher

PEACE OF SOUL – Fulton J. Sheen

THE PERFECT JOY OF ST. FRANCIS – Felix Timmermans. Trans. by Raphael Brown

THE POWER AND THE WISDOM – John L. McKenzie

THE POWER OF LOVE – Fulton J. Sheen

POWER TO THE PARENTS! – Joseph and Lois Bird

THE PRACTICE OF THE PRESENCE OF GOD – Trans. with an Intro. by John J. Delaney

THE PSALMS OF THE JERUSALEM BIBLE – Alexander Jones, General Editor

RELIGION AND WORLD HISTORY – Christopher Dawson. Ed. by James Oliver and Christina Scott

A RELIGIOUS HISTORY OF THE AMERICAN PEOPLE (2 vols.) – Sydney E. Ahlstrom

OTHER IMAGE BOOKS

RENEWING THE EARTH – Ed. by David J. O'Brien and Thomas A. Shannon

REVELATIONS OF DIVINE LOVE – Trans. with an Intro. by M. L. del Mastro

THE ROMAN CATHOLIC CHURCH – John L. McKenzie

THE RULE OF ST. BENEDICT – Trans. and ed., with an Intro., by Anthony C. Meisel and M. L. del Mastro

ST. FRANCIS OF ASSISI – G. K. Chesterton

ST. FRANCIS OF ASSISI – Johannes Jorgensen

SAINT THOMAS AQUINAS – G. K. Chesterton

SAINTS FOR ALL SEASONS – John J. Delaney, editor

A SENSE OF LIFE, A SENSE OF SIN – Eugene Kennedy

THE SEXUAL CELIBATE – Donald Goergen

SHOULD ANYONE SAY FOREVER? – John C. Haughey

THE SHROUD OF TURIN (Revised Edition) – Ian Wilson

THE SIGN OF JONAS – Thomas Merton

THE SINAI MYTH – Andrew M. Greeley

SOMETHING BEAUTIFUL FOR GOD – Malcolm Muggeridge

THE SOUL AFIRE: REVELATIONS OF THE MYSTICS – Ed. by H. A. Reinhold

THE SPIRIT OF CATHOLICISM – Karl Adam

SPIRITUAL CANTICLE – St. John of the Cross. Trans. and ed., with an Intro., by E. Allison Peers

THE SPIRITUAL EXERCISES OF ST. IGNATIUS – Trans. by Anthony Mottola, Ph.D. Intro. by Robert W. Gleason, S.J.

THE STAIRWAY OF PERFECTION – Trans. and ed. by M. L. del Mastro

STORM OF GLORY – John Beevers

THE STORY OF THE TRAPP FAMILY SINGERS – Maria Augusta Trapp

SUFFERING – Louis Evely

SUMMA THEOLOGIAE – Thomas Aquinas. General Editor: Thomas Gilby, O.P.

   Volume 1: The Existence of God. Part One: Questions 1–13

A THEOLOGY OF THE OLD TESTAMENT – John L. McKenzie

THE THIRD PEACOCK – Robert Farrar Capon

THIRSTING FOR THE LORD – Carroll Stuhlmueller

THIS MAN JESUS – Bruce Vawter

THOMAS MERTON, MONK – Ed. by Brother Patrick Hart

THOMAS MERTON ON MYSTICISM – Raymond Bailey

THOMAS MERTON ON PRAYER – John J. Higgins, S.J.

A THOMAS MERTON READER – Revised Edition – Ed. by Thomas P. McDonnell

A TIME FOR LOVE – Eugene C. Kennedy

OTHER IMAGE BOOKS

TO LIVE IS TO LOVE – Ernesto Cardenal

TOWARD A NEW CATHOLIC MORALITY – John Giles Milhaven

THE TWO-EDGED SWORD – John L. McKenzie

UNDERSTANDING MYSTICISM – Ed. by Richard Woods, O.P.

THE VARIETIES OF RELIGIOUS EXPERIENCE – William James

THE WAY OF PERFECTION – St. Teresa of Avila. Trans. and ed. by E. Allison Peers

THE WAY OF A PILGRIM (AND THE PILGRIM CONTINUES HIS WAY) – Trans. by Helen Bacovcin

WE AGNOSTICS: On the Tightrope to Eternity – Bernard Basset, S.J.

WE ARE ALL BROTHERS – Louis Evely

WE DARE TO SAY OUR FATHER – Louis Evely

WHY CATHOLIC? – Ed. by John J. Delaney

THE WIT AND WISDOM OF BISHOP FULTON J. SHEEN – Ed. by Bill Adler

WITH GOD IN RUSSIA – Walter J. Ciszek, S.J., with Daniel L. Flaherty, S.J.

A WOMAN CLOTHED WITH THE SUN – Ed. by John J. Delaney

THE WORLD'S FIRST LOVE – Fulton J. Sheen

THE WOUNDED HEALER – Henri J. M. Nouwen

A 80 – 6